Praise for *The Girls of Murder City*

"It turns out that behind *Chicago* there was a sexy, swaggering, historical tale in no need of a sound track. Liked the movie. Loved the book."
—*The Wall Street Journal*

"Douglas Perry . . . tells their stories in delicious and devilish detail."
—Glenn C. Altschuler, NPR

"A well-researched and skillfully crafted time capsule about Chicago-style justice (or lack thereof) . . . Fans of true crime and popular history will enjoy the book's oversized female characters and its hardboiled background of crime and no punishment."
—*The Boston Globe*

"Captivating."
—*The Christian Science Monitor*

"This one has it all—and in the title, no less. What more could you want?"
—*Asbury Park Press*

"The book's a romp, an enjoyable read about the seamy tales that held the world's attention as jazz, guns, post-WWI energy, and Prohibition made the United States a country riven and riveted by flappers, gangs, and murder."
—*Eugene Weekly*

"[A] wickedly fun read."
—*The Brooklyn Rail*

"A helluva time for Chicago, and Perry captures the sensationalism, sexism, and wantonness of Chicago's take on the Prohibition Era."
—*Newcity* magazine

"A vivid mix of biography and history . . . an excellent and enjoyable account."
—*PopMatters*

"Fueled by rich period detail, a narrative voice that perfectly channels the pulse of Jazz Age Chicago, and a cast of characters that seem destined for the stage, Perry has written a crackling history that simultaneously presents the freewheeling spirit of the age and its sober repercussions."
—Chickagoan.com

"Perry neatly tracks the stories that splashed across the front pages of the Chicago papers in 1924. . . . [A] fascinating piece of social history."
—blogcritics.org

"Captivating . . . [Perry's] bouncy, exuberant prose perfectly complements the theatricality of the proceedings, and he deftly maneuvers away from the main story without ever losing momentum." —*BookPage*

"Oh good lord is this a fun book. . . . [Perry] perfectly balances surprise and expectation. Here's the truth: Douglas Perry is a master."
—*Corduroy Books*

"Perry presents readers with a picture of the delirious three-ring circus that took over the press and the courts when 'Gangsterism, celebrity, sex, art, music—anything dodgy or gauche or modern boomed in the city.'"
—*Shelf Awareness*

"Lusty, feisty, intriguingly unique." —*Barnes & Noble Review*

"Consistently entertaining . . . A chronicle of the wild spring and summer of 1924, when Chicago was afflicted with a seeming epidemic of female murderers." —*Kirkus Reviews*

"Entertaining . . . wised up . . . savvy, flamboyant social history."
—*Publishers Weekly*

"Vivid. [The] fast-paced story behind the story."
—*Booklist* (starred review)

"Douglas Perry takes the reader back to the glitzy Chicago days when beauty trumped bad behavior, criminal acts earned celebrity status, and reporters were freewheeling. *The Girls of Murder City* is a rip-roaring, fast-read visit to a fascinating time and place in American history; a book that is destined to become a Jazz Age classic."
—two-time Edgar Award winner Carlton Stowers

"Vividly written, scrupulously researched, Doug Perry's *The Girls of Murder City* brings the legends of Chicago back to clamoring (and calamitous) life."
                    —Michael Lesy, author of *Murder City: The Bloody History of Chicago in the Twenties*

"In *The Girls of Murder City*, Douglas Perry magically mixes true crime, sociology, psychology, romance (of a sort), and near-slapstick comedy into an incredible book. This is one of those rare opportunities for readers to learn and be royally entertained at the same time."
                    —Jeff Guinn, author of *Go Down Together: The True, Untold Story of Bonnie and Clyde*

"Crime doesn't pay for *The Girls of Murder City*, but it sure pays off for Douglas Perry's readers. This is a consistently page-turning, highly entertaining, and very intriguing story."
                    —Howard Blum, author of the *New York Times* bestseller and Edgar Award–winner *American Lightning: Terror, Mystery, the Birth of Hollywood, and the Crime of the Century*

"An intriguing account of the two murder cases that provided the inspiration for the musical *Chicago*. Perry conveys a sense of the 1920s and its notorious murders with flair and panache. A must for everyone interested in the history of the city."
                    —Simon Baatz, author of *For the Thrill of It: Leopold, Loeb and the Murder That Shocked Chicago*

ABOUT THE AUTHOR

Douglas Perry is coauthor of *The Sixteenth Minute: Life in the Aftermath of Fame*. An award-winning writer and editor, his work has appeared in the *Chicago Tribune*, *The San Jose Mercury News*, *The Oregonian*, *Details*, and many other publications. He lives in Portland, Oregon.

THE GIRLS OF MURDER CITY

Fame, Lust, and the Beautiful Killers
Who Inspired *Chicago*

DOUGLAS PERRY

PENGUIN BOOKS

PENGUIN BOOKS

Published by the Penguin Group

Penguin Group (USA) Inc., 375 Hudson Street, New York, New York 10014, U.S.A. • Penguin Group (Canada),
90 Eglinton Avenue East, Suite 700, Toronto, Ontario, Canada M4P 2Y3 (a division of Pearson Penguin Canada
Inc.) • Penguin Books Ltd, 80 Strand, London WC2R 0RL, England • Penguin Ireland, 25 St. Stephen's Green,
Dublin 2, Ireland (a division of Penguin Books Ltd) • Penguin Books Australia Ltd, 250 Camberwell Road,
Camberwell, Victoria 3124, Australia (a division of Pearson Australia Group Pty Ltd) • Penguin Books India Pvt
Ltd, 11 Community Centre, Panchsheel Park, New Delhi—110 017, India • Penguin Group (NZ), 67 Apollo Drive,
Rosedale, Auckland 0632, New Zealand (a division of Pearson New Zealand Ltd) • Penguin Books (South Africa)
(Pty) Ltd, 24 Sturdee Avenue, Rosebank, Johannesburg 2196, South Africa

Penguin Books Ltd, Registered Offices: 80 Strand, London WC2R 0RL, England

First published in the United States of America by Viking Penguin,
a member of Penguin Group (USA) Inc. 2010
Published in Penguin Books 2011

10 9 8 7 6 5 4 3 2 1

PHOTOGRAPH CREDITS
Insert pages 2 (top left), 6 (top left), 8 (top): Author's collection. • Page 2 (top right), (bottom): Courtesy of Drew
Messmann • Page 3 (top left): Courtesy of Transylvania University • Page 8 (bottom): *Chicago Tribune* file
photo. All rights reserved. Used with permission. • Page 4 (top left): Billy Rose Theatre Division, The New York
Public Library for the Performing Arts, Astor, Lenox and Tilden Foundations • Page 4 (top right): Courtesy of
Ron Dixon • Page 4 (bottom): Courtesy of Wendy Teresi • Page 5 (bottom): Copyright 2009 The Fresno Bee.
Reprinted with permission. All rights reserved. • Page 6 (top right): Helen Cirese Papers, 1915–1974, University
of Illinois at Chicago Library, Special Collections • Page 7 (top): Courtesy of Western Springs Historical Society,
Western Springs, Illinois. • Page 7 (bottom): Abraham Lincoln Presidential Library & Museum
(Credits for other photographs appear adjacent to the respective images).

Map: U.S. Geological Survey

THE LIBRARY OF CONGRESS HAS CATALOGED THE HARDCOVER EDITION AS FOLLOWS:
Perry, Douglas, 1968–
    The girls of Murder City : fame, lust, and the beautiful killers who inspired Chicago / Douglas Perry.
    p. cm.
    Includes bibliographical references and index.
    ISBN 978-0-670-02197-0
    ISBN 978-0-14-311922-7 (pbk.)
    1. Women murderers—Illinois—Chicago—History—Case studies.   2. Murder—Illinois—Chicago—
History—Case studies.   I. Title.
    HV6517.P475 2010
    364.152'309227731—dc22   2010003980

Printed in the United States of America
Designed by Carla Bolte • Set in Warnock Light

FOR DEBORAH

Contents

Characters

MAURINE WATKINS, *aspiring playwright—"blonde, comely and chic: a pleasant way to be."*

BELVA GAERTNER, *double divorcée—"Cook County's most stylish murderess."*

WALTER LAW, *Belva's boyfriend—"a man who couldn't say no."*

WILLIAM GAERTNER, *Belva's millionaire ex-husband—"the most patient soul since Job."*

BEULAH ANNAN, *"the prettiest woman ever charged with murder in Chicago."*

HARRY KALSTEDT, *Beulah's boyfriend—"the other man."*

AL ANNAN, *"Beulah's meal-ticket husband."*

W. W. O'BRIEN and WILLIAM SCOTT STEWART, *Beulah's attorneys— "best in the city, next to Erbstein."*

GENEVIEVE FORBES, *reporter on the* Daily Tribune.

IONE QUINBY, *"The* Evening Post's *little bob-haired reporter."*

SONIA LEE, *sob sister on the* American.

HELEN CIRESE, *girl attorney—"headmistress of 'Jail School.'"*

WANDA STOPA, *the bohemian—"Little Poland's love-foiled girl gunner."*

KITTY MALM, *"the Tiger Girl"—convicted because she wasn't quite refined.* ⎫
                                ⎬ *Inmates of Murderess Row*

SABELLA NITTI, *"Senora Sabelle"—the first woman ever sentenced to death in Cook County.*

ELIZABETH UNKAFER, *"the queer one."* ⎭

NATHAN LEOPOLD, *"the Master."* ⎫
                               ⎬ *The Thrill Killers*
DICK LOEB, *"his dutiful friend."* ⎭

ADDITIONAL PLAYERS: *Judge, Jury, Bailiffs, Jail Matrons, Police, Reporters, Editors, Attorneys, Court Fans.*

CHICAGO: SPRING AND SUMMER, 1924

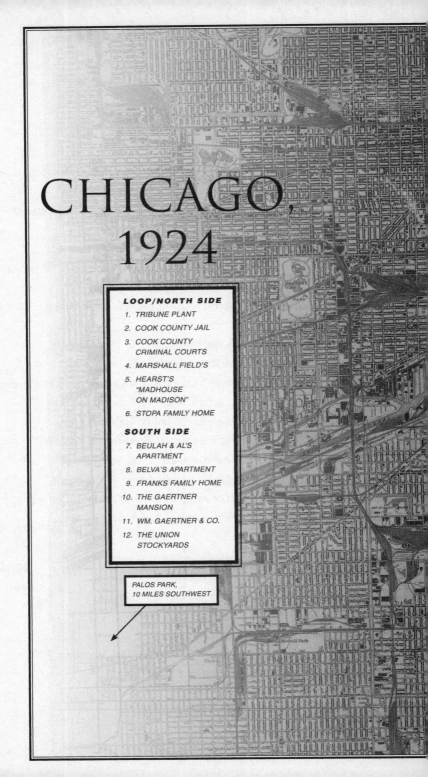

CHICAGO, 1924

LOOP/NORTH SIDE

1. TRIBUNE PLANT
2. COOK COUNTY JAIL
3. COOK COUNTY CRIMINAL COURTS
4. MARSHALL FIELD'S
5. HEARST'S "MADHOUSE ON MADISON"
6. STOPA FAMILY HOME

SOUTH SIDE

7. BEULAH & AL'S APARTMENT
8. BELVA'S APARTMENT
9. FRANKS FAMILY HOME
10. THE GAERTNER MANSION
11. WM. GAERTNER & CO.
12. THE UNION STOCKYARDS

PALOS PARK,
10 MILES SOUTHWEST

The Girls of Murder City

Prologue

Thursday, April 24, 1924

The most beautiful women in the city were murderers.

The radio said so. The newspapers, when they arrived, would surely say worse. Beulah Annan peered through the bars of cell 657 in the women's quarters of the Cook County Jail. She liked being called beautiful for the entire city to hear. She'd greedily consumed every word said and written about her, cut out and saved the best pictures. She took pride in the coverage. But that was when she was the undisputed "prettiest murderess" in all of Cook County. Now everything had changed. She knew that today, for almost the first time since her arrest almost three weeks ago, there wouldn't be a picture of her in any of the newspapers. There was a new girl gunner on the scene, a gorgeous Polish girl named Wanda Stopa.

Depressed, Beulah chanced getting undressed. It was the middle of the day, but the stiff prison uniform made her skin itch, and the reporters weren't going to come for interviews now. They were all out chasing the new girl. Beulah sat on her bunk and listened. The cellblock was quiet, stagnant. On a normal day, the rest of the inmates would have gone to the recreation room after lunch to sing hymns. Beulah never joined them; she preferred to retreat to a solitary spot with the jail radio, which she'd claimed as her own. She listened to fox-trots. She liked to do as she pleased.

It was Belva Gaertner, "the most stylish" woman on the block, who had begun the daily hymn-singing ritual. That was back in March, the day after she staggered into jail, dead-eyed and elephant-tongued, too drunk—or so she claimed—to remember shooting her boyfriend in the head. None of the girls could fathom that stumblebum Belva now. On the bloody night of her arrival, it had taken the society divorcée only a few hours of sleep to regain her composure. The next day, she sat sidesaddle against the cell wall, one leg slung imperiously over the other, heavy-lidded eyes offering a strange, exuberant glint. Reporters crowded in on her, eager to hear what she had to say. This was the woman who, at her divorce trial four years before, had publicly admitted to using a horsewhip on her wealthy elderly husband during lovemaking. Had she hoped to make herself a widow before he could divorce her? Now you had to wonder.

"I'm feeling very well," Belva told the reporters. "Naturally I should prefer to receive you all in my own apartment; jails are such horrid places. But"—she looked around and emitted a small laugh—"one must make the best of such things."

And so one did. Belva's rehabilitation began right there, and it continued unabated to this day. Faith would see her through this ordeal, she told any reporter who passed by her cell. This terrible, unfortunate experience made her appreciate all the more the life she once had with her wonderful ex-husband—solid, reliable William Gaertner, the millionaire scientist and businessman who had provided her with lawyers and was determined to marry her again, despite her newly proven skill with a revolver. He believed Belva had changed.

Maybe she had, but either way, she was still quite different from the other girls at the jail. She came from better stock and made sure they all knew it. Even an inmate as ferocious as Katherine Malm—the "Wolf Woman"—deferred to Belva. Class was a powerful thing; it triggered an instinctive obeisance from women accustomed to coming through the service entrance—or, in this lot's case, through the smashed-in window. Belva, it seemed, had just the right measure of contempt in her face to cow anybody, including unrepentant murderesses. She was not beautiful like perfect, young Beulah Annan. Her face was a sad, ill-conceived thing, all the features slightly out of proper proportion. But arrogant eyes shined out from it, and there was that full, passionate mouth, a mouth that could inspire a reckless hunger in the most happily married man. She'd proved that many times over. When Belva woke from her blackout on the morning of March 12, new to the jail, still wearing her blood-spattered slip, she'd wanly asked for food. The Wolf Woman, supposedly the tough girl of the women's quarters, hurried to bring her a currant bun.

"Here, Mrs. Gaertner," she'd said with a welcoming smile, eyes crinkled in understanding, "eat this and pretend it's chicken. . . . It makes it easy to swallow." With that, Katherine Malm set the tone. By the end of the week, the other girls were vying for the privilege of making Belva's bed and washing her clothes.

∾∾∾

To her credit, Belva adapted easily to her new surroundings. The lack of privacy didn't seem to bother her. The women's section of the jail, an L-shaped nook on the fourth floor of a massive, rotting, rat-infested facility downtown, was crowded even before her arrival, and not just because of the presence of Mrs. Anna Piculine. "Big Anna," the press said, was the largest woman ever jailed on a murder charge. She'd killed her husband when he said he'd prefer a slimmer woman. Then there was Mrs. Elizabeth Unkafer, charged with murdering her lover after her cuckolded husband collapsed in grief at learning of her infidelity. And Mary Wezenak—"Moonshine Mary"—the first woman to be tried in Cook County for selling poisonous whiskey. Nearly a dozen others also bunked on what was now being called "Murderess Row," and more were sure to come. Women in the city seemed to have gone mad. They'd become dangerous, especially to their husbands and boyfriends. After the police had trundled Beulah into jail, the director of the Chicago Crime Commission felt compelled to publicly dismiss the recent rash of killings by women. The ladies of Cook County, he said, were "just bunching their hits at this time." He insisted there was nothing to worry about.

The newspapers certainly weren't worried; they celebrated the crowded conditions on Murderess Row. Everyone in the city wanted to read about the fairest killers in the land. These women embodied the city's wild, rebellious side, a side that appeared to be on the verge of overwhelming everything else. Chicago in the spring of 1924 was something new, a city for the future. It thrived like nowhere else. Evidence of the postwar depression of

1920–21 couldn't be found anywhere. The city pulsed with industrial development. Factories operated twenty-four hours a day. Empty lots turned into whole neighborhoods almost overnight. Motor cars were so plentiful that Michigan Avenue traffic backed up daily more than half a mile to the Chicago River. And yet this exciting, prosperous city terrified many observers. Chicago took its cultural obsessions to extremes, from jazz to politics to architecture. Most of all, in the midst of Prohibition, the city reveled in its contempt for the law. The newly elected reform mayor, witnessing a mobster funeral attended by thousands of fascinated citizens, would exclaim later that year: "I am staggered by this state of affairs. Are we living by the code of the Dark Ages or is Chicago part of an American Commonwealth?"

It truly was difficult to tell. Gangsterism, celebrity, sex, art, music—anything dodgy or gauche or modern boomed in the city. That included feminism. Women in Chicago experienced unmatched freedoms, not won gradually—as was the case for the suffragettes—but achieved in short order, on the sly. Respectable saloons before Prohibition didn't admit women; speakeasies welcomed them. Skirts appeared to be higher here than anywhere else. Even Oak Park high school girls brazenly petted with boys, forcing the wealthy suburb's police superintendent to threaten to arrest the parents of "baby vamps." Religious leaders—and newspapers—drew a connection between the new freedoms and the increasing numbers of inmates in Cook County Jail's women's section.

❧❧

> *I can hear my Savior calling,*
> *I can hear my Savior calling,*
> *I can hear my Savior calling,*
> *"Take thy cross and follow, follow Me."*
> *Where He leads me, I will follow,*
> *Where He leads me, I will follow,*
> *Where He leads me, I will follow,*
> *I'll go with him, with him, all the way.*

Those killer women made a sweet sound. Belva, the "queen of the Loop cabarets" before Mr. Gaertner came along, knew how to carry a tune, and she gave herself the solos. And now that she had grown accustomed to "jail java" instead of gin, and the tremors had subsided, she sang with confidence. Katherine Malm was game, too, her voice soaring, dueling for the light, right up there with Big Anna's booming alto.

Not everyone, though, had the spirit of the Lord. Beulah Annan didn't see anything uplifting about being in jail. "How can they?" she'd bleated on her first day in the pen, shuddering at all those raspy voices trying to sound angelic. The hymns made her think of her childhood in rural Kentucky. She was an angel, for sure, back then, leaning her cheek against her mother's elbow during services, the prettiest little girl in town. She was an angel still, as far as her husband, Al, was concerned. All she had to do was turn those big eyes on him, her mouth puckering as she began to cry, just as she had when he came home to a dead man on the floor and learned that his wife had been running around on him. She'd done a lot of crying since that day—to no avail. Her dear Harry—the man she should have married—was still dead. Beulah could hide alone in her cell, she could squeeze her eyes shut and bury her face in her bunk in the middle of the day, but she could not get her brain to change what had happened.

The jail itself was an effective reminder. It assaulted newcomers with its simple reality. The bare stone walls that rose into sticky blackness. The small, steel cells, one after another, each one interlaced with string for drying wet towels, underwear, and uniform blouses. A smell permeated the block—an institutional smell, old and irretrievably unclean—as though vomit had perpetually just been wiped up somewhere nearby. Plus the smells and sounds of the women themselves, the sudden blasts of argument, the hawking up of phlegm, the moronic giggles and beany toots. A choir hardly made up for it all. On that first day, having exhausted herself from hours of desperate babbling to the police and the state's attorney and reporters—confessing volubly, endlessly, reenacting her crime over and over—Beulah barely moved for hours. She took no food and confessed no more, just cried alone in her cell, softly but monotonously, like

a faucet that wouldn't quite turn off. At one point Sabella Nitti, an immigrant woman convicted of killing her husband with a six-pound hammer,
stopped in front of the cell and stared in at the weeping young woman.
There was not a great deal of sympathy in Sabella's old, worn face. "The
writer who visits these prisoners week after week noticed a faint atmosphere of resentfulness when pretty Beulah Annan recently was added
to the group," one reporter wrote soon after Beulah arrived on April 4.
"The others thought of the effect her beauty might have on the jury which
tried her."

It was a legitimate grudge. Only men made up the jury pool in Illinois,
and when it came to judging women, it seemed men only truly cared about
one thing: beauty. And Beulah was a vision. She knew it, too. At every
opportunity she posed for the news photographers. She would rub her
lips into a respectable frown, pull her shoulders in and down to highlight
her fragile frame. The image proved irresistible: the thin straight nose;
the high cheekbones, so high and sharp they seemed to force her eyes
wide open; the gorgeous red hair that rolled off her head like a prairie fire.
Once Beulah's wistful gaze began staring out at newspaper readers, fan
mail arrived by the bucketful, along with flowers and even a steak dinner.
Odds were, she wouldn't be convicted. The pretty ones never were—not
once in Cook County's history. Maybe that was why Beulah didn't make
a run for it. She'd just washed the blood off her hands and waited for the
authorities to show up.

"Sorry? Who wouldn't be?" Beulah liked to say when asked how she felt
about killing her boyfriend, shot squarely in the back. "But what is there
to do? We can all be sorry after it's done. If only we could go back. If only
we could! It's so little we get out of cheating. But the pleasure looks big, for
the moment, doesn't it?"

≈≈≈

The singing in the rec room went on without Beulah every day, but it barely
got started on this Thursday afternoon before petering out. Everyone's
thoughts were elsewhere. The hymns would have to wait. The inmates,

instead of singing, started to debate, laying out the possible fates for beautiful Wanda Elaine Stopa, the next girl to join Murderess Row. Assuming the police ever found her. The cops had no idea where she was. This morning she had shot her boyfriend, or maybe she shot his wife, and then she disappeared. The whole cellblock seemed to be leaning forward, expectant. When the evening papers arrived in a couple of hours, the inmates would find out what had happened. They'd get to see pictures of this girl the entire city was talking about.

Beulah couldn't bear it. She sat in her cell in a pique. Ever since she'd arrived, it had been all about her and Belva. They were the stars of Murderess Row, and Beulah, the pretty one, always took pride of place. Now, suddenly, there was real competition. "Another Chicago girl went gunning today," one newspaper blared across the front page of a special edition, which was blasting through the presses at this very moment. Outside the steel bars of the Cook County Jail, out in the free world, Wanda Stopa was on the run. Beulah wanted her to keep on running—far, far away.

Part I

❧

A MAD ECSTASY

Beulah Annan, unselfconscious at the
Hyde Park police station despite wearing little more than a slip,
provides a killer look for the camera.

1

A Grand Object Lesson

Out in the hallway, young men stood in a haphazard line, trying to look eager and nonchalant at the same time. They were regulars outside the *Chicago Tribune* newsroom, waiting around each day, hoping a big story would break so that they might get a fill-in assignment, a chance to prove themselves. They usually waited for hours and then went home disappointed. Maurine Watkins stepped past them, quiet as a breath. She kept her head down in modesty, obscuring her face in an explosion of dark locks. No one seemed to notice her. Wearing a long, loose-fitting dress, she didn't look like the fashion-conscious young women who typically came through the building seeking positions. She looked like a country girl. She walked into the room; the men stayed in the hall.

It was the first day of February 1924, and Maurine had come to the local room, the *Tribune*'s main newsroom, for an appointment. Nerves played havoc with her vocal cords as she stood before the reception desk, but that was to be expected. She'd never tried for a job like this one before. Her parents, her teachers and friends back home, could hardly imagine why she would want it.

Maurine, after all, wasn't applying to be a switchboard operator, the position most frequently sought by women coming to the *Tribune*. The company had fifteen operators who handled some twelve thousand calls a day, a volume that took them to the edge of exhaustion every shift. She also wasn't hoping to sell want ads. This was another job considered suited to women, because the ad taker, like the switchboard operator, had to be helpful and considerate. The *Tribune* received hundreds of want-ad orders each day, continuous evidence of the paper's absolute dominance in the Middle West's largest advertising market. Ads could be placed not just at the *Tribune*'s two downtown buildings but also in many groceries and drugstores in the city. And anyone in the metropolitan area with telephone access could reach the paper's classified desk by calling Central 100. Keeping track of all of this advertising activity was a mammoth undertaking. Each want-ad order, before being filled, had to be checked against the advertiser files in the Auditing Division to make sure the customer had no outstanding payments, another task handled by women. They spent all day, every day, flipping through huge audit books, which were anchored to the tops of desks by steel poles, allowing the pages to revolve for easy searching.

These were all good jobs for a respectable young single woman, jobs important to the welfare of one of the preeminent companies in a city that boasted of dozens of nationally important enterprises. But Maurine, at twenty-seven years of age, was here for something different. She wanted to be a reporter. A police reporter, no less, something only one woman at the paper—the formidable Miss Genevieve Forbes—could claim as part of her beat. Maurine didn't know how difficult it was to achieve what she wanted—the men out in the hall would have done anything just for an editorial-assistant position—but now, standing inside the doorway, she shrank at the sight of the reporters' den laid out in front of her. This was hardly like the newspaper they had back in Crawfordsville, the small town in west-central Indiana where she grew up. The *Tribune* claimed to be the World's Greatest Newspaper, and now Maurine saw why.

The Tribune Plant Building, inside and out, always impressed first-time visitors, even if it wasn't quite in the heart of Chicago's roaring downtown. Its six stories rose up at Austin Avenue and St. Clair Street, with its loading docks now barricaded from Michigan Avenue by a construction site. Railroad tracks ran along the building's south side for easy distribution of bulk materials. Wagons rumbled out of its eastern cargo bays. The Plant stood at the southern terminus of a mile-long stretch of industrial and warehouse buildings that began in Little Hell, the Italian slum. South of the Plant, across the Chicago River in the "Loop," was where the real action could be found. That was where the Board of Trade went full tilt every weekday. That was where Marshall Field, so wealthy he could give a million dollars to endow the Columbian Museum of Chicago, operated his grand department store. Just a few miles farther south, in the Stockyards, the Armours and Swifts bought, prepared, and packed meat for the entire nation. Even farther south was the Pullman Company and its celebrated model town, now incorporated into the city. The *Tribune*'s board, however, believed in the North Side's future. The new Wrigley Building sat directly across the street from the Tribune Plant, proof that the four-year-old Michigan Avenue Bridge had become the natural spillover point for the increasingly crowded Loop. In fact, the Plant Building, which opened for business on December 12, 1920, was only the beginning for the Tribune Company. In front of it, facing Michigan Avenue, stood the skeleton of a thirty-six-story tower, what the company insisted would be "the world's most beautiful office building."

The Plant Building may have been only a temporary corporate headquarters, destined ultimately to be the haunches of the "Tribune Monument," but it nevertheless had been built to make an impression. In 1924, most people still did business in person, and that meant management wanted customers to walk away from an encounter with the *Chicago Tribune* with the certainty that great things happened there. Each of the half dozen viciously competitive daily newspapers in the city endeavored to ensure, by sheer physical impressiveness, that every citizen who walked into its building would want to be a part of the enterprise, if only as a reader. The young writer Theodore Dreiser, seeking employment at a Chicago newspaper before the turn of the century, was poleaxed by the sumptuousness on display in the lobbies:

> Most of them—the great ones—were ornate, floreate, with onyx or chalcedony wall trimming, flambeaus of bronze or copper on the walls, lights in imitation of mother-of-pearl in the ceilings—in short, all the gorgeousness of the Sultan's court brought to the outer counters where people subscribed or paid for advertisements.

Dreiser, given to flights of fancy, imagined that beyond those royal lobbies were veritable "wonderlands in which all concerned were prosperous and happy." He thought reporters the equivalent of "ambassadors and prominent men generally. Their lives were laid among great people—the rich, the famous, the powerful—and because of their position and facility of expression and mental force they were received everywhere as equals." If he could only secure a position at a newspaper, he was certain he would be happy for the rest of his days.

Maurine wasn't so naive as that, but she nevertheless expected something memorable—and she wasn't disappointed. The *Tribune*'s local room hummed and trembled like a train car. All the best men worked here: the managing editor and city editor, the police, county building and political reporters, the rewrite battery and senior copyreaders. Urgency and efficiency dominated. Pneumatic tubes popped with incoming reports from the City News Bureau and with outgoing ad copy to the Old Tribune Building in the Loop. Nine steam tables, weighing more than seven tons each, hissed violently from the next room, as if some terrible sea creature were being tamed in a cage. Basket conveyors rolled between the local room and the composing room a floor below, metal crossties for the pulleys squealing. Fifty-five Linotype machines, in double and triple rows next to the composing room, could be heard clacking away like cast-iron crickets, a sound so relentless it invaded dreams.

And everywhere—literally, everywhere—men. Maurine had never seen so many men in one place. They barked into telephones, leaped up, slammed hats on their heads, and strode from the room. They whooped and hollered and smoked cigarettes. They used foul language. The managing editor sat in the middle of the maelstrom and gave orders, without ever raising his voice. He had no reason to yell: The reporters, editors, and copyreaders feared and admired him. Edward "Teddy" Beck was a Kansan by upbringing but a Victorian gentleman by temperament, which meant he knew that such a manly shambles as a newsroom should be off-limits to delicate womanhood.

It wasn't Beck, though, whom Maurine had to convince. She had written a letter to the city editor, Robert M. Lee, a smart and challenging letter, and he had responded that she should call on him at the paper. Not that she could expect Lee to be an easy sell either, especially once he got a look at her. Most of the women who wanted to work at newspapers were tough girls, with the necessary "large and commanding" physical presence to match their attitudes. Maurine, on the other hand, was tiny—barely over five feet tall. She was also beautiful, with iridescent blue-gray eyes in a face as round and sweet as a baby's. Still more set her apart. All the girls today wore their hair bobbed in mock-boy style—"cropheads," Virginia Woolf derisively called them—but not Maurine. Her hair billowed off her forehead in confused revolt, twisting and spinning until corralled into a mangled cloud in the back. The fashionable girls also wore short skirts that showed off their calves, and thin blouses that fell directly on the skin. Maurine dressed only in conservative outfits. And if all of that wasn't strange enough, there was something else, something that made her especially unsuited to the position she sought. Her shyness was palpable.

No, she had never been a reporter before, she admitted, sitting across from the city editor. She barely got the words out.

"Had any newspaper experience at all?" Lee asked.

"No."

"Know anything about journalism?"

"I took it in college."

Lee looked the young woman over, trying to get a bead on her. The appraisal unnerved Maurine. She forced her hands to stay in her lap, took a deep breath. Lee tried another tack: He asked her why she thought she could make it as a police reporter at a professional paper, specifically at one of the country's most admired and aggressive papers. Maurine's mouth ticked open, but no words came out. She was too frightened to answer. Lee's gaze remained impassive, and Maurine realized she had made a terrible mistake by coming. This was a serious operation, employing trained and dedicated staff. A *Tribune* reporter had famously tracked the absconding banker Paul Stensland to Africa and brought him back for trial. Finley Peter Dunne, whose Mr. Dooley sketches had been a favorite of President Roosevelt's, had worked for the *Tribune*. Ring Lardner was a *Tribune* man. The dashing Floyd Gibbons lost an eye covering the World War for the

Tribune. Who was she, Maurine Watkins of Crawfordsville, Indiana, to think she could be a reporter here? She stood up and tried to get an apology unstuck from her throat.

Lee stood, too, and insisted that she sit back down. He knew how to treat a lady. He wouldn't have her running off to the toilet in tears. Maurine crouched on the edge of her seat. The editor sat and looked her over again. She was so small. Her body had a sullen prepubescence about it, as though it had been stunted by cigarettes or some dread childhood disease. It was thrilling.

"I don't believe you'll like newspaper work," he said.

Maurine nodded. "I don't believe I will."

They understood each other, then. Lee told her she was hired. Fifty dollars a week; she could start the next day, Saturday. He rose again and showed her out.

Maurine must have left the building in a daze. She surely knew it never happened like this. Just getting to interview for a reporter position in Chicago was an impressive feat. The typical job seeker, standing around in the hall day after day for an editor who never came out, "began to feel that the newspaper world must be controlled by a secret cult or order." The *Tribune*, the biggest, most successful paper of all, was the toughest place to secure a slot, especially for women who wanted to be in the newsroom. Unlike William Randolph Hearst's rags, the *Tribune* didn't run sob stories. It didn't play to its women readers' innate decency with sentimental tales of woe. That was what Maurine liked about it: It was "a real hanging paper—out for conviction always." The *Tribune*'s crime reporters had to be fearless and hard-hearted. They had to have all the skills of the police detectives they were trying to stay a step ahead of. (Indeed, reporters often impersonated officers to get witnesses to talk.) Most police reporters were hired from the City News Bureau, which handled routine crime news for all of the local papers, or from the suburban dailies. Or they first proved themselves as picture chasers, which sometimes involved breaking into the homes of murder victims and grabbing family portraits off walls. Young Miss Watkins, so angelic-looking and proper, could hardly be expected to do such a thing.

In fact, that was what her new editor was counting on. Reporters had to be tough. Sometimes they had to shake information out of sources. It was necessary, but it also made people distrust and fear newspapermen. Robert Lee sensed that Maurine Watkins could crack the nut a different way. He bet that thieves and prostitutes and police sergeants would be drawn to this lovely, petite woman, to her small-town manners and "soft, blurred speech," and would confide in her without truly realizing they were talking to a reporter. Who would expect such an attractive young lady to be a police hack? That wasn't what newspaperwomen did. Almost all of the women to be found in newsrooms "languish over the society column of the daily newspaper," pointed out *New York Times* reporter Anne McCormick. "They give advice to the lovelorn. They edit household departments. Clubs, cooking and clothes are recognized as subjects particularly fitting to their intelligence."

Clubs, cooking, and clothes. Those were women's spheres—no one would argue that. But, as with most things, Chicago was different. In the nation's second city, more and more women were showing up in the dock for murder and other violent crimes. These were the subjects Maurine would be writing about. Male reporters often took offense when assigned to a "girl bandit" or husband-killer story, but somebody had to cover the female-crime phenomenon. The number of killings committed by women had jumped 400 percent in just forty years, now making up fully 10 percent of the total. This was a significant cause for concern to many newspaper readers. It suggested that something about Chicago was destroying the feminine temperament. Violence, after all, was an unnatural act for a woman. A normal woman couldn't decide to commit murder or plot a killing. This was why, argued an Illinois state's attorney, when one did abandon the norm, "she sinks lower and goes further in brutality and cruelty than the other sex." The violent woman was by definition mentally diseased, irreparably defective.

That was one theory, anyway. Another, far more popular one held that men, more brutal than ever in this terrible modern age, pushed them into it. William Randolph Hearst embraced this position. In the pages of his two Chicago newspapers, the *Herald and Examiner* and the *American*, women didn't kill out of anger or greed or insanity. They were overwhelmed by alcohol or by feminine emotions, or both, and so were not responsible. Even the fallen woman was, at heart, good and could be saved. Hearst hired "sob sisters" like Patricia Dougherty (who wrote under the pseudonym Princess Pat) and Sonia Lee to warn girls to keep out of trouble. "It's a grand object lesson in steering clear of life, my job is," Hearst reporter Mildred Gilman would lament in her autobiographical novel, *Sob Sister*. Perhaps so, but it made for heart-tugging journalism. Who could forget Cora Orthwein crying out to the police after killing her cheating sweetheart back in 1921? "I shot him," she wailed. "I loved him and I killed him. It was all I could do." The sob sisters at the *Herald and Examiner* described Cora's sorrow-filled beauty and pointed out how, during her exclusive interview with the paper, she unconsciously "touched a scar on her lip" caused by her late boyfriend's fist. "I never drank as much as I have, lately," she said. "He kept wanting me to drink. Friends argued with him not to keep piling the liquor into me." As was widely expected, it worked out for her in the end. The *Tribune* noted before she went on trial that "Cook County juries have been regardful of women defendants" for years, especially when there was any hint of physical or emotional abuse by a man. Less than an hour after closing arguments, Cora Orthwein was acquitted.

◦◦◦

Maurine wasn't supposed to be interested in such depraved women. She wasn't a girl from the neighborhood, like Ginny Forbes. She had been raised by doting, respectable parents in a quiet town, far from the big city. Her father, George Wilson Watkins, Crawfordsville's minister, had sent his only child to Transylvania University in Lexington, Kentucky, a school affiliated with their Disciples of Christ faith, to study Greek and the Latin poets.* The Reverend Watkins wanted to keep his daughter in a religious, cultur-ally conservative environment, as well as cultivate her Southern roots. She had been born in Louisville, about seventy-five miles from Lexington, at her grandmother's house.

---

*Ninety years before Maurine, Jefferson Davis studied the same texts in the same classrooms.

For years Maurine thought she wanted the same things for herself that her father did. She had been a dedicated, obedient student throughout her life, with a particular facility for languages and a deep devotion to the study of the Bible. From a young age she envisioned a quiet life of academic and religious accomplishment. She had headed back north after her junior year, to be closer to home, and in 1919 graduated first in her class from Butler University in Indianapolis.

That fall Maurine moved to Cambridge, Massachusetts, to do graduate work in the classics at Radcliffe College. Greek, the language of the New Testament, would be her focus. "If more people knew the Greek, they wouldn't misinterpret the Bible," she told her cousin, Dorotha Watkins. Maurine intended to get an advanced degree at the well-regarded women's college and then move to Greece to commit herself to research work. But it took only a matter of days in Cambridge before the plan's foundation cracked and started to crumble. Walking to and from classes on Radcliffe's verdant campus, she "began looking at some of the people who had their Ph.D.s and decided I wasn't as keen about it as I had imagined." Her course work barely under way, she had a sinking feeling that she'd committed herself to the wrong path.

The spark for this abrupt change in attitude came from one simple administrative action: her acceptance into George Pierce Baker's prestigious playwriting workshop. Baker, a professor in the English department at Harvard University, was Eugene O'Neill's mentor and the best-known drama teacher in the country. Maurine had held out little hope of acceptance when she applied for the workshop. She dared not dream of a life as a writer. During her high school years and into college, she enjoyed writing short stories and plays, but the activity's most powerful draw was simply that it was something she could do alone. Maurine had always felt easily overwhelmed in social situations. Her shyness sometimes physically paralyzed her. Even now, in her twenties, she was happiest when holed up in her room at her parents' house, lost in thought, writing down high-minded stories about morality and personal responsibility in perfect, looping script. Most of the stories went directly into a drawer, never to be read by anyone. When she found out she was one of Baker's chosen few, however, she viewed it as a sign—a belated turning point in her life. Baker brought her into a workshop where some of the students had already had plays professionally produced, and all of them had dedicated themselves to serious writing.

George Pierce Baker's passion for the theater, for its power and social purpose, thrilled her. Through dramatic interpretation, Baker said, writers made the world better. Nothing could have focused Maurine's interest more. It spoke to her evangelizing background. Living on the East Coast for the first time, she found herself wondering, "What on earth has happened to religion!" The country had become godless and corrupt. She was convinced "the only thing that will cure the present condition is a real application of Christianity." Suddenly her quiet writing avocation, for years a sideline to her academic pursuits, seemed not just a legitimate ambition, but an urgent one. Art was an obligation, Baker told her. The fifty-four-year-old professor warned his students against bogging down in academic theories. He advocated finding out about "your great, bustling, crowded American life of the present day."

Maurine took this as a literal call to action. Baker was encouraging her to get out of her own head, to experience life, but for Maurine, her professor's exhortations also acted as a spur to engage evil—the real thing, out in the real world. It was a relief finally to be given permission to do what she'd always felt called to do. Baker likely suggested newspaper work. He believed it was excellent training for a serious writer. (His prize student, O'Neill, had worked as a reporter.) Once that seed had been planted, Maurine knew where she had to go. Chicago was Bedlam: debauched, violent, unimaginable—and full of exciting opportunities. It was a city, Theodore Dreiser wrote in his 1923 memoir, *A Book About Myself,* "which had no traditions but which was making them, and this was the very thing which everyone seemed to understand and rejoice in. Chicago was like no other city in the world—so said they all."

So Maurine went to Chicago. She withdrew from her classics program, packed up her small wardrobe, and left, just like that. Scared but determined to overcome her fears, she arrived in her new city knowing not a soul, a true missionary for God and for art. She picked out an apartment to rent on the North Side, across the street from St. Chrysostom's Episcopal Church on North Dearborn. It wasn't her church, but the proximity to a holy place surely eased her anxiety at settling in such a large, dangerous city. St. Chrysostom's was a gem, with its stone courtyard, its low-slung Gothic cathedral, and its triangular stained-glass windows. Lying in bed on the morning of her first day as a police reporter, listening to the bell clang with sonorous vitality from the top of the church's tower, Maurine could have been back in Crawfordsville, her mother a moment from bursting through the door to roust her in excited anticipation of the day's sermon. Except now Maurine knew that when she sat in church on Sunday, she wouldn't be a passive receptacle. She would be an avenging angel. Or she could be, if given the chance by her editors. She needed a murder—one good murder.

"Being a conscientious person, I never prayed for a murder," she later said. "But I hoped that if there was one I'd be assigned to it."

She wouldn't have to hope for long. This was Chicago.

2

The Variable Feminine Mechanism

In the first hour of Wednesday, March 12, a new Nash sedan rumbled down Cottage Grove Avenue on Chicago's South Side. It was the only car on the road. Belva Gaertner slouched low in the passenger seat and pulled her knees up toward the glove box. She wanted Walter Law to have a glimpse of her calves. Belva was thirty-eight years old, nearly ten years older than Walter, and twice a divorcée, but she still had beautiful legs. She would allow Walter to reach out and massage them. In fact, she would allow him to do anything he wanted to do. But he didn't stroke her leg. Instead, he gripped the steering wheel and refused to look at her.

The headlights blurred into blackness as the car hurtled through the night. They could have been anywhere. Not just anywhere in the city, but anywhere in the world. They swung onto Forrestville Avenue, the sedan shaking as if being turned by a can opener. This was the Grand Boulevard neighborhood sleeping around them. The men and women here had to get up in just a couple of hours; many of them worked in the Stockyards. But the neighborhood was far enough east—past Back of the Yards, Canaryville, and Gage Park—that these people had dreams. You couldn't smell the slaughterhouses out here, at least not all the time. The car stopped at the curb, the engine heaving. Walter heaved, too. He and Belva were both drunk, lost in a thick fog. Belva should have known better. The bootlegger had been out of pints by the time they got to him, at midnight; he only had the larger bottles, the quarts. They'd already been drinking for hours, but they bought a bottle anyway.

Walter still wouldn't look at her, though she begged him to. Later, she realized the quart might have been a bad batch, cut too heavily with fusel oil and coal tar dyes. Walter couldn't hold his liquor very well, but this bottle hit him harder than usual. Belva got out of the car in a mood, slamming the door and stomping away. But she came back; she always came back. She climbed into the machine and leaned over the gearbox. She wanted to make up. Walter still didn't. Booze—and Belva—made him crazy, suspicious. The orchestra had been playing "The One I Love Belongs to Somebody Else" when they left the Gingham Inn, and Walter was especially susceptible to suggestion. He finally turned to her. He told her she had to mind herself better when they went out. Belva didn't like the sound of that. She pulled out her pistol.

"I bet I'm a better shooter than you are," she said.

Walter laughed at her, slapping his hand on the steering wheel. He told her that of course *he* was the better shot. He may be an automobile salesman—he'd sold her this sedan—but he knew how to handle a gun. Belva's mind focused as he was laughing. Walter didn't know that she carried the gun with her everywhere. Sometimes she'd sit with it at her vanity in the morning. She'd grip the handle, stretching out her long fingers to manage its weight and then extending her arm and squinting, taking aim. But she never went to a shooting range to practice. She knew it didn't matter how good a shot she was—or how good a shot Walter was. You couldn't compete with the gangs. They were on the front page of the newspaper every day. They roamed the streets like madmen. Nothing scared them—not even the police. Especially not the police. That was a good reason, she thought, for the two of them to go up to her room.

"Think of it," she told Walter. "What if some bandit stopped and robbed us and maybe tried to get rough with me, what would we do?"

∽≈∾

More than an hour later, Belva still didn't have an answer to that question. She sat naked on a couch in her apartment, thinking about it. She stared at the blood-soaked clothes steaming on the floor in front of her. Her coat, dress, shoes, and hat were laid out as if she couldn't decide what to wear. The caracul coat bothered her the most.

Belva stood up and began to pace. A coat like that sold for a couple of grand at the fine downtown stores. Belva fired up a cigarette and paced some more. She didn't know how this could have happened. She had gotten drunk early in the day, before Walter had called on her. Just pleasantly buzzed, as usual, the kind of tingling warmth that held you like a new mother. Usually that worked in her favor. No one took her too seriously when she was sloshed. Being passed out at her flat or at the Gingham Inn meant she couldn't get in trouble. Usually.

There was a knock on the door. Belva looked toward the back of the apartment. Her mother stayed in her bedroom. Belva had never been able to count on her mother, not once in her whole life, so she didn't expect tonight to be any different. She managed to stay hopeful as she put on a robe. Maybe William had come to check on her. That was possible. Her ex-husband would have been waiting for her to telephone. She called him every night when she got home; it was their ritual. He'd certainly be worried by now. William didn't go out to the cabarets anymore. Their last couple of years of marriage, she couldn't get him to go anywhere. But now he wanted her back. He bought her expensive clothes and diamonds. He'd just bought her that Nash sedan. All so she'd come back.

Belva couldn't decide if she should marry him again. A lot had changed since their divorce. William was more successful than ever: He had just won the Franklin Institute Gold Medal for designing a serum-injection system that made blood transfusions safer. But he was an old man now. Soon he would be sixty, and he looked a decade older. It wasn't difficult to picture him being carried off on a stretcher, never to return. Of course, a lot had changed for her, too. She sometimes felt like she was sixty. She hated looking in the mirror in the morning, watching gravity slowly taking her away, back to the earth.

Belva opened the door and found two policemen staring at her. They stepped inside at her invitation, but they didn't know where to stand. The room was stuffed to the gunwales. Belva had gotten most of the furniture in the divorce, so the little apartment was stacked with couches and chairs, dressers and tables and love seats. She always had somewhere to sit. The policemen checked the place out; they checked *her* out, the large diamond rings on her fingers, the watch on her wrist that was set with precious stones. Belva realized the watch face was shattered and the time had stopped at 1:15.

The policemen asked her if she had a gun. Yes, she said. She always carried a gun. She added that it was a present from her husband—William Gaertner, the scientific-instruments manufacturer. She figured they would know the name. "He gave me that coat, too," she said. She pointed with her toes to the wet heap on the floor: a green velvet dress, a white butterfly hat, a lamb's-wool coat, scuffed-up silver slippers.

The policemen told her they'd found a dead man in her car, an automobile salesman named Walter Law. Belva nodded. They said she'd been seen leaving the car and then returning. They asked if she had gone to her flat to get a gun. She denied it. Then she amended the answer: "I don't know," she said. "I was drunk."

Belva's head had begun to clear by this point. She realized these policemen were real, and that Walter really was dead. The officers took her to the Fiftieth Street station house. They sat her down, offered her a cup of coffee, and began to interview her. She and Mr. Law had spent the evening drinking, she told them. They'd been seeing each other for a couple of months and had developed a sort of routine. His wife didn't seem to mind that he'd go out with another woman a few times a week. Tonight, around midnight, they were saying good-bye when something happened—a gunshot, she didn't know from where. Belva remembered calling out "Walter! Walter!" and receiving no response. Naturally, she was scared. It might have been stick-up men. Walter had fallen against the steering wheel, and Belva tried to move him. Panicked, she fumbled for the door handle, stumbled out of the car, and ran—ran for her life.

Assistant State's Attorney Stanley Klarkowski introduced himself. Belva smiled up at the prosecutor. She appreciated a courteous man. He was also a good-looking man, young and tall. But then Klarkowski began talking, and Belva sighed. More questions.

The assistant state's attorney knew how to get answers out of people. Soon Belva admitted she and "Mr. Law" had been fighting. At the Gingham Inn she'd snuck a dance with another admirer while Walter was away from their table, and she worried he'd seen them. She didn't want another scene like one they'd had a few nights before. "I was frightened," she said. "Last Sunday night when he took me home he wouldn't talk to me all the way home, just sneered and said, 'If I ever see you with anybody else I'll wring your neck.'"

Klarkowski pushed her for specifics about the evening and the shooting, but Belva had nothing more to offer. Her mind was a muddy hole. "Oh, Mr. Attorney," she finally cried out, her eyes wild, "I can't remember anything—not if I have to hang for it."

"Did you shoot Law?" he asked.

Belva chewed at the inside of her cheek, tears dropping from her face like boulders. "I don't see how I could," she said. "I thought so much of him."

⚡⚡⚡

So far, Maurine Watkins felt like a flunky. In her first few weeks at the paper, she had mostly stood around at suburban police stations miles from the action, calling in brief reports on petty burglaries and car crashes. Her name appeared nowhere in the *Tribune*. Bylines were reserved for the top reporters, and you had to land a big story—and successfully milk it for days or weeks—to qualify. After only a few days on the job, Maurine tried to show initiative by jumping into a taxi with Al Jennings, the famed outlaw turned politician.* She got the interview, but nothing came of it in the paper. If she were lucky, she might be assigned an innocuous soft feature about "bobbed wigs" or a theater reopening and see her work manhandled by copyreaders who had an aversion to modifiers or any phrase they could identify as possibly being an original thought. It hardly helped to know that all the cub reporters got the same treatment, including the *Tribune*'s coeditor in chief, Joseph Medill Patterson, back when he was a young hack.

Maurine didn't dare complain. The *Tribune* local room had a faintly militaristic air about it. Robert Lee's predecessor had been a cavalry officer during the Spanish-American War and insisted on being called Captain Stott. The newsroom's majordomo was a profane, hulking, middle-aged

---

*Jennings had been a notorious train robber in the late 1890s. After serving five years in prison, he worked on silent-film Westerns and later ran for governor of Oklahoma.

man-child by the name of Jimmie Durkin, who would answer the phone and then order a reporter to hop to it: "Shake a leg! Take them dogs off that desk and give 'em a workout. You ain't doin' nothin.'" Lee, like the captain before him, wanted only team players on his staff. "The prima donna is one who will not understand that a newspaper is bounded by steel hoops—literally, not just speculatively," the city editor told a group of Northwestern University students, referring to the huge metal molds used to print mass-circulation newspapers. "It is surprising what little elasticity there is in the metal page of type. And yet the prima donna will weep bitter tears, resign, curse the editor and classify him among the most unspeakable of blundering upstarts because the sacred brainchild of the prima donna has been trimmed to fit."

These were just words, the kind of scare-'em-straight words a newspaper editor was expected to drop on impressionable journalism students, but the family-run paper's two editors in chief, Patterson and his cousin, Robert McCormick, strove to have the *Tribune* live up to them. Teamwork, not individual star reporters, would make their newspaper great. For the most part, it was working. By the middle of the century's second decade, the *Tribune* had become the undisputed top dog in the city, having broken the back of the old *Chicago Record-Herald* with want-ad innovations that made the *Tribune*, in its own words, the "world's greatest advertising medium." By the early 1920s, the *Tribune*'s daily circulation topped five hundred thousand. On Sunday, it was well over eight hundred thousand. This was double the newspaper's circulation just a decade before. As a result, William Randolph Hearst's *Herald and Examiner* was now the *Tribune*'s only morning competitor.

McCormick and Patterson were Ivy League boys, grandsons of Joseph Medill, the man who made the *Tribune* a powerful player in the city and state by helping put Abraham Lincoln in the White House. They took their stewardship of the paper seriously. They were determined that it be the best. When the country committed to the World War, for example, the Tribune Company, with a full recognition that it would lose money, launched a Paris-based edition of the newspaper. It debuted, appropriately and not at all coincidentally, on July 4, 1917. Throughout the rest of the war, soldiers at the front often found out what had happened to other units nearby not from the army but from the *Chicago Tribune.*

This kind of ambition impressed readers—and competitors—but it didn't faze Hearst. Rather than trying to match the *Tribune's* depth, he sought to bring his rival down to his level. The country's biggest newspaper baron moved into Chicago in 1900 with the launch of the *Chicago Evening American.* The *American,* soon to be joined by its sister morning paper, fought to gain the workingman's pennies with blatant populism and the kind of sensationalist reporting that had worked so well for its owner in New York. Serious journals called the Hearst style "the new black plague" and an "unholy blot on the fourth estate—bawdy, inane and contemptible." His reporters, the critics said, "mock at privacy and finger in glee all the soiled linen they can discover." A cartoonist labeled Hearst the Wizard of Ooze.

Hearst didn't care. His newspapers served a larger purpose than gaining the favor of the intelligentsia or, for that matter, making money. Twice elected to the House of Representatives from New York, Hearst dreamed of the presidency. A Democrat, he supported the eight-hour day and woman suffrage, and so did his newspapers. His papers also vocally supported him, and he believed he had to have a presence in Chicago to build a serious national political organization. Hearst epitomized the "journalism of action" that seethed in Chicago like nowhere else, New York included. He emphatically was the Wizard of Ooze, but he also crusaded against the powerful and privileged. He dug out government corruption, and when he couldn't find or invent proof, he screamed about it in editorials.

When Hearst entered the Chicago market, the *Tribune,* fearful of yellow journalism's appeal, fought to keep the new papers off the city's newsstands, setting off more than a decade of violence that served as hands-on training for many of the thugs who later became beer runners during Prohibition. The hardball tactics in the circulation war reached their apex one day in 1912 when two of Hearst's men jumped onto a streetcar at Washington and Wells and noticed that not one of the riders was reading a Hearst paper. The bullyboys snapped; they pulled out revolvers and pumped bullets into two men who were reading the *Tribune.* They then killed the conductor.

By the 1920s, however, Hearst was in his seventh decade and had mellowed. Having lost bids for both the New York City mayoralty and the New York governorship, he had come to accept that he would never live in the White House. So instead he turned his attention to building an outrageously grand estate in California and pumping up the Hollywood career of his mistress, actress Marion Davies. This meant his newspapers were more important than ever. He needed cash flow—a lot of it. Politics and the boss's aggrandizement no longer drove the papers' news judgment. Drama did. Now more than ever, to secure their circulation goals, the two Hearst newspapers in Chicago sought to mold news to their liking, which meant the commonplace blown up bigger and better than in any of their competitors.

Fortunately for Hearst, he had thought ahead by luring one of the city's best editors, Walter Howey, from the *Tribune* shortly after coming into Chicago. Howey's charge was, "Beat the *Trib.* That's your only job. Just beat the *Tribune.*" The ambitious editor planned on doing exactly that, by whatever means necessary. "Don't ever fake a story or anything in a story," Howey told one young reporter, summarizing his journalistic credo. "That is, never let me catch you at it."

It was one piece of advice everyone under Howey diligently followed. No one ever got caught at anything, as long as first-rate copy came in. In contrast to the *Tribune*'s culture, the Hearst papers boasted such notoriously out-of-control reporters that their headquarters at Madison and Market, which the *American* and the *Herald and Examiner* shared, was known as the Madhouse on Madison Street, with no hyperbole intended. Editors at the two newspapers worked their reporters fourteen hours a day and told them daily journalism and marriage couldn't coexist. Their crime reporters practically lived at police stations. They bribed officers to sit in on interrogations, and they sometimes took an active part, yelling at suspects, tricking them, threatening violence. Jailers let them into cells, where for hours they would play cards with accused murderers, jotting down quotes between games and phoning them in to rewrite men. The toilet was right there in the cell, and interviews and card games would continue while one of them sat on the can.

Boorish behavior may have been tolerated at the other papers, but the Madhouse enthusiastically encouraged it. Hearst's women police reporters covered only women criminals, and they sat in their own isolated area of the newsroom. This was for their own good, for Howey believed that drinking put men in the best frame of mind to produce superior copy. Everyone drank on the job—the newsroom frequently reeked of vomit. Howey's most memorable physical characteristic was a glass left eye, which supposedly was necessitated after he drank too much during a breaking story, blacked out at his desk, and impaled the orb on a copy spike. Maybe that useless eye was one of the reasons the papers' headline type got so big on the front page—often a whopping six inches high. But that was doubtful. The heads also got consistently racy. Howey trained headline writers to boil down a story to a single shocking phrase. If he didn't find it in the story, the headline writer went to the rewrite man and pressed him: "What do you mean, the man was shot dead in the street? That happens daily. What makes this shooting differ from all others?"

Howey roamed the newsroom, looking over the shoulders of his rewrite men, constantly reminding them that he didn't want a rundown of facts—that was the job of the "leg man" who called in the story. The rewrite specialist at a Hearst paper provided the emotional context, the bang that forced a reader at a newsstand to pick out the *American* or the *Herald and Examiner* instead of the *Tribune, Daily News, Evening Post,* or *Daily Journal.* "Hype this up!" the editor would demand, over and over. "Hype this up!"

≈∞≈

It wasn't easy for the *Tribune* to match the sometimes questionable details that poured daily out of the rewrite bank at the Madhouse on Madison. "A newspaper man need have only a spoonful of brains to dip his journal in blood and wave it before a morbid mob," Robert Lee said defensively, when comparing the *Tribune*'s "steady hand" to the Hearst papers' sensation. But Lee was happy to wave blood around too, if only a little more decorously, and on a Tuesday night in the middle of March, a report came in that wouldn't need to be hyped up to attract the morbid. Maurine Watkins learned that a man had been found shot dead in a car over on Forrestville Avenue. Possible suicide. She set out for the Fiftieth Street police station. It was after one in the morning—more than three hours after deadline for the earliest edition.

In the station's booking room, reporters from the various newspapers waited for more information. No one thought the dead man in the car was a suicide. The new widow, Freda Law, came through, stunned and shuffling, a pretty young thing. Not long after, two officers brought in a middle-aged woman from the back room—the woman who'd been with the dead man. She was wide-eyed drunk, scared into some semblance of clarity. Her hair was twisted into origami; her hands trembled. She'd been crying. Maurine, on the job for only a few weeks, already understood what this was all about. A drunken fight that went too far—you got them every night.

The woman listed in her seat as detectives waited on a cell assignment for her. Maurine hovered, hoping for a chance to get in some questions. There was something about the woman, something that didn't quite fit with an address on the wrong side of Washington Park and a domestic dispute ending in gunshots. The woman stank, but she was wearing beautiful jewelry—huge hunks of diamonds—and she had a way of holding herself that got your attention. None of the founders of the Anti-Saloon League, which had driven the dry movement for twenty years before it took hold, could have foreseen that someone like this, a woman of means and sophistication, would be a victim of their efforts. That was what Prohibition did—it pulled everyone down into the pit.

She and Walter were so drunk, they'd gotten giddy, the woman was telling the policemen minding her. She had been worried about their safety, going home so late. It was very dark out, she said. Even drunk, the woman knew how to tell a story, how to build suspense. She propped her elbows on shaky knees, made eye contact. "On our way to my home we began talking about stick-up men," she said. "I jokingly remarked, 'I'll bet I'm a better shooter than you are.' Mr. Law said I was mistaken. 'I'm a wonderful marksman—I never miss,' he said, laughing out loud and patting me on the shoulder. I suggested, jokingly, that we toss up a coin and that the winner shoot the loser. I said if the winner missed the loser, the latter would get a chance to shoot, and vice versa, until one of us was shot. There were nine bullets in the pistol. And then—oh, I don't know just what did happen. I was too drunk."

A group of reporters had gathered around, as if the woman were a scout leader sitting in front of a crackling fire. In the days ahead, the papers would refer to her as the Flip-Coin Murderess. A veteran officer at the station, a Lieutenant Egan, pressed her to continue, to *try* to remember. "Mr. Law said something about hold-up men . . . said he was afraid of them," the woman insisted. Her nose, too big for her face in the best of circumstances, had been engorged by drink. It looked like a deformity. Her eyes bulged. "I remember seeing him collapse over the wheel, but I had no idea what was the matter," she continued. "I looked at Wallie closer and saw blood streaming down his face. I put up my hand to stop the flow, but I couldn't. 'Walter, Walter,' I called. But he did not move or answer me. Then I tried to pull him out of the driver's seat so I could drive the car home, but I couldn't budge him; he was so limp. His head fell on my arms and that is how my clothing came to be spattered with blood. I became frightened and ran home." Tears had started during the story, and they rolled down the woman's cheeks and hung from her jowls. She sat back. She seemed to cave in on herself in exhaustion, her mottled face sliding into her neck.

It was quite a performance. Reporters were left wondering what to make of it—and what to make of her, this drunken rich woman who carried a pistol. She was a mess, a grotesquerie, but everyone seemed to recognize there was something special about her, something . . . *appealing*. Was she a gangster's mistress? A bit old for that, maybe, but when first brought in she had the same look that all the gangster girls had, the ones who stood around outside the central police station waiting for their men to come out. It was the vacant, bemused look of someone watching a rinky-dink neighborhood parade go by.

Finally somebody recognized her: She was Belle Gaertner, a popular cabaret dancer before the war. She'd left the stage to marry William Gaertner, one of the country's leading manufacturers of scientific instruments. There'd been a scandalous divorce—Mrs. Gaertner had been caught committing adultery. That was all before Maurine's time, but the young reporter liked what she was hearing. She had a big story.

৯৫৯

Maurine had page-one material, there was no doubt about it. But there was a problem. "Girl reporters"—that was what everyone called women hacks—almost never made it to the front page. The biggest, most challenging assignments went to the best reporters, and that meant men. A girl reporter simply couldn't be counted on—even many women in the newsroom believed that. "On the big story her vision is apt to be [too] close and her factual grasp inadequate," insisted *New York Herald Tribune* reporter Ishbel Ross. Editors demanded "complete reliability" on breaking news, Ross noted. "They can't depend on the variable feminine mechanism."

Women on newspaper staffs who wanted to knock down such notions rarely got the opportunity. Despite the dramatic rise in "gun girls" and women bandits in Chicago, some of the city's newspapers still wouldn't send girl reporters out on nighttime assignments. "I would rather see my daughter starve than that she should ever have heard or seen what the women on my staff have been compelled to hear and see," exclaimed one editor. Other outfits—like the Hearst papers—employed only sob sisters, who were allowed out after dark but whose charge was to write heartbreaking stories of personal tragedy, no matter what the circumstances.

The *Tribune*, at least, wanted a true "feminine perspective" on women criminals. It sought strong, unsentimental women who could write crime stories "with a high moral tone." To no one's surprise, the paper had had limited success so far. One of its first hires was a young woman not long out of the University of Chicago. On her first assignment, Fanny Butcher interviewed a woman whose son had attempted to kill her. The fledgling reporter was so shaken by the events the woman described that she barely made it back to the local room without collapsing. Next, Butcher spent a week in the morals court, watching as men and women were arraigned on prostitution and related charges. She had to listen, she said, "to the intimate details of sexual intercourse, abnormal as well as normal, of amounts paid and demanded as refund by dissatisfied customers, of friskings during lovemaking, and of young girls hounded by procurers. I went home every night and promptly lost whatever dinner I had been able to get down (I weighed ninety-eight pounds when it was over)." Butcher wasn't able to take it, just as the *Tribune*'s managing editor, Teddy Beck, had foreseen. He sent her to women's features to save her from having to write any more "tales of depravity."

Maurine was certainly aware of the widespread doubts about her gender's ability to cut it under pressure, but she didn't have time to worry about perceptions. Knowing that a replate would be necessary for a final street edition, she began to write as soon as she had the bare-bones facts. She was so rushed that she didn't even get all of those facts right. She called Belva by her popular nickname, her old stage name, and misspelled her first husband's surname. She called the dead man Robert, instead of Walter. She misnamed the café where Belva and Walter had sat drinking. Nevertheless, she had a feel for the story. She knew it was leading somewhere good. She wrote:

> Mrs. Belle Brown Overbeck Gaertner, a handsome divorcee of numerous experiences with divorce publicity, was arrested at an early hour this morning after the police had found the dead body of Robert Law, an automobile salesman, in her automobile.
>
> Law had been shot through the head. His body was found slumped down at the steering wheel of Mrs. Gaertner's Nash sedan, a short distance from the entrance to Mrs. Gaertner's home, 4809 Forrestville avenue. On the floor of the automobile was found an automatic pistol from which three shots had been fired, and a bottle of gin. . . .
>
> From the license number of the automobile Mrs. Gaertner's name and address were found. The police went to her apartment at 4809 Forrestville avenue and found Mrs. Gaertner hysterically pacing the floor. She readily admitted she had been with Law, but steadfastly denied she knew anything of the manner of his death. . . . She finally admitted the gun was hers, saying she always carried it, because of her fear of robbers. When pressed concerning the actual shooting, she answered all queries with:
>
> "I don't know, I was drunk."

Maurine, probably nervous about how her first big story would be received by the copyreaders, reined in her personality, sticking to the facts at hand. There was nothing special about the finished product, nothing like what the *Herald and Examiner* would surely come up with, though Maurine did linger on the infidelity that caused Belva's divorce back in 1920. The story had the feel of being rushed. Considering the late hour when Belva arrived at the police station, it's possible Maurine called the story in, with a copyboy running to the "morgue," the paper's archives, to pull information on Belva's divorce for her. But the young reporter knew she'd done a competent job. It was a start. The typewritten pages, pounded out by her or a rewrite man, were sent down to the composing room in a basket. The story had been designated for a page-one position in place of another item already on the presses; once the story was ready, the remade pages would be cast, the presses shut down, the new plates inserted and the presses sent flying again, all within minutes. All Maurine could do now was wait. In the composing room, a copyboy took the pages over to the copy cutter's desk. The cutter sliced the story into sections for the copyreaders and marked each "take" with a number to keep it in order. Everybody worked quickly, and soon the Linotype operator began to knock away at his keyboard, transferring Maurine's words into hot type.

The *Tribune* was a massive operation, a city institution, and any reporter was just one very small part of it. This fact was represented perfectly by the Linotype, which differentiated not a whit between sports or crime, star columnist or suburban reporter. The machine operator read every word of every story that was dropped onto his holding plate, but he didn't comprehend any of it—there wasn't time. He simply shoveled it into the mechanical maw.

The Linotype, or line-casting, machine was part typewriter, part foundry. The machine had revolutionized newspaper publishing late in the previous century, allowing a small team to swiftly set page after page of metal type, resulting in casts that could be used on multiple presses at the same time. With this innovation, along with the electric-powered rotary press, newspapers suddenly could be far more than a handful of pages each day. They could cover the whole world, with as many pages per edition and copies every day as readers and advertisers made economically feasible. The *Tribune*'s maximum capacity for a forty-page edition was well over one million copies. Yet there was nothing glamorous about the technological triumph that made this possible. An operator sat before a ninety-character keyboard, the rest of the Linotype machine rearing up before him at close range, making him look like a disobedient child being forced to face the wall. A pot of molten metal was attached to the back of the machine, providing the source material for the lines typed out by the operator. The Linotype was, quite simply, a large, dangerous beast, with various safety mechanisms built in to keep the 550-degree liquid metal from spraying through gaps between the letter molds. As the operator typed, little mechanical arms swung just above eye level, releasing matrices—small pieces of metal—on which letters were stamped and then arranged into completed lines of hot type, spitting them out one by one with a satisfying *tick-tick-tick* and then distributing the letter molds back to their magazines for the next line. On the fourth floor of the Tribune Plant Building, dozens of these machines stood side-by-side, clicking and humming in unison as deadline approached, the operators one with their Linotypes.

Maurine's story may have been treated just as dispassionately by the Linotype operator as every other item going into the paper, but Maurine recognized that hers—and similar stories about Belva "Belle" Gaertner in the city's other newspapers—was going to make a greater impact than anything else on the page. Every Chicago reporter knew that a gun-toting girl was a guaranteed public obsession, an instant celebrity, at least for a few days. Newspaper readers couldn't get enough of them. The really interesting or beautiful girl gunners could spike circulation for weeks. Maurine was sure that Belva was a really interesting one. These initial tidbits laid out before readers undoubtedly would only pique interest; all of Chicago's sob sisters and girl reporters were going to be after the story for days and perhaps weeks—right up until Belva Gaertner stood before a jury to hear her fate, if it came to that.

The thrill of it, the anticipation, gripped Maurine. Excited by making it onto page one, she now wanted to lead the way on the story. She wanted to best the sensationalist Hearst operation without faking anything. Maurine had pored over the *Herald and Examiner* and the *American* for weeks; she understood them and their readers. The Hearst papers knew how to do melodrama. Every crime story was instantly recognizable: the plot, the characters, the narrative arc and moral code. Tragedy was glamorized, ordinary individuals romanticized. Those ordinary individuals had to be remade into dramatic caricatures and easily identified by consistent phrases: Katherine Malm, whose trial in February had made all of the front pages, wasn't a snuffling ex-waitress who'd fallen in with the wrong crowd. She was the "Two-Gat Girl"—the "Wolf Woman." Likewise, one of Malm's cellmates, Sabella Nitti, wasn't a terrified illiterate immigrant who didn't understand what was happening to her. She was "Senora Sabelle, alleged husband-killer." Maurine had studied drama under George Pierce Baker. She got it. Life would be so much better, so much more *alive*, if it could be stripped down to its essentials, like in a play.

Maurine ended her first page-one story with a tantalizing question posed by Belva's ex-husband, William—one that suggested there was much yet to be written about this woman.

> Mr. Gaertner said last night at his home, 5227 Kimbark avenue, that he knew Mrs. Gaertner's whereabouts and that he had seen her occasionally in the three years since their divorce. "What has happened to her now?" he inquired.

Set in type, it sounded like an accusation, a weary, dismissive retort by a bitter ex-mate. That was undoubtedly how Maurine meant it to sound. She knew she could create a page-one serial on "Belle Brown Overbeck Gaertner," the wild former cabaret performer who'd wrecked a marriage to a wealthy man and now found herself in a much worse stew. But that wasn't how William Gaertner had meant the question. He was a scared old man, woken in the middle of the night by a reporter. He wanted to know what had happened to his incident-prone ex-wife, who also happened to be the love of his life.

Maurine didn't have a good answer for him. The last she had seen of her,

Belva Gaertner was headed to a jail cell. "Call William," Belva had pleaded to an officer. "William will know what to do."

William Gaertner would have been surprised to hear his former wife say such a thing. When it came to Belva, he never knew what to do. Throughout their marriage, it seemed that nobody, and nothing, could make her happy. But William would keep trying. After the reporter disengaged the line, he hung up the phone, dressed, and headed down to the police station.

3

❧❧❧

One-Gun Duel

The horses had almost made the marriage worthwhile for Belva. William maintained his own stables, which rivaled even those of the city's most exclusive riding clubs. Belva, like William, loved to ride, and she did so effortlessly, moving her body to match her horse's stride, a simple clench of her thighs goading the steed into a trot, another and she was racing across Washington Park's expansive South Open Green. One observer noted that the "suppleness and litheness acquired in the dance added to her grace in the saddle," a conclusion seconded by her husband. William gave her a present during their courtship, a handmade horsewhip with a fitted grip perfect for her long fingers. On almost every day of her marriage, she moseyed across Sixty-first Street on one of William's black hunters and into the park, the cherished whip vibrating against her palm. With her trim torso and her penchant for opulent headwear, Belva cut a striking figure on the bridle path, galloping past the adjacent White City Amusement Park, with its screaming, happy children.

Belva Gaertner should have been happy, too. Hyde Park was a glorious place to call home in the years immediately after the war, when she was married to William. It was one of the most exclusive neighborhoods in the city. A lawyer named Paul Cornell had purchased three hundred acres of land in the 1850s and developed what was then a suburb, using the name of the elegant New York and London neighborhoods in hopes of creating the same atmosphere for his new burg. After the Civil War, he and a group of well-to-do men who'd bought lots in fledgling Hyde Park inveigled the Illinois legislature into forming a South Park Commission to sell bonds and levy taxes. Cornell and the commission had no small plans. They hired the country's most acclaimed landscape architect, Frederick Law Olmsted, to create a grand "aristocratic landscaping" design for what would become the 523 acres of Jackson and Washington parks, plus their connector, the Midway Plaisance Park. Olmsted's original plan was never carried out, but nevertheless the area's ugly prairie scrubland was quickly transformed. The parks, opined a visitor, were among the best in the world, with "broad drives and winding alleys, ornamental trees, banks and beds of flowers and flowering shrubs, lakes and ornamental bridges, and turf that cools the eye under the fiercest noon." This attraction, along with the 1893 World's Columbian Exposition in Jackson Park and the launch of the University of Chicago a year earlier, began a new wave of fevered development, adding a commercial component and greater self-sufficiency to the area. It also became, in practical if not official terms, the southernmost point of the metropolitan area. Cable Court on South Lake Park Avenue was so named because it was the turnaround for cable cars heading to and from downtown. Later the city built an elevated line. Despite the college students and increased activity, the wealthy held tight, adding more large, elegant homes to the neighborhood. The parks, along with Lake Michigan, made Hyde Park wonderfully insular, hemming it in on three sides in a gorgeous parabola. Hyde Parkers—especially the wives, who didn't have to trek downtown to work each day like their husbands—had good reason to believe they lived in their own exclusive world.

It wasn't enough for Belva. She had dreamed her whole life of being among the idle rich, but it turned out she bored easily. Not just in the depths of winter, when she found herself shut inside. She was bored in June. She was bored in July. In the great rooms and hallways of the Gaertner household, boredom trailed her like an annoying corgi, always there, underfoot.

Her husband's wealth and position offered diversions, without question. William, who'd founded his Wm. Gaertner & Co. in 1896, regularly bought her beautiful clothes, the best in the city. And Belva did her own shopping, too, with open accounts at Marshall Field and the most exclusive couturiers. Every day gorgeous accessories hung from her ears and fanned out across her collarbone. Her rings could slice watermelons, and she wore a lot of them, sometimes one on every finger. The glittery rocks caused the other society ladies of Hyde Park to gape. Belva enjoyed the gewgaws and quickly expected only the best, but unlike so many of the wives of wealthy industrialists and bankers, she couldn't squeeze forth much passion for acquiring things. Passion was to be had, Belva Gaertner knew, but not in Hyde Park and not out in the open. Its time was late, very late. Only late at night would strangers put away their stifling formalities and inhibitions, come together, and do things with other strangers they'd never dare do with their loved ones. Belva had found a place for herself in the late-night cabarets and roadhouses of Chicago. She'd created an identity for herself in them, years before she ever met her husband. She wasn't Mrs. William Gaertner to these men and women. She wasn't even Belva. She was Belle . . . oh, how she missed Belle!

That was the name she had been using when she met William, back in 1911. William was forty-six at the time and one of Chicago's most eligible bachelors, not that this designation influenced his actions. Despite excellent manners, he mostly steered clear of the society ladies and lawn parties of his Hyde Park circle, preferring instead the dancing girls in the down-market Loop cabarets that promised "revelations of the female form divine and the portrayals of passion." Here, wearing molded breastplates and a feathered headdress, Belva, at twenty-five, stood out. She was far from the most beautiful girl in the cabaret, yet all of the regulars seemed to be in love with her. It helped that she was admirably built, with a broad chest and long legs, but she really won men over with her personality. Belva would approach a table after one of her performances and take over the conversation. She dazzled men with her dancing eyes, the roar of her laughter, her windmilling limbs as she told a story—she always had a story. Only when she was caught in repose, a still life, might an admirer recognize that she was really quite an ugly duckling. William Gaertner never did recognize it.

Not long after making her acquaintance, William commissioned a full-length portrait of Belva in cabaret dress and gave it prominent wall space at his residence. It was the image seared into his mind, the moment he first saw her on stage, her body turning with erotic languor beneath her clothes, arms rising up like a succulent baby's. She'd introduced herself as Belle Brown that night, but William hadn't been fooled. He soon discovered her given name, Belva Boosinger, and that she also answered to Mrs. Ernest Oberbeck. She was a married woman. That wasn't all. Outside the cabaret, some men called her Eleanor Peppol. Sometimes, when settling delinquent accounts, they also called her Sweet Baby or other, dirtier names. The array of monikers, along with frequent address changes, should have sent up a red flag for a man of William Gaertner's means. But by the time this information came in, it was too late. He had to have her.

Belva, it turned out, was easy to have—one quick divorce was all it took. She just wasn't easy to control. This would prove to be a problem, especially after they married in 1917. William, who'd come to Chicago in his twenties from his native Germany, ran his business however he wanted. He ran his household however he wanted. He expected to be in control. He controlled the universe, in a sense. In 1907 he'd accomplished a singular and acclaimed breakthrough, successfully building a giant "gun camera" that could photograph the canals and polar caps of the planet Mars. So why couldn't he control his own wife? She lived her own life. She made her own plans. She snubbed him when it suited her. It infuriated William, and it excited him too. He had a basset-hound face that turned beet red at the slightest provocation, the face of a small-time carnival barker. It must have been red all the time around Belva. He was caught in a miserable, unbreakable circle: Lust. Desperation. Hatred. Love.

Belva never seemed to get caught in that cycle herself. After the first flush of marriage had worn off, William often would come home from work and find the house empty. Sometimes Belva simply would be out riding. She'd come in at a gallop with a broad grin on her face. After a couple of hours in the saddle, her thighs and buttocks glowed, radiating from the inside out like a clay pot right out of the fire—a beautiful soreness that would leave her short of breath all evening, desperate to go out on the town. William, exhausted from a full day in the lab and the boardroom, rarely wanted to join her, and so she'd set off into the night on her own or with a young man who came to the door. Belva always invited William along, but he would demur. He had to get up early. "You go, dear," he'd say. "Enjoy yourself."

"You are one husband in a million," an escort supposedly told him one night as the man and Belva headed for the door.

William didn't believe the man. Surely a larger percentage of husbands were getting the shaft, not that confirmation of this hypothesis would have appeased him. There was no way he could ever understand Belva's generation. The rules he grew up with had all been rubbed away. Even the good girls now danced close, oblivious to chaperones. Young women—proper, well-raised young women—encouraged party diversions like Sardines, a hide-and-seek game in which the whole point wasn't actually to hide or seek but for everyone to end up mashed tantalizingly close together in a tight space. On top of such frivolities, girls now revealed flesh in public—bare ankles and arms and, worse, the unfettered outlines of much more through thin summer clothing. In his deepest heart, William probably never truly expected fidelity from Belva. She was more than twenty years his junior and came from the lower classes. She had a temperament wilder than any stallion he'd ever had. She had to run. He surely did expect something, however. Some discretion, for one thing. And frankly, some taste in lovers. Men of means, like him. Men of talent and accomplishment. Men with ambition beyond bagging a society lady. More important, he hoped that, in time, Belva would settle down and settle in, become a companion.

When it didn't happen, he had no idea how to handle it. He would reprove Belva when she came in at three A.M. smelling of alcohol, pointing out that he had to be up early every morning and didn't appreciate being woken. He'd lecture her when she would collapse in bed, half paralyzed before her head touched the pillow. "Thanks for the advice," she'd answer groggily. She'd then come home later the next night and playfully pinch and slap her husband as he tried to sleep. She was no longer just a social drinker—or, at the very least, she was doing entirely too much socializing.

Time and again she came home drunk. William became so frustrated that he'd try to simply blot her out. "It wasn't unusual for him to get angry at me and refuse to speak for weeks at a time," she later complained.

Being a scientific-minded man, William Gaertner chose scientific methods to solve the problem. He hired celebrated detective W. C. Dannenberg, the city's former Morals Squad director, to track and chart her progress through the days. Almost immediately, this approach showed results, for Belva didn't have to go far to find fun. The neighborhoods to the west of Hyde Park had filled up with rail-yard workers and clerks and shoe salesmen, and with them came a burgeoning entertainment district that was beginning to suck the life out of the Loop's nights. In Plaisance Park, the Frank Lloyd Wright–designed Midway Gardens originally featured elegant music and dancing for the South Side's finest, but now it catered to the masses. It held more than a thousand dancers at a time and was often packed. Outside there were three raised dance floors, each separated by tables that allowed men on their own to sit and survey the night's female offerings. Inside, built along Japanese architectural lines, a maze of nooks allowed philandering men and women to hide themselves away just blocks from home. Next door to the Midway Gardens was the Sans Souci Amusement Park, with its always-crowded beer garden rolling out from a band shell where musicians filled the air with popular tunes night after night. The White City Amusement Park also had a ballroom, this one popular with residents of the nearby "honeymoon flats" along the western border of Washington Park.

It was along this stretch of small residential houses facing the park that Belva got caught. On March 30, 1920, Dannenberg asked William to come along on his wife's trail. The detective and his men had been tracking her for a while. They'd watched her cozy up inside Midway Gardens and rub bellies on the dance floor at Dreamland Café. She had an established routine; Dannenberg knew full well that this outing would prove to his client beyond any doubt that Mrs. Gaertner was no good. They pulled up to 5345 Prairie Avenue, two blocks west of Belva's favorite bridle path in the park, barely a mile from the Gaertner home. Dannenberg made clear to William that they should approach quietly, as silent as Indians. The redheaded detective, who'd made his name a decade earlier by arresting the white slavers Maurice and Julia Van Bever, took the lead. Once he got the front door open, he burst in and rushed into the bedroom. Belva shrieked and dived for the floor, where she'd left her clothes. Another naked body skittered in the opposite direction. William, trailing in behind the detectives, didn't have the heart for a scene in this strange house. He turned and ran out.

❧

Belva munched on a sandwich as she waited in a corridor at the Wabash Avenue police station. Reporters stood around her, jockeying for position. Someone asked what happened the previous night, and she sighed.

"I tell you I can't recall what happened," she said. "Somebody must have shot him, but I can't remember how it was done." Belva shifted in her seat. She sat with her legs crossed, face regally impassive. She'd gotten some sleep, and William had brought her fresh clothes, so she was beginning to feel like herself again. Watching her, some of the hacks began to wonder if the whole thing was a big mistake, if this well-bred woman simply had been in the wrong place at the wrong time. Belva took a swig of milk and looked up.

"I think I can get my coat cleaned so it will look all right again," she said to no one in particular. The strange comment hung in the air. A reporter asked what she meant, and she described the beautiful caracul coat that now had blood all over it. The police took it, she said. "It's an expensive coat, you know. Sometimes a coat like that is worth as much as $2,800."

Nearly three thousand dollars for a coat? Her ex-husband really was loaded. The reporters scribbled furiously.

Nearby, Walter Law's wife—widow—also waited on this cool Wednesday afternoon. She sat with her father-in-law and other family members. "Walter died at his work," Freda Law told a *Chicago Daily News* man, who'd asked about her husband being out so late with another woman. She stared at the reporter. She was in shock; it had only been a few hours since she'd heard about her husband's death. "He had sold Mrs. Gaertner that car, and he was demonstrating to her how to drive it," she said. "He did that with almost all his customers. I never heard of the Gaertner woman until I read about Walter's death in the papers. I do not believe she killed him. The bullet that caused his death came from the outside, and probably never was meant for him. Walter was devoted to me. I never suspected him of doing anything that might give me cause to be jealous, and I don't suspect him now."

A policeman stepped into the hall. "All ready now," he said. The inquest was about to start. Belva rose and took a last drag from a cigarette she'd bummed from her guard. The *Chicago Daily Journal* reporter noted the casual way she smoked in front of them. "There was nothing brazen about it, nothing defiant," he related in wonderment. It was one thing to see your typical girl pickpocket sucking on a cigarette in public, but a classy lady like Belva Gaertner—that was something to talk about. Belva pulled a powder puff from her handbag and buffed her face, then stepped purposefully into the room. Mrs. Law was already inside and sitting.

Maurine Watkins also found a seat. She may have been the *Tribune* reporter on the scene last night, but she was going to have to fight to keep the story. Genevieve Forbes had been sent out to the inquest, too. Robert Lee had realized he had a potentially big story and a rookie reporter covering it. Maurine took no mind of Forbes; they didn't sit together.

Belva, sitting with Tom Reilly and Marshall Solberg, two of the lawyers provided by her ex-husband, looked gorgeous. It was a remarkable transformation. When William was allowed to visit with her in the morning, he must have been shocked by what he saw. Belva, his beautiful Belle, seemed to have aged dramatically in the week since he'd last seen her. Her face, always so pleasantly plump, had gone slack. Those alluring, sleepy eyes that had captivated him were fogged up and rimmed in red. And yet here she was now, just a few hours later, fully restored. William, managing to think things through, had brought her a conservative outfit: a brown full-length dress, a simple black coat with a fur collar, a brown hat. He'd also brought her seven rings to choose from, but she didn't bother making up her mind; she wore them all. With the hat and the fur collar cropping her face in a perfect box frame, with makeup expertly applied and her naturally unabashed smile back in place, she was young again, a vamp. She pulled the hat down over her forehead, the brim edging toward one brow, giving her eye a dashing glint. William Gaertner couldn't help it: He was besotted anew. "I hope for a reconciliation just as soon as possible," he told reporters.

The inquest, or coroner's jury, was a pro forma proceeding that laid out the basic facts of a possible crime and served as a prelude to a grand jury. It rarely attracted much attention. But on this dreary afternoon, the benches were full of reporters and other observers. The lawyers weren't surprised. The afternoon *Daily News*, which had hit the street less than an hour before, crashed the story across the entire front page in mammoth type: "One-Gun Duel Tragedy Told by Woman." It held pride of place even over a gangland-murder story about the notorious bootlegger Dean "Dion" O'Banion, the Torrio gang's chief rival, who was supposedly planning to surrender to police for questioning about the assassination of a fellow bootlegger. That morning, Maurine's story in the *Tribune* had also gone on page one, but in a smaller slot and with a more demure—and incorrect— headline: "Mystery Victim Is Robert Law; Hold Divorcee."

Everyone expected the follow-up stories, with the benefit of evidence from the inquest, to be juicier, and they wouldn't be disappointed. Walter Law, the state pointed out, was younger than Belva Gaertner, a good ten years younger, which was how she liked her boyfriends. But the younger ones were getting harder and harder to come by, so she had been desperate to hold on to this one. "The motive which the state believes lies behind the case is this," declared Assistant State's Attorney Stanley Klarkowski. "Mrs. Gaertner had ensnared Law. He tried to break away, to stick to his wife and family. She killed him rather than lose him."

Klarkowski walked through the details of the events that led Belva Gaertner to be in custody today. Sometime after midnight she and Walter Law, who had been seeing each other for about three months, parked near her apartment in a black Nash sedan. Belva left the car, presumably to go up to her apartment. At about one in the morning, two policemen walking their beat saw a woman open the passenger-side door and disappear into the Nash. Pausing, the cops noticed that the automobile didn't go anywhere, but that was hardly unusual. Everyone had a closed car these days, especially cheating husbands. The morals court had recently called the closed car "a house of prostitution on wheels," and that meant this was a situation for Vice. The officers quick-stepped to the corner to use a police call box. That was when they heard the shot.

Hustling back to the car, they discovered a man—shot through the head—and no sign of the woman they'd seen. The man's body lay crumpled against the steering wheel, his arm dangling, a trickling bottle of gin just out of reach. There was an automatic pistol on the floor next to it.

Bert "Curley" Brown, manager of the Gingham Inn, at Sixty-eighth and Cottage Grove, stepped up to the stand. He was a big man with an easy, knowing smile. He acknowledged that Walter Law and Belva Gaertner had been in his establishment. "They didn't have any gin," he said. "Just ginger ale. We don't allow gin. They didn't display any gun in the café—though they may have talked about one—for I've always got my eyes peeled for guns. They were such a nice couple—I'm certainly shocked."

Maurine didn't think much of Brown, dismissing his testimony as "satire." She wrote down the key questions the inquest brought up: Did Belva Gaertner murder Walter Law? Did she shoot him in self-defense? Did she accidentally shoot him? Did he kill himself? Did a third person do the slaying?

This much was clear: The officers, patrolmen David Fitzgerald and Morris Quinn, had no idea what they were dealing with when they called their station with the car's license-plate number. It could have been a suicide or a robbery gone awry. It could have been a gang shooting—it was certainly gruesome enough to be an underworld hit. When the deputy coroner, Joseph Springer, arrived at the scene that morning, he checked the man slumped over the steering wheel. A bullet had punched through the man's right cheek and exited through his left ear. Blood had flowed down the deceased's chest and out the open car door, pooling on the cold ground. Springer picked up the automatic pistol on the car's floor and opened the chamber. One shot had been fired. He retrieved the dead man's wallet from his coat: Walter Law, automobile salesman.

The sedan, however, wasn't Law's. It belonged to one Belva E. Gaertner. Detective Sergeant William Corcoran testified that officers Fitzgerald and Quinn found Belva in her apartment, pacing the floor. There was a large bruise on her cheek, and it was clear that she had recently backed off from a state of hysteria. "We got drunk and he got killed—I don't know how," she told the officers. That was pretty much all she had to say.

While Maurine focused on the testimony, Forbes, more experienced than her younger colleague, found another angle. She made sure to sit near the widow, who was surrounded by family and friends. Much of what Mrs. Law was hearing surprised her, and she periodically sent forth small, quivering moans of distress. She squeezed her fists together at her sides and glared at Belva. She murmured something to her father-in-law that Forbes didn't quite catch.

"No, daughter," said Harry J. Law, patting Freda Law's back while trying to maintain a stoic expression. "It's not that woman's fault entirely. Walter ought not to have gone out with anyone. He had a lovely wife and a fine baby. No, he did wrong, and we know it."

Mrs. Law muttered again, and tried to stifle a sob.

"No, daughter," Mr. Law whispered again, calm but forceful. "No, the times aren't getting worse. Things were this way when I was a boy back in the Carolinas. But it was more quiet. A man has to stand up and fight against it. That's all."

The rundown of events took two hours, and Freda Law squirmed and muttered through all of it. Belva's attention flagged early. Others, too, quickly lost interest: Yawns popped up here and there as the police testimony became redundant. Finally, a detective whispered in Klarkowski's ear. "Bring him in quick," the prosecutor replied. A well-groomed man in his thirties entered the room, his eyes darting, and took the oath. He said his name was Paul E. Goodwin and that he worked with Law, selling cars. It was clear that Belva and her lawyers had no idea who this man was or what he would say.

"Walter told me Monday that he planned to take out more life insurance because Mrs. Gaertner threatened to kill him," Goodwin testified. "In a joking way he said he was afraid Mrs. Gaertner might shoot him. Three weeks before, he told me she locked him in her flat with her and threatened to stab him with a knife unless he stayed there."

The testimony was better than Klarkowski could have hoped. The assistant state's attorney had planned to have the inquest continued to the next day, so the police would have more time to tidy up their investigation, but Goodwin provided everything he needed. After that damning testimony, this case was definitely moving on to a grand jury and trial. Klarkowski turned to Joseph Springer, who was running the inquest. "The state is willing to let this case go to the [coroner's] jury at once, without further delay," he said.

The deputy coroner looked to the defense table. "Does Mrs. Gaertner wish to take the stand?"

Reilly rose, with Belva's eyes following him up to his full height. "She does not, on advice of counsel," he said. "Her statement to the police has been admitted in evidence. That is all she cares to say."

With that, Klarkowski closed the show, adding the key pieces of Goodwin's testimony to his summation. "I believe that when Law and Mrs. Gaertner returned from the café she tried to make him enter her apartment," he said. "He, remembering the time she locked him in and held him there at the point of a knife, refused. Then she pulled the gun, perhaps. He tried to stop her, but couldn't." The prosecutor asked for a verdict.

As soon as the jury and the deputy coroner left the room, reporters swarmed over Belva, Klarkowski, and Freda Law. Klarkowski waved off questions, but Belva and Mrs. Law welcomed them. The two women sat in the bare-walled room of the police station, separated by only a few seats, answering questions, seemingly oblivious to each other. Back and forth they went, each serving as background noise for the other.

"At first, I felt rather sorry for that other woman because she was guilty of killing and everything. But did you see her come in? She was almost giggling. Oh, I never knew I could hate anyone so much."

"Walter never did get along with his wife. He often told me that if it weren't for his little boy he'd never live with her."

"We had been married for four years and my husband was devoted to me. We celebrated our fourth wedding anniversary only last Friday."

"He was always a perfect gentleman, and I certainly never had any occasion to threaten his life. . . . He told me that the reason he wanted his insurance increased was because his wife had asked him to. About three weeks ago she went to a fortune teller and found out that her husband was going to die suddenly within eighteen days."

"No, I don't want her to hang. But I don't want her to go to jail for a month or two and then step out."

The two women could have gone on this way for some time, offering details and opinions about Walter Law, his marriage, and what should happen next, but after only twenty minutes, the coroner's jury returned. The interviews ended abruptly.

"Walter Law," the jury declared, "came to his death in the automobile of Mrs. Belva Gaertner from a bullet fired by Mrs. Belva Gaertner."

Freda Law buried her head in her father-in-law's embrace. Belva stared straight ahead and then blinked slowly. A reporter asked her a question, but she didn't hear him. If she had come in giggling, she wasn't going to leave that way.

❧❧❧

The day after William caught her in bed with another man, Belva returned home as if nothing unusual had occurred. Over the three years of their marriage, she never showed any sign of feeling guilty. She never offered a hint that she regretted any of her actions. She did what she wanted, and that made it right.

Belva strolled up the front walk of the Gaertner estate, her head high, as expertly put together as always. She had no plans to talk to William about the events of the previous night; she was just going to go on with her life—with *their* life. But on this morning she was met with a surprise. The front door was locked. She knocked but received no reply. She banged and banged, and finally she heard shoes stepping toward the door. When it was opened, she found not a familiar, apologetic servant but a hard, strange face—a private detective—staring out at her. He wouldn't let her enter.

Belva, steaming with such fury that her floppy hat risked burning to a cinder on her head, stomped downtown, where she employed a burly guardian of her own. They returned to the house and forced their way inside. William, hiding upstairs, called the police in a panic.

A car rolled up not long after. "What's the matter?" the officer asked when he found a standoff in the marbled foyer.

Belva wheeled on the uniformed policeman, startled at the extreme measures her husband was taking. First a private bullyboy, now an official one. "I don't know of any reason why we need the services of the police force here," she snapped.

William gave her a reason: This wasn't her home anymore. "She wants to stay in the flat," he told the officer.

"Who is she?"

"My wife," William said.

Ah. With that, the officer decided it was time to move on. The police hated domestic disputes, especially when they involved wealthy men who had influence. He advised them to take it up with their lawyers, then turned and beat a quick retreat back to the station house.

William already had a lawyer on retainer. He would be filing for divorce, citing cruelty. Belva went out and got her own lawyer—Charles Erbstein, perhaps the best-known attorney in the city. She also hired a set of private eyes to match those that William had. The dispute, inevitably, hit the papers. The *Tribune*, breaking the story on April 9, 1920, assumed the necessary mocking tone:

> Eight detectives are comfortably ensconced at the home of Mr. and Mrs. William Gaertner, 5474 Hyde Park boulevard. Mr. Gaertner filed suit for divorce last week and invited Mrs. Gaertner to leave. When she declined, he summoned the police. They were neutral.
>
> Then he retained a private detective to watch the home. Mrs. Gaertner retaliated by employing one to protect her interests and watch the other. The husband came back with one more. She then supplemented hers as

an assistant. That made it two and two. But Mr. Gaertner added a couple more and so did Mrs. Gaertner.

Now she is consistently followed as was Mary by her little lamb. The eight sleuths accompany her to the theaters, the shopping district, the telephone, even to the mail box.

"It's a rather trying situation," Belva told the *American*. "You see, between my husband's corps of detectives and my own crew I hardly know where I'm at. I need help."

She admitted she was "having a deuce of a time" remembering which detectives were hers and which his, and, bonding with a female reporter from the *Chicago Evening Post*, she asked how the reporter would handle the state of affairs. Ione Quinby, a cherubic twenty-eight-year-old with fashionable black bangs, took the question seriously. She looked about the expansive manse, with its high ceilings, marble floors, and expensive furniture beyond her imagination. There was a lot of territory to cover in this one building and a lot of opportunity for a bad apple to nick some pretty finery. "It seems to me," Quinby said, "you should get a couple of neutral dicks to keep an eye on both crews."

It wasn't the best advice. Neutrality was hardly practical—loyalty went to whomever signed the checks, and private detectives didn't come cheap. So the status quo prevailed, and that meant William had the upper hand. But Belva would not be driven from the estate. She took a small room in the house for herself and the few things that were truly important to her. William's detectives didn't dare go in there, but they lingered on the lawn outside her window at night, smoking cigarettes and watching for movement behind the curtain. The detectives kept copious notes of her activities, and when she wasn't doing much, they lolled on the plush furniture. If Belva headed for the front door unexpectedly, a mad scramble would bunch up the Kermanshah rugs behind her. "Don't overexert yourselves," she'd tell them. "I'm going to my sister's. The phone number is Kenwood 137586."

Soon enough, the story went national. It was too amusing to pass up. Wags called the Gaertner estate "the House of a Thousand Detectives." The *Courier and Reporter* of Waterloo, Iowa, trilled that Belva now had "no more privacy than a goldfish. There are detectives to the right of her, 'dicks' to the left of her, sleuths in front of her. They follow her about like conscience, making notes of everything she does, checking the routine of her daily life like so many eager Boswells."

Belva, enjoying the attention and always good for a laugh, joined right in. "I've gotten so used to detectives that if they were to be called off I'd miss the dear things," she said. The reporters loved Belva: She was a hoot, and she treated them as guests, offering tea and snacks.

She treated her "dicks" better. She knew that bought companions could still be enjoyable companions, and so she embraced them as long-lost friends and playmates. The detectives joined her on shopping trips, ostensibly to keep an eye on William's watchers, who were trailing behind, but really so she'd have someone other than the salesgirls to talk to. They would "promenade on each side of her" down Michigan Avenue, trying to look professional while Belva cracked wise and smiled broadly at anyone who gave them a funny look. She even played billiards with her detectives—and showily not with William's detectives—until William, in a snit, hid the balls.

It wasn't all just fun and games for Belva. She was playing to win. Shortly after the newspapers took up the story, Belva announced that she would prove in court that her husband had beaten her with a horsewhip. The whip would be presented, she said, as "Exhibit A." More than that, the beatings went both ways, because William wasn't just an abusive husband, he was a sexual deviant. "Sure, I whipped my millionaire husband," she said, ratcheting up the story's salaciousness, "but it was he himself who gave me the whip and begged me, yes, even forced me, to do it." She showed reporters the whip, turning it over and over in her hand. "It was he who made me use it," she said. "It was he who forced me to the terrible and disgusting task of beating him. Twice I consented. After that I refused. If that is cruelty, his charges are true."

No doubt William considered this a low blow, but Belva believed she had no choice. However much she joked and laughed with reporters, she thought she was fighting for her life. She had earned her marriage to William Gaertner. And she had convinced herself—almost—that it wasn't her infidelity that undermined the union but William's jealous company men.

She publicly accused Robert McGearald, Gaertner's secretary, of trying to break her and William up.

It was scandalous stuff, and reporters girded for an explosive court case that could run on the front page for days. But then, on May 6, the first day of the divorce trial, Belva suddenly pulled back. She decided she couldn't do it. She would not be testifying, she said. She would not contest the suit. She gave no reason, not even to her lawyer, maybe because, after everything that had come out, she realized the truth would be too hard for people to believe. She had married William because he loved her, truly loved her, and to Belva "that was everything." It had been a shock when she discovered it wasn't. She had broken William's heart—and her own as well. That was enough.

In answering questions posed by his lawyer, William Gaertner talked about the last straw. "My wife had been away from home for three nights," he said in open court. "She told me she had stayed at the home of women friends. On the night of March 30, with W.C. Dannenberg and others, I trailed her to 5345 Prairie Avenue, where we found her with a man who said he was Edward Lusk."

"Where was Mr. Lusk?"

"Behind a door," William said.

The judge had heard all he needed to hear. William Gaertner, a respected man in the community, an important man, had been humiliated by his wife. The court granted the divorce. Belva received $3,000, a car, and a selection of the household's furniture. Not much of a settlement when your husband was worth, excluding his thriving business, more than half a million dollars.

❧❧❧

Belva sighed extravagantly. She gazed off into the distance, annoyed that she had to answer the question. In the past, she always had been able to win over the press with her gaiety, as she did during her divorce from William. But this was different. After the things that were said at the inquest, she recognized that happy flirtatiousness wasn't appropriate.

"The story is simply ridiculous," she told the reporter from the *Daily News*. She was sitting in a ten-by-five cell at the Cook County Jail, her new home now that the coroner's jury had pronounced judgment. Reporters surrounded her. "I never threatened Law," she said. "True enough, I was fond of him—" Genevieve Forbes, incredulous, cut in. She asked Belva if she was saying she hadn't menaced Walter Law with a knife.

Belva turned from the *Daily News*'s hack to the *Tribune*'s. "Me threaten him with a knife? That's crazy. He was always a courteous gentleman to me. Why should I ever be angry with him?"

Belva leaned back against the bare cell wall. She'd been surprised at the coroner's jury's decision but had recovered quickly. After the inquest ended, she put her shoulders back and strode out of the Wabash Avenue station, an officer on each arm. A pack of reporters followed them over to the jail. Now Katherine Malm, her new cellmate, sat nearby, listening intently, a look of admiration on her face. Belva was the only inmate "dressed up" in the women's section of the jail. She wouldn't receive her gray jail uniform, and thus have to give up her stylish outfit, until later in the day. To the *Daily News* reporter's eyes, she "was a picture of self-possession, a woman of the world," especially compared to the Malm girl.

"It gives me an awfully blank feeling to be accused of murdering another woman's husband," Belva said. Caught up in defending herself, she hadn't noticed how the male reporters were drinking her in, but now suddenly she did. She apologized for how she looked. "You see, they have taken away all my powder and makeup and my rings and money, too," she said.

A stout Italian woman walked past the cell hefting a basket of laundry. Belva glanced up. She knew who the inmate was. Sabella Nitti had been convicted of murdering her husband and sentenced to die. She would be the first woman ever to hang in Illinois. Sabella now awaited an appeal before the state Supreme Court.

"I hope they won't put me to work," Belva said, watching the condemned woman disappear around the corner with the laundry. "I hate to work."

4

Hang Me? That's a Joke

Katherine Malm, "Kitty" to her friends, was happy to have a new cellmate. When the jail matrons brought Belva in, closely followed by reporters, Kitty made herself useful, squeezing through the crush of bodies to fetch a stale currant bun for her.

Belva tore into the bread with barely an acknowledgment of her attendant. It may have taken her a minute to recognize that this pale, black-haired girl, dressed in the formless striped uniform issued by the jail, was the same young woman who had dominated every front page in the city just two weeks before. Everybody—all of Chicago—knew who Katherine Malm was. Her trial had been a sensation. After the reporters left, Belva looked her cellmate over. Kitty didn't seem to be anything like how the papers described her. They called her the Wolf Woman and the Tiger Girl, but Belva could see nothing vicious about this small-boned nineteen-year-old, who sat as still as the air and offered a hopeful smile every time Belva looked her way.*

Prosecutors had finally ended the embarrassing string of girl-gunner acquittals in Cook County when they convicted Kitty Malm. The streak had stood at twenty-nine in the summer of 1923 when Sabella Nitti was convicted of murdering her husband, but the newspapers didn't consider that a true win for the state. Sabella was a poor, rough-looking, middle-aged ethnic woman who spoke almost no English. In the *Tribune*, Genevieve

*The nicknames had nothing to do with Kitty's alleged crime. They simply made for good headlines.

Forbes derided her as "seamy-faced," "gibbering," and a "cruel animal." Many reporters barely considered her human. Like Negro defendants, Sabella was an easy target for any prosecutor. There was simply no comparison between her case and the trial of a white, *American* woman. There'd never been a time when it was easy to convict a white woman in Cook County, especially a young white woman. An earlier streak, this one of husband killers, had stretched to thirty-five consecutive acquittals before finally ending in 1919, when a middle-aged Swedish immigrant was found guilty. The acquittals were so consistent, year after year, that a reporter could state baldly that "women can't be convicted of murder in Cook County." So Kitty Malm—young and white and at least not unattractive—was the state's prize catch. She and her man, Otto Malm, had tried to rob a sweater factory back in November and ended up killing a security guard. Otto, who had a long rap sheet, confessed, but not Kitty, who decided to trust in Illinois' all-male juries. To the state's attorney's office, her conviction was public proof that the days of women getting away with murder were finally over.

Belva Gaertner, the well-mannered society divorcée, and the ragamuffin Tiger Girl seemed an odd pair, but their backgrounds actually had a lot in common—more than Belva would ever publicly admit. They both had had emotionally perilous childhoods. At fourteen, Belva found herself dumped at the state orphanage in Normal after her widowed mother slipped into abject poverty. At twelve, Kitty dropped out of the fifth grade to work in a factory, instructed by her mother that there was "no need for girls to go far in school." They both also had a weakness for men that got them in trouble. The day after Belva arrived at the jail, Kitty received a divorce summons from her legal husband, Max Baluk. (She'd married Otto Malm illegally after leaving Max.) "Defendant Katherine Baluk, for a considerable time past, has given herself over to adulterous practices, wholly regardless of her marriage vows," the bill read. It went on to accuse her not just of committing adultery with Otto Malm, but also with "divers [*sic*] other lewd men, whose names are to your orator unknown." Kitty understood enough of what she was reading that she burst into tears. She got the gist: Max hated her. This shouldn't have surprised her—Max had beaten her throughout their relationship, until she took their new baby and fled to a flophouse—but it still hurt to see it written down on paper. Max now claimed that their two-year-old daughter, "Tootsie," wasn't his, that Kitty had left him because "she had a good time with another fellow" and got pregnant. Kitty showed the legal document to Belva, and the two women, despite a nearly twenty-year age difference, bonded over their poor treatment by men. "Fellows, always fellows," Kitty said.

Soon Belva and Kitty were playing cards together in their cell, smiling and laughing for news photographers, Kitty talking endlessly about her travails. The younger woman had just one piece of advice—a warning, really—for Belva: Get ready to hear everyone you know lie about you. That was what happened to her, she said. In November, Otto had told police the truth—that he had killed Edward Lehman, the watchman at the Delson sweater factory on Lincoln Avenue, during the botched robbery attempt. He even admitted he'd accidentally hit Kitty with one of his shots, leaving her with a raw wound on her head where the bullet grazed her. For her part, Kitty, still desperately in love with Otto, went further for her man. To show her devotion to Otto after his confession, and to help him get free of the law, she tried to commit suicide shortly after being arrested, hanging herself with a bedsheet. A jail matron cut her down just as she was starting to turn blue. "You can now tell them that I done the shooting so they will let you go to take care of baby forever, but please quit the racket and raise Tootsie in an honest way for your departing mama's sake," she wrote to Otto in a suicide letter. A few days later, Otto discovered he might be executed for murder. He quickly adjusted his memory about what had happened at the Delson factory. Kitty had been shooting too, he now said, and "it was the shot from her gun that killed the watchman; she done it." Otto sold her out, just like that.

"Men are quitters," Kitty told Belva in disgust, her lip curling into an ugly sneer. "They're long on talk, but, Lord, when it comes to the showdown, they're yellow."

⁂

Even with Otto turning on Kitty, her lawyer, Jay J. McCarthy, had gone into her trial feeling confident. He pointed out to her that Otto was the career criminal, not her, and that Otto had confessed to the Delson shooting, again not her. Plus, Kitty was the young mother of a two-year-old girl, who would sit in court beside her grandmother each day looking adorable and sad. Most important of all, McCarthy reminded his client that Illinois' all-male juries were averse to punishing women, even when they weren't young mothers. The lawyer figured Kitty would be free in a couple of days. He was so confident of it that he rejected a prosecution plea offer of fourteen years.

The lawyer's confidence was contagious. "Hang me? That's a joke," Kitty told a group of reporters as jury selection began. "Say, nobody in the world would hang a girl for bein' in an alley with a guy who pulls a gun and shoots." The *Tribune*'s Genevieve Forbes noted how the former waitress sashayed into court as if she didn't have a care in the world.

She flopped her abundant fur wrap over the back of the chair as if she were making herself comfortable before the feature picture in a motion-picture house started. And the purple silk lining sprawled over the knees of the bailiff behind her, much as it might have swept over another seat in a theater.

Then Kitty took off her hat, a small black straw, in the favored cloche shape, with a bit of lace veil over her large brown eyes. She shook her black bobbed hair, jiggled around in her seat, and settled down to wait, and to read.

That breezy attitude didn't last long, however. On Thursday, February 21, the trial got under way. The first sign that this one might turn out differently than other girl-gunner cases was the simple fact that the newspapers' nicknames worked. Everyone wanted to get a look at the dangerous Wolf Woman, the ferocious Tiger Girl. Dozens of men and women assembled in the corridor of the Criminal Courts Building for the trial's start. When the doors to Judge Walter Steffen's courtroom opened, the crowd pushed forward, jamming the doorway and blocking the hall outside. The room quickly filled. It's likely that Maurine Watkins was one of the spectators who squeezed into the packed room. It would have been hard for her to resist going over to the courthouse whenever her work schedule allowed (and it typically did, for she often worked the night shift). She'd started her new career as a police reporter right when one of the most sensational "girl slayer" trials in Chicago history was starting. But Katherine Malm was Genevieve Forbes's story; Forbes had stayed on top of it ever since the night of November 3, when Lehman, the young watchman at the Delson sweater factory, was shot down. The boy uttered his last words at the Alexian Brothers Hospital that night, with a policeman and a prosecutor leaning over him and Forbes a step behind, a pencil hovering over her notepad. From her first day on the job, Maurine dreamed about getting this kind of story—and worried she never would. How often did a Kitty Malm come along?

With his opening statement, Assistant State's Attorney Harry Pritzker tried to preempt any ideas Hearst's sob sisters might have had about presenting Kitty as a victim. "Mrs. Malm is the hardest woman ever to walk into a courtroom," he said. "The evidence will show that she fired the shots that killed Lehman. We will ask that she receive the heaviest penalty the state can inflict." Kitty was struggling to keep her attention on this attack when the prosecution brought in a .38 caliber revolver for the jury to see, the one she was supposed to have used to kill the watchman. They placed a holster next to it. Uninterested in the gun, Kitty turned away—and caught sight of Blanche King standing in the back of the room. Kitty, surprised, smiled. She had figured she'd never see her friend again. King started down the courtroom aisle supported by a nurse. Three months before, Kitty had avoided a police dragnet after Otto's capture and escaped to Indianapolis. That was where she'd met King; they shared a room at a boardinghouse. The two young women hit it off right away. Before returning to Chicago and surrendering in hopes of saving Otto and seeing her daughter, Kitty tearfully said good-bye to Blanche, she thought forever. Pritzker stood up and announced that Miss King, despite ill health, had come from Indianapolis to testify in the interests of justice. Kitty looked at her attorney in confusion.

King was sworn in, and Pritzker asked her how she knew the defendant.

The witness sat up straight. "The twenty-second of last November," she said, her voice full of pep, her head swiveling to take in the dozens of eyes gazing upon her. "I was boarding at 128 West Walnut Street, in Indianapolis, and the landlord, Victor Capron, took me to the 'Chicago girl's room' and said, 'Blanche, meet Kitty.'"

"Did you ever see the defendant with any guns?" Pritzker asked.

"Yes, two."

"Where?"

"In my room."

"Did she have any names for them?"

For a moment King looked as though she were about to laugh. Her heart rate spiked at the excitement. The nurse stood just a couple of steps away. "Yes," King said, her breath coming in rapid bursts, "'Little Betsy' and 'Big Bertha.'" She identified the gun on display as "Big Bertha."

"Tell us about this revolver."

"She had it strapped around her waist part of the time in that holster."

"How many times did you see her with it?"

"Every day."

McCarthy, unprepared for the surprise witness, offered no objections. It was his first murder trial. When the witness was asked whether the defendant had ever said anything about being on the run, King answered with a happy child's blurt: "You bet!" She said that Kitty announced to her, "I hate coppers, and I'll kill any who comes to take me." The only times Kitty didn't have her hand on one of her pistols, she added, was "when she was eating, when she was sleeping, and one other time." King looked to the reporters in the front row, smiling.

Kitty, unbelieving, sat throughout the testimony with her eyes riveted on King. She wanted to scream. She wanted to jump up and yell, "Liar!" but she didn't. She sat there in shock, her mouth wrenched open. Blanche King, on the other hand, was exuberant. After her testimony ended, she waited around in the hallway until every reporter there had a chance to talk to her. Her nurse stood nearby. Along with a variety of long-standing physical ailments, King also had mental problems.

Assistant State's Attorney Pritzker no longer had to worry about the Hearst papers. King's testimony was so dramatic, and so damaging to the defense, that the sob sisters never got a chance to do their work. The reports that splashed across Chicago's front pages were straightforward, in-your-face crime writing worthy of coverage of the city's most vicious gangsters.

"Katherine Baluk Malm, on trial for her life in the court of Judge Walter P. Steffen, carried two guns on her hip like a girl in a dime novel, and wore a dress with buckles that enabled her to slip in, open quickly and draw her weapons. Moreover, she hated 'coppers' and swore that if she saw one he'd drop."

That was the normally staid *Daily News.*

The imagery was simply too good to pass up. All of the city's papers used variations on King's dramatic description of how the Tiger Girl carried her guns. (Forbes, in the *Tribune,* declared that Kitty "carried a gun where most girls hide their love letters.") Kitty read some of the coverage the next day and spent the weekend in her cell crying uncontrollably.

On Monday, Kitty arrived in court to find chaos. Public interest in the trial, high from the start, had turned fanatical. Reporters fought their way into the courtroom. The *Evening Post* reported that "some 200 would-be spectators thronged the corridors of the Criminal Courts building" in hopes of seeing Kitty Malm in the flesh. Once bailiffs cleared the way, the defendant entered with her head down. She wore a sexy new black dress, procured by her lawyer, that emphasized her small waist and ignored her smaller bosom. But she walked stiffly to the defendant's table. There was nothing extra to her gait, no oomph to catch the eye of the average jury-man, as McCarthy undoubtedly had hoped when he picked out the dress. The crowd gaped anyway. Kitty, they now believed, was the real thing after all: a killer.

Kitty, stepping up to the stand on shaky legs, did her best to knock down her former friend's testimony. "I never carried or fired a gun in my life," she said, her voice quavering. She acknowledged that she had been friendly with Blanche King but denied saying any of the things King attributed to her. Just thinking about Blanche's betrayal caused her eyes to well up, and she knew Otto was waiting out in the hall to say even worse things about her. She began to hyperventilate. Judge Steffen had to stop the testimony over and over so that the defendant could gain control of her emotions and make her answers intelligible to the jury. The *Tribune* wrote that "Mrs. Malm's testimony came as the sensation of the trial," but most spectators left disappointed. They didn't want denials and tears. They didn't want to hear about Kitty's love for her daughter. They had taken time off from work or household chores to listen to the Wolf Woman tell exactly how she shot that watchman dead.

The jury wanted the same thing. After just an hour and twenty minutes, the foreman, Walter H. Harper, rapped softly on the door of the jury room. After four ballots, they were ready with a verdict. The lawyers, the defendant, and a still-large contingent of court fans filed back into the courtroom. Harper handed a piece of paper to the court clerk. The clerk unfolded it and read: "We, the jury, find the defendant, Katherine Baluk Malm, guilty of murder in manner and form as charged in the indictment, and we fix her punish—"

The rest of the word was drowned out by Kitty's scream. She clutched her arms and fell in on herself, as if she'd taken a blow to the stomach. McCarthy steadied her. The clerk, who'd looked up at the sound, returned to the piece of paper. "Fix her punishment at imprisonment in the penitentiary for the term of her natural life."

"Expressions of surprise were heard all over the courtroom," wrote the *Post.* It had finally happened: a conviction. Kitty screamed again, deeper, angry. She shook her head violently. When McCarthy and the bailiffs tried to calm her, she threw them off: "Keep away! I don't want to see anybody." The circuitry in her brain suddenly snapped. She dropped in a dead faint, hitting the floor as if she'd jumped from a third-floor window. Spectators in the crowded courtroom pushed forward, oblivious to Judge Steffen banging his gavel. Kitty lay rigid, lost in blackness. Despite repeated efforts, lawyers and guards couldn't revive her. "While the confusion was at the height, deputy sheriffs lifted the woman from the floor and put her on a chair," Forbes wrote. They carried her to the prisoners' elevator and then hefted her across the street. She woke in her cell, confused, trying to sort out what had happened.

"My God! What did they do?" she asked.

❧❧

That was a good question. All of the women on Murderess Row had to be wondering exactly what that jury had done. Was everything different now because of Katherine Malm? Were juries now willing to convict women of murder, after years of refusing to do so? The state's attorney's office said yes: Murderous women would now—at last—pay the penalty in Cook County just as men did.

For prosecutors, however, building on this single verdict surely would be problematic. Yes, Kitty was a young white woman and she'd been convicted, but she wasn't like so many of the women who'd been set free in recent years, especially the high-profile ones. Cora Orthwein had been a St. Louis society lady before divorce and booze caused her to "fall" from respectability and ultimately to shoot down her low-life boyfriend. Then there was Anna McGinnis, who'd been acquitted of knocking off her husband the previous summer. She was young and beautiful and had perfect manners. Times may have been changing, but the Victorian feminine ideal still loomed large in the typical juryman's psyche. He couldn't help but be disposed toward demure ladies with pretty figures and good pedigrees. Poor, uneducated girls like Kitty Malm, on the other hand, were a grave social danger. They were "physically and mentally contaminated," insisted one of the first scholarly reports on female criminality, *The Cause and Cure of Crime*. The social activist Belle Moskowitz declared that "the girl whose temperament and disposition crave unnatural forms of excitement is nearly beyond the bounds of salvation. . . . She may affect the well being of others."

That was Kitty in one pithy statement, and the newspapers knew it. For weeks she had stared at reporters through the jail's bars, defiant, seemingly without comprehension. Her hair was amateurishly hacked short, arcing across the left side of her forehead like a scythe. When the reporters arrived each day for interviews, she approached the front of her cell slowly, indirectly, like a wary animal—every time the same way. To male reporters in particular, there was no denying that Kitty Malm was a lewd, diseased girl. She'd stare right into a man's eyes, her face scrunched up as if she were working on a tough math problem. Her attitude and language were vulgar. Men looked at Kitty Malm and thought of the whores who walked North Clark Street after dark.

So had anything really changed? Two weeks after convicting Kitty, Assistant State's Attorney Pritzker announced that Belva Gaertner was "as guilty as Kitty Malm" and should receive the same treatment from a jury. But the *Tribune* stated the situation bluntly: Katherine Malm was "the only really young woman who's ever gone over the road"—that is, been convicted of murder. And the reason was that she "wasn't—well—quite 'refined.'" A respectable lady who shot her husband or boyfriend, on the other hand, a woman like Belva Gaertner, still didn't scare men: She was a romantic figure, a representation of how much women in general, with their overflowing emotions, loved and needed their men. "My experience makes me know how unreasonable men can be and makes me give the woman every advantage of the doubt," said one man interviewed about the rash of women shooting their men in Cook County.

It could all be explained through simple biology, newspaper readers were told in the aftermath of the conviction. Kitty Malm—and, needless to say, Sabella Nitti—was not like ordinary, decent women. You could tell simply by looking at her. A woman prone to crime and violence had a "broad nose and cheekbones, full chin and lips, contracted upper frontal skull development and prominent bulging development of the forehead just over the eyes and nose." That was the conclusion of noted phrenologist Dr. James M. Fitzgerald. His description tended to fit ethnic women more than Anglo women, but the doctor was a little subtler than that in his analysis. Asked by newspapers to examine photographs of murderous women, Fitzgerald insisted that they "all have broad heads. You can put it down as a basic principle that the broad-headed animals eat the narrow-headed ones. . . . All these women are alike in having single-track minds, with imperfect comprehension of consequences. They are 'show me' people who have to experience to understand, and the jails are full of this type. Food and sexual interests make a strong appeal to them."

So which was Belva Gaertner: a broad-headed animal or a narrow-headed one? Being a respectable lady, she planned on keeping a hat on in court, but she knew her life likely depended on her ability to shape the answer to that question, to make men—both jurors and reporters—see what she wanted them to see.

5

No Sweetheart in the World
Is Worth Killing

Maurine's desk sat on the east side of the local room, squeezed between the photo department and the file room. A battered typewriter, a castoff from another reporter, came with it. If she needed anything else, she could call out to a copyboy, though she didn't like to raise her voice. Genevieve Forbes enjoyed a desk in a more central location, within easy sight of Robert Lee, who handed out the most important assignments. Forbes would thump in and out of the room without a glance toward her junior colleague.

Maurine could hardly have expected anything else from Forbes. Only a handful of girl reporters covered crime in Chicago, and none did so exclusively. This did not engender feelings of sisterhood or cliquishness among them. Being the best female police reporter in a newsroom carried very little cachet, which meant being second best might be cause for transfer to the fashions beat.

Besides, Forbes, thirty years old and unmarried, had some reason for jealousy. The paper's star reporters, the men who always got the stories Forbes wanted, no longer walked straight through the center of the room. They meandered, weaving their way around to the far corner, where they paused to tie a shoe or laugh at a joke they'd just remembered. Maurine was "so lovely to look at that the men in the local room managed to have to walk by her desk, and of course stop for a cheery word," observed Fanny Butcher, who worked in the adjacent Sunday room. Butcher amused herself day after day by watching men bump into each other as they looked for something to do near the new girl reporter. Maurine tried to ignore the hovering men, but that rarely discouraged them. If she were tapping away on her typewriter, she could count on someone leaning over her shoulder, perusing a line, and offering a suggestion for improvement.

The attention directed at Maurine couldn't be entirely attributed to her beauty. She represented a rare challenge in the newsroom. The men dared not pinch her behind or make crude suggestions for assignations, as they would to Fanny Butcher or Forbes. She was different from the other young women on staff. Maurine had never even seen a poker game before joining the *Tribune.* She didn't drink or smoke. She had trouble meeting a man's eye. It brought out the romantic spirit—and good manners—in her male coworkers. Teddy Beck, the managing editor, became so frustrated at seeing his reporters crowded around Maurine all the time that he laid down a diktat: "There will be no more women in the local room." One of the few other women with a desk in the room, Margery Currey, thought that meant she had been fired. She began cleaning out her desk, avoiding eye contact with other reporters to keep from crying, before being told the edict didn't apply to her. Settled back in front of her Underwood, she noted, "This is one time when my face was my fortune." Currey, Butcher pointed out, was an excellent journalist, "but ravishingly beautiful she was not."

Forbes got to stay too. She had proven her value many times over, but there was also simply too much work to do for Beck's order ever to be implemented: too many murderesses knocking off their boyfriends, too many girl pickpockets and pretty little con artists, too many young women snatched from respectable lives by white slavers or their own dark curiosity.

More than anything else, Forbes and Maurine could thank the Eighteenth Amendment for their burgeoning career opportunities. No one had foreseen that Prohibition would have such disastrous consequences. Chicago's newspapers had all supported the constitutional amendment and its enforcement law, the Volstead Act, which went into effect in January 1920. But their support hardly convinced anyone that the law was right. Prohibition's timing had simply been awful. The 1920s began, wrote Burton Rascoe, the *Tribune*'s former literary editor, "in a general atmosphere of cynicism, disillusion and bitterness." The unprecedented carnage of the World War had touched everyone in one way or another; now few people, especially those under forty, had any tolerance for the tin-eared moralizing of the temperance folks. After Prohibition got under way, alcohol consumption spiked—and continued to rise even as the quality of the spirits plummeted. For a whole generation, across class lines, defying the dry law became an act of self-definition—a necessary rebellion against a sordid, hypocritical ruling class. Illegal production and distribution of alcoholic beverages, centered in Chicago, became one of the biggest industries in the country, with beer sales in the city topping $30 million a month by one accounting.

The official corruption that came with this unprecedented criminal expansion was similarly outsize. Gangsters funneled a million dollars in bribes each month to Chicago's police, prosecutors, and elected officials. It made the whole city—at least to Maurine's suddenly jaded eye—a "grand and gory comedy." When it came to bootleggers, those charged with enforcing the law, at every level, became blind and dumb. Reporters who didn't overlook this rampant graft suffered. Fred Lovering, of the *Daily Journal*, foolishly broke a story about bribery at the Cook County Jail. The next time the reporter walked into the lockup, guards grabbed him and held him down while prisoners pummeled him. Lovering's nose was reduced to a blob of flaccid flesh, leaving him with breathing problems, a severe speech impediment, and constant pain for the rest of his life. Maurine was stunned to learn that a warden at a smaller facility called in federal agents "to stop bootlegging in his jail so that he can bring his prisoners to trial sober"—stunned, that is, to discover an honest man running a jail in the county. She found that in every kind of crime—"hijacking and graft scandals . . . frequency of murders, percentage of acquitted, etc."—Chicago stood out, and that most of it was related to booze.

※※※

Bootlegging was an overwhelming problem in Cook County Jail—with the exception, for the most part, of the women's section. Sitting in a cell less than forty-eight hours after her arrest, Belva Gaertner's hands shook, and she gulped cup after cup of stale coffee to settle her nerves. This may have been rough on the new inmate, but she quickly recognized it was for the best. The newspapers thrived on Prohibition as much as the bootleggers, though in an entirely different way. For the sob sisters, no story line was more reliably popular than that of the reformed sinner. Belva, with the drinking and the gunplay and the high-profile divorce, was sure to be a huge story, and almost all of the city's papers began working on her potential redemption.

On March 14, the day after the inquest into Walter Law's death, the *Daily Journal* declared that Belva had turned to the Lord and gathered the other women inmates to sing hymns. "One number on the programme was a pianologue," the paper wrote. "The words were spoken by Mrs. Belle Gaertner, held in connection with the killing of Walter Law, and the accompaniment was the tune and faint plaintive words: 'Where He leads me, I will follow.'" Once the singing was over, the *Journal*'s reporter pulled Belva aside:

> Mrs. Gaertner, clad in a sober but hopeful black canton dress with Spanish lace sleeves, refused to "talk." Her attorneys had been there early in the day and left rules to be followed. . . . Mrs. Gaertner admitted reluctantly that she feels well, although the jail cots are not the most comfortable in the world.

The *Journal*, as expected, provided the conventional premise for a girl-gunner story: the predatory man. "Law is to blame for the trouble my daughter is in," Belva's mother, Mary Leese, said from the apartment she shared with her daughter. "He was crazy about her and always after her. He came here nights and took her out, and not content with that, he came here often in the daytime. He wouldn't let her alone." The elderly woman told the paper that she didn't understand how Mrs. Law could have been so "hoodwinked" by her husband.

The Hearst papers also stayed with the tried-and-true formula for their coverage of Belva, though their approach differed from the *Journal*'s. They created glamour out of blood and misery. The photo retouchers at the *American* and the *Herald and Examiner* were experts at buffing up pictures of women criminals: painting out wrinkles, eye bags, double chins.

In the original photos from the night of the shooting, Belva looked old and exhausted, her skin loose, eyes drooping. This was a woman who'd seen way too much life. Those same photos in Hearst newsprint, however, showed a woman transformed, a lean and fetching beauty—maybe even beautiful enough to be innocent. With their emphasis on sensation and sentimentality, the Hearst newspapers had a stake in their murderesses looking more beautiful than those in the staid *Tribune* and *Daily News*, and their artists competed with each other like rival funeral-home directors.

Following Walter Howey's imperative to "hype this up," the *American* and the *Herald and Examiner* further goosed their story packages about Belva with bulging headlines and captions that sported purple prose, all seeking to get the reader emotionally involved in the ongoing drama. The *Herald and Examiner* warned that poisonous alcohol had accounted for more than two hundred deaths in Cook County in 1923. Worse, the fusel oil and industrial solvents in the bootleggers' "reckless mixtures has created a new type of alcoholism and insanity." Could this be the reason Belva shot? The *Herald and Examiner*'s sister paper took the possibility seriously, or at least half seriously. The *American* re-created the gin-soaked events leading up to the shooting in a series of cartoon panels. This kind of strip, popular for girl-crime stories, promoted moral behavior—modesty, abstemiousness, familial love—while at the same time wallowing in its opposite. It always featured drawings of a wild-eyed, scantily clad woman holding a smoking gun and an empty bottle of liquor. The typical murderess, one panel exclaimed, "like all girls, faced the old problem of whether to follow the conventions of the world or her own desires." Belva Gaertner, the reader was told, had had plenty of fun, but now she regretted it.

The *Tribune* officially remained above such sensational treatment of the news, but Maurine felt confident she had the ability to match Hearst anyway. Even without imaginative photo retouchers and headline writers helping her, she could still break out of the standard *Tribune* style and be creative on her own. Her colleague at the paper, Genevieve Forbes, was already stretching the boundaries of newspaper form—"for an editor may give you your assignment, but you give yourself your style," the veteran newswoman said. Forbes's style was often clumsy, but at her best she expertly combined the hang-'em-now attitude the *Tribune* took with all accused killers and the sob-sister sentimentality of the Hearst papers. With her report on the Law inquest, the intense, insecure Forbes, who had started out at the *Tribune* as an editorial assistant, showed Maurine how it was done. Her story focused not on the inquest itself, like Maurine's report, but on Freda Law's reaction to the cool, smirking woman who'd killed her husband. She wrote:

> When they talked of gin and blood, Mrs. Law trembled as if she might faint, huddled close to her father-in-law, and tried to keep from crying. It was her grief for her dead husband, she indicated. When they spoke of the divorcee's nocturnal visits with Law to south side cabarets . . . Mrs. Law pushed herself forward and sneered across the table at the older, more vivacious woman with the seven diamond rings. It was her hatred for her husband's alleged slayer, she admitted.

Forbes, whose stories about Kitty Malm and Sabella Nitti helped lead to convictions, went on to describe how Belva was plainly dressed at the inquest because her "best caracul coat, her chic white hat and her modish green dress are ruined with blood. So she wears a brown sport dress, a plain black coat with a fur collar and a brown sport hat. Seven diamond rings and a wristwatch have been washed clean of Walter Law's blood. They sparkle more brightly from that cleaning, as she uses her hands to gesture."

Maurine understood the lesson: If a girl reporter wanted to compete for the front page of the *Tribune*, she had to write tough, hard-hitting prose while also being as entertaining as the "sensation sheets," even if that meant taking occasional liberties to make a strong case. (Belva, for example, wasn't wearing her wristwatch at the inquest. The faceplate had been cracked, and it no longer worked.) As it turned out, in both temperament and experience, Maurine was ideally suited to this approach. Her companion inquest article, straightforward and factual, paled in comparison with Forbes's, but she wasn't cowed by having a veteran reporter encroach on her story. The next day, with her third piece on

Belva in as many days, Maurine found her voice. Having sat with Belva in her cell for much of the evening, she let the alleged murderess tell her own story, while the omniscient and unseen reporter narrated. Instead of going for pathos, like the *Journal* and the Hearst newspapers, Maurine allowed Belva's unconscious self-absorption to take center stage. She slyly poked fun at—and holes in—everything her subject said. "No sweetheart in the world is worth killing—especially when you've had a flock of them—and the world knows it," Maurine began in the Friday, March 14, edition.

That is one of the musings of Mrs. Belva Gaertner in her county jail cell and it is why—so she says—a "broad minded" jury is all that is needed to free her of the charge of murdering Walter Law.

The latest alleged lady murderess of Cook county, in whose car young Law was found shot to death as a finale to three months of wild gin parties with Belva while his wife sat at home unsuspecting, isn't a bit worried over the case.

"Why, it's silly to say I murdered Walter," she said during a lengthy discourse on love, gin, guns, sweeties, wives, and husbands. "I liked him and he loved me—but no woman can love a man enough to kill him. They aren't worth it, because there are always plenty more. Walter was just a kid—29 and I'm 38. Why should I have worried whether he loved me or whether he left me?"

Then the double divorcee of frequent newspaper notoriety turned to the question of juries.

"Now, that coroner's jury that held me for murder," she said. "That was bum. They were narrow-minded old birds—bet they never heard a jazz band in their lives. Now, if I'm tried, I want worldly men, broad-minded men, men who know what it is to get out a bit. Why, no one like that would convict me."

It was a breakout performance for Maurine—incisive and brutally effective, an exemplar of the *Tribune*'s executioner's style. Most of all, the story proved to Robert Lee that his instincts about Maurine had been right. Everyone wanted to confide in her and help her out, including a high-profile murder suspect. Belva had revealed herself to the young *Tribune* scribe in a way she hadn't to anyone else, providing the most beautiful quotes any crime reporter could hope for.

"I wish I could remember just what happened," she said to Maurine, just as she had to so many other reporters when pressed for details of the bloody night. Except then she offered something more: "We got drunk and he got killed with my gun in my car. But gin and guns—either one is bad enough, but together they get you in a dickens of a mess, don't they? Now, if I hadn't had a gun, or if Walter hadn't had the gin . . ." Belva let the thought go unfinished. "Of course," she added, "it's too bad for Walter's wife, but husbands always cause women trouble."

Belva must have been surprised when she read the story the next morning. She thought she'd been careful, and she no doubt thought she and Maurine had had an understanding. But the sweet-faced little reporter showed her subject no consideration in exchange for opening up to her; Maurine made clear to her newspaper's tens of thousands of readers that Belva caused as much trouble as the worst possible husband. She highlighted Belva's gay laughter during the interview—how she "chortled in jail, [while] plans were completed for young Law's funeral today." More than that, Maurine purposely did not acknowledge that Belva actually made a decent point in the interview. Walter Law was married and almost a decade younger than Belva. Why *should* she have worried whether he loved her or not? Belva surely knew Walter wasn't going to leave his wife and son for her. And if her history proved anything, it was that she knew there was always another man waiting down at the end of the bar.

It made for a compelling argument, and Belva's lawyers—and the Hearst papers—were giving it a good, hard look. But that simply didn't matter to Maurine. She worked for the paper that was "out for conviction always," and she believed in her mission. Belva Gaertner, one way or another, had led a man to his moral destruction and death. Whatsoever a woman soweth, that shall she also reap.

❧

Maurine stuck mostly to the courthouse, the jail, and the police stations on her beat. This was the established, safe way for a woman to cover crime, and it served her strengths. She wasn't really a reporter, after all—she'd never been trained. She was a *writer.* The problem was that Belva Gaertner and the world in which the stylish divorcée lived existed almost entirely in Maurine's head. Maurine took in what Belva said, studied her while she said it, and then used her imagination to fill in the details.

Maurine's (and Genevieve Forbes's) chief competition on the girl-crime beat, on the other hand, had no qualms about getting out on the street. Ione Quinby of the *Evening Post* was a familiar face in the Levee, the vice district in the near South Side's First Ward. There'd been hundreds of brothels, saloons, and opium dens operating in the district at its height, before the war, when Quinby started her journalism career. A young woman walking in the Levee always had to worry about being thumped on the head by a white slaver, but Quinby did it anyway. The upside was too big. The 1911 Vice Commission calculated that "Chicago's vice annually destroys the souls of 5,000 young women." Some of those five thousand souls each year became Quinby's most titillating stories. The reporter even embraced the entrepreneurial spirit of the Levee. In her purse, unknown to her employer, Quinby kept mimeographs of a legal document. Coming upon a newly arrested girl at the Wabash Avenue or Harrison Street police station, she'd place the contract before the suspect and ask her to sign. It gave Quinby permission to write and sell the woman's life story. Most suspects, uneducated and scared, would sign without realizing they had a choice. A couple of months later a "My Life in Crime" story—often written in the first person—would appear in *True Detective* or *Master Detective* magazine. The story was always a cracker. Quinby had a way, a colleague said, "of prying the details of unhappy marriages, unrequited love, and secret sex experiences out of the most non-communicative murderesses; they would confide facts to her which they had withheld even from their own attorneys."

Maurine must have been surprised—and heartened—upon meeting her competitor. The thirty-two-year-old Quinby was Chicago's foremost chronicler of "murderesses," rivaled only by Forbes. But like Maurine, there was nothing imposing about her. "The *Post*'s little bob-haired reporter," as Quinby's paper promoted her, stood barely five feet tall and had a chubby, little boy's face, with crinkling eyes and a grin that split her mouth like a gorge. She reveled in police sergeants and competing reporters underestimating her. She'd march through the *Post*'s newsroom when she had a good story going, pumping herself up by repeating over and over to herself: "Hoo-boy, hoo-boy!" One fellow scribe remarked that there "is a certain little toss of her head when she talks and a tiny little compression of her lips that denote a strength that one might not suspect in one so small."

Despite Quinby's pleasant, open-faced personality, Maurine didn't try to befriend her. The two reporters recognized each other as budding rivals, particularly on the Belva Gaertner story. Quinby had become friendly with Belva during the suspected murderess's divorce case in 1920, a big advantage for the *Post* hack. Indeed, back then, just before woman suffrage became law, Quinby saw "Mrs. Belle Gaertner" as a kind of feminist heroine. When her divorce from William was finalized that spring, leaving her with a paltry settlement, Belva didn't go in search of another millionaire husband, as would be expected. Instead, she undertook a new career: taxi driver. It was a novel—to some, a scandalous—choice for a woman. Motor cars were booming in popularity, but many people still couldn't fathom driving one. They were terrifying, futuristic machines. Driving a car was certainly unladylike. But Belva, always cheerful and stubborn, took no mind of such fuddy-duddy thinking. A taxi was a grand idea, she thought, especially as she was the rare woman who had a bead on her true nature. "Well, I just can't take orders from anyone," she said. "Therefore I can't hold a job. I must be my own boss. So I decided that as a taxi driver I'd be my own boss, make enough to live on, and still have the pleasure of the car."

A woman who couldn't take orders—*that* was a story. Quinby spent a day with Belva soon after she got her livery license. Any man walking by the taxi stand where Belva stood beside her machine, "clad in a trim chauffeur's suit of green," had to stop and stare, the reporter wrote. "What else could he do, under the combined barrage of two impelling dimples, a row of perfect pearly teeth in their cherry-lined frame and two laughing, lustrous eyes?" In the spring of 1920, Belva was a symbol of a daring, new, "modern" way of life—one in which automobiles whisked girls out of their neighborhoods, out of their parents' orbit, and into the world; one where jazz pounded and thumped in clubs every night, working people into a dangerous, animal state. Almost everything about this modern life seemed to be fast—breathtakingly fast, sometimes scary fast—and that included young city girls like Quinby herself, the "flappers." They talked fast; they walked fast. They smoked furiously and flirted constantly. They wore rouge and lipstick—their "cherry-lined frames"—and skirts that showed their legs. They went out to the dance halls on their own. None of them wore corsets. It was, said one commentator, "sex o'clock in America."

Maurine, growing up in her small Midwestern town and going to school in the South and in Indianapolis (Chicagoans derided the Indiana capital as Nap Town), experienced almost none of this churning change that so thrilled Belva Gaertner and Ione Quinby. Maurine could have stayed in Crawfordsville and avoided it almost altogether. Proponents of the old ways, after all, weren't simply giving up. Doctors warned that the "flapper lifestyle"—such as wearing makeup and spending late nights dancing and petting—threatened "severe internal derangement and general ill-health." School boards across the country put the hammer down on female teachers, with contracts that required them to be in bed by eight P.M. and prohibited them from wearing skirts above the ankle, bobbing their hair, or smoking cigarettes. The *Evening American* reported that the "faculty at Northwestern University has decided that for a pretty coed to display a pretty knee in a picture is 'unfavorable publicity.'"

This was the side Maurine's parents were on, and Maurine never contradicted her parents. She certainly never considered bobbing her hair or displaying a pretty knee. She didn't like to think of herself as beautiful. Beauty was for the Divine, and Maurine, a devout girl, a minister's daughter, could never think of herself as Divine. Young Crawfordsville ladies strove to be respectable, not beautiful. Maurine went to church every Sunday and prayed for guidance. Her parents could be proud of her.

And yet . . . here she was in Chicago—the Jazz Capital, the "abattoir by the lake." The city had a way of overwhelming the individual, of breaking down his or her opposition. Young men and women arrived in Chicago from across the world and promptly lost their identities—or reforged them into tougher, more vital versions of themselves. There was little use in resisting. Already Maurine had decided that she would make an awful wife and so told suitors she "would not do that to anyone." In Chicago, she found she could be freer than she ever thought possible, more open-minded and outgoing. Soon after starting at the *Tribune,* she wrote a glowing profile of Aletta Jacobs, a radical doctor from Holland who vigorously supported birth control, something Maurine's church just as vigorously opposed. Maurine knew all about how birth control was "race suicide"—it had been one of Theodore Roosevelt's pet issues—but she now appeared unconcerned. She also attended a conference for the Women's International League for Peace and Freedom, where the fervor of the socialist group's members impressed her, especially a "smiling blonde with brilliant blue eyes" who told her of the "beautifully moral pacifistic resistance of the laborers."

The foundation on which Maurine had been raised seemed to shake with every passing day, more so than her parents back in Crawfordsville possibly could have imagined. The fledgling reporter wasn't just exposed to controversial reformers like Aletta Jacobs and socialists. She had swiftly developed a new, wholly unexpected interest: murder. It was a fascination that would have horrified everyone she grew up with. Just a few weeks earlier, it would have horrified Maurine, too. It still did, in fact, but now she tamped down that horror with the kind of twinkling bravado all of her fellow reporters seemed to sport so easily. She didn't have it in her to demand information from battered victims or grief-stricken family members as if it were owed to her, but she could pretend to be unmoved by the bloody events she wrote about. And sometimes—after hours of standing around at police stations and battling for the phone to call in reports—she actually was. She became numb, and it was liberating. Maurine decided that murder was more accepted in Chicago than anywhere else in the country. Gun-toting gangsters—Johnny Torrio, Dean O'Banion, the Capone brothers—were among the biggest celebrities in the city. Chicagoans rejected the notion, common in Crawfordsville, that a man had to be a sociopath or brain-damaged to kill another person. Instead, violence could simply be a necessary response to the environment. One of Maurine's early assignments was the case of fifteen-year-old Dominick Galluzzo, a "sober, earnest-eyed" boy who'd been pushed to his limit by an abusive father and so shot him down. The coroner's jury determined the shooting a justifiable homicide. So did Maurine, who enthusiastically listed the dead man's transgressions, such as calling his wife "an ugly old thing" in front of her coworkers at a candy factory. In Chicago, the young reporter had noticed, murder "doesn't put anyone in a flurry." Thanks to the newspapers, it was a part of daily conversation, and as often as not, that conversation included an approving nod or laugh.

Maurine nodded and laughed, too. She couldn't help it. She liked the Chicago attitude. She liked nerve. Chicagoans certainly had that. On the East Coast, titled Europeans and wealthy industrialists still dominated the public eye. But in this wild city, democracy ruled. To get star treatment in "Murder City," Maurine noted, all you had to do was pull a gun, for "Chicago, bless her heart, will swallow anything with enough gore and action." Maurine herself eagerly gorged on as much as she could. Being a reporter in a big city, a city where no one knew her, gave her courage. She would even develop a kind of crush on a gangster, later saying that the "nicest man I met during the time I was doing newspaper work was supposed to be the toughest gunman in Chicago's West Side. He was like something you read about, such a charming, courteous man. . . . I might add that he was the only man I ever met in the newspaper world who, when he swore, apologized for it." Maurine interviewed the gangster in a hospital room after he'd been shot three times, noting that he got out of bed to greet her "with as much casual grace as any continental actor in lavender pajamas."

"I had to ask him a lot of questions that were none of my business," she said. "He acted so sorry not to be able to answer them that I felt like weeping. I asked him who shot him, but the only way we could ever have found out was by watching to see who was the next man 'bumped off.'"*

The gangster's matter-of-fact attitude toward violence was awful, and

*Maurine never named her tough West Side gunman, but it may have been Myles O'Donnell (of the West Side O'Donnells), who was shot three times in November of 1924 but survived.

she knew it, but at the same time there was something in Maurine—in her need to idealize, to glamorize—that found it immensely appealing. Gangsters thrilled her. Chivalry and romanticism, those forgotten Victorian ideals, weren't dead; they simply belonged to the underworld now. "Gunmen are just divine," Maurine took to saying. "They have such lovely, quaint, old-fashioned ideas about women being on pedestals. My idea of something pleasant is to be surrounded by gunmen."

⋙⋘

Maurine couldn't say the same about gun girls. She would never find Belva Gaertner interesting in the same way Quinby did. Despite setting off on her own path, despite eschewing marriage, Maurine's feminism remained inchoate. Gangsters like Dean O'Banion could be romantic figures, but not violent women. More than that, she found murderous women—God forgive her—funny. Standing around at the Criminal Courts Building, she could get her fellow reporters laughing about the city's latest murderess going down in history as "a little sister of Lady Macbeth, Salome and Lucrezia Borgia," further ingratiating herself with the men and putting off the women scribes.

The zingers that Maurine tossed out when talking about Belva (or Kitty Malm or Sabella Nitti) undoubtedly were a means of coping with what she was experiencing. Underneath the snide remarks about "charming murderesses" pulsed a deep-seated fear of what it all meant. The British war hero Ian Hay Beith, just landed in the United States for a speaking tour, worried that "the privileges that young women have enjoyed since the war have reduced the happiness that life holds for them, and men today lack the old-fashioned reverence for women that was the most sacred thing in life."

Maurine, cynical jokes and her own liberation aside, agreed. Freedom came with responsibilities, and too many of the women in Chicago were being overwhelmed by their choices. That much she understood very well.

6

The Kind of Gal Who Never Could Be True

On Thursday, April 3, Beulah Annan heard a rap on the screen door at the back of her apartment. She pushed aside the newspaper, padded barefoot through the little kitchen, and opened the inner door. She found Harry Kalstedt standing there, as she knew she would. He was smiling that laconic smile of his.

"Oh, hello, Anne," Harry said. "You all alone?" He always called her Anne. Not Beulah. Not May, her middle name. It made a nice sound in his mouth: Anne. Sweet, but also teasing, damp, seductive. She'd told him on the phone just an hour ago that she wouldn't be around today, but he came over anyway, and here she was ready for him, wearing only her camisole. Harry Kalstedt's smile widened. He said she looked like she could use a drink. Beulah smiled back at him. She said she reckoned she could.

Harry stepped into the kitchen. "I hate to do this, but I need money," he said, spoiling the mood they had going. He had a good job delivering for Tennant's Laundry, but Beulah had noticed that he never seemed to have any money. She twisted the doorknob back and forth in her hand. Harry smelled like he'd already been drinking. He hadn't saved her a drop.

"How much do you need?"

"Six dollars."

Beulah frowned. "I can't let you have that much; I haven't got it."

Harry said he'd take whatever she had, and Beulah tramped into the bedroom to retrieve her pocketbook. Harry took a dollar and was gone, the screen door clattering as punctuation. It was a little after twelve.

Beulah drifted into the living room, leaving the newspaper on the table. There was no news from Murderess Row again. She followed coverage of Belva Gaertner closely in the papers, but the last couple of days hadn't offered much. It seemed Belva, after nearly three weeks without booze or boyfriends, had lost some of her joie de vivre. The fancy divorcée now let her lawyer do the talking for her. The others were even worse. Kitty Malm, defeated and scared, had put away her bluster for good and didn't bother with reporters anymore. Sabella Nitti waited for the hangman with mindless stoicism. Boring, boring, and boring.

The men, fortunately, had picked up the slack. The *Tribune* that morning carried a death notice for Frank Capone, "beloved son of Theresa and the late Gabriel, brother of James, Ralph, Alphonse, Erminio, Humbert, Amadea, and Mafalda. Funeral Saturday at 9 A.M. from late residence, 7244 Prairie Avenue." The April Fool's Day shootout in suburban Cicero that had killed the bootlegger was on the city's front pages for a second straight day. The Capone family home, a few blocks south of Washington Park, wasn't far from Beulah's building. Already, truckloads of flowers overwhelmed the house, covering the terrace and hanging from trees in the front yard. Many of Beulah's neighbors, reading the notice, planned to walk over on Saturday to watch the funeral procession glide slowly toward Mt. Olivet Cemetery. That was the kind of thing Beulah liked to do, too, but right now she wasn't thinking about the funeral or the exciting gangland events that precipitated it. She wasn't thinking about Belva Gaertner or the other girls at Cook County Jail, either. The newspaper was forgotten. Now that she'd seen Harry Kalstedt, now that she'd smelled him, Beulah's thoughts were entirely in the moment. She couldn't stand how long it was going to take him to get back to the apartment.

She put on her favorite record: "Hula Lou." *Her name was Hula Lou, the kind of gal who never could be true.* Beulah got so lonesome being in the flat by herself when her husband, Al, was at work. That was why she took a job at Tennant's Laundry. What else was she going to do? It wasn't as though she'd get more housework done if she were home every day. She hated doing housework. She much preferred sitting around dreaming about Harry.

It had been six months since she and Harry Kalstedt met, and Beulah remembered the very moment of it. His eyes had lingered a long time, drawing a smile out of her. She knew how she looked. The women in the newspaper ads had the same large, enchanting eyes, the same perfectly marcelled hair, the same curvy torsos dropping into tight little hips. Beulah was a thing of beauty in every way. She took pride in it. And not just in her looks. Her mother had taught her how to act around a man: the gaze always so soft and clinging, the mouth always bowed into deep interest as he talked of the weather or the stock tables or hats. She would sometimes take Harry's hand and hold the back of it against her breast and sigh.

Harry returned with two quarts of wine. Back in October, when Beulah had a bad reaction to booze, she wrote in her diary, "No more moonshine for me." But she didn't mean it. Whenever she got really sick from drinking, she'd just skip work for a couple of days. She knew a doctor who'd give her morphine to get her through the worst of it. How alcohol felt as it spread through her—her head light and fizzy, her extremities tingling—always made the possible fallout later worthwhile. She and Harry settled in on the couch, filled the glasses she'd set out. Beulah snuggled into his chest. She knew she ought to feel ashamed when she was with Harry, kissing and loving him in the middle of the day, her day off from work, but she never did. She felt it was a woman's prerogative "to keep a card up her sleeve," especially a card as strong and good-looking as Harry Kalstedt.

They sat there and drank and listened to the record player. That was fine for a while, the wine sweet and warm, the jazz more so, but when she and Harry drank and kept their clothes on, they only wanted to make each other mad. It never took much drinking. Sure enough, that dollar she'd given him started to grate on her. She looked at the flowered paper on the walls, the sawdust-stuffed furniture. Everything in her life was cheap. She sat up and accused Harry of lying about having money to spend on her. He always said he was going to take her places, throw some money around, but he never did. Harry was awfully tight with a dollar.

When he didn't respond to her, just took another drink, Beulah became furious. She was certain he had other girlfriends. Why else would he never have any money? *There's another man,* she said suddenly, the only thing that came to her mind to say. A real Southern gentleman, a man who knew how to act, who took her out dancing. Johnny was his name.

Now Harry sat up. *Johnny?* Who was this Johnny? He glared at her. He wanted to know what she had been doing with this other man. Had she been with Johnny on the bed in the next room—the bed where she had lain down for *him* so many times? Harry never asked her that question about Al. Maybe he assumed she never did it with Al anymore. "If that's the kind of a woman you are," he said, spitting out the words. He called her a vile name.

"Well, you're nothing!" she yelled, her face filling with heat, her beautiful eyes cut into deep, angry slits.

"To hell with you!" he barked.

Beulah screamed louder: *You're nothing but a dirty goddam jailbird!* Harry's eyes jumped and he got up. Even in the big city, that was an insult that burned like hot coals.

Something's going to happen, Beulah thought. She bit her lip. Maybe he would take her now, right here on the couch. Yank her underthings off and split her open, with the breeze from the window rolling over them and her husband soon to come home from work. Her chest felt tight, the heart desperate to get out. Harry stepped forward, "with a look in his eyes." Beulah turned toward the bedroom.

⌒⌒

At 4:10 she decided to call the laundry. It had been more than two hours since her fight with Harry. She turned down the volume on the Victrola. *Hula Lou . . . she's got a pretty form, it's pretty every place, you never get a chance to look her in the face.* Her boss, the head bookkeeper, answered the phone. "Hello, Betty," she chirped, "what are you doing?"

Betty Bergman sighed. It was Beulah. "I'm awfully busy," she said.

"Is Billy there?" Beulah thought it'd be good to talk to Harry's brother-in-law, just for a minute.

Betty cocked her head to hold the phone in place against her shoulder. He's been in and out, she said.

There was a pause, then a small voice: "Is Moo there?" Beulah held her breath: Why'd she use one of her pet names for Harry?

Betty sighed again. Stupid, silly girl. "You know he hasn't been here all day long," she said.

Beulah gripped the receiver until her hand hurt. "That's funny," she said. "I had an appointment with him for a quarter after twelve and he hasn't shown up!" She was triumphant.

"What's the matter, Red? You sound kinda stewed."

"No, I haven't had a drink all day," Beulah insisted. "I talk queerly because I'm trying to talk to you and read the telephone directory at the same time."

Beulah hung up. She wandered to the window and looked over the ledge. Schoolgirls had been playing out there earlier, but they were gone now. Beulah slowly rotated her hips to the music, waggled her knee. She'd been dancing around the room for an hour before she called Betty, and now she was exhausted. Tears suddenly sprang from her eyes and she buckled, almost retching.

The record scratched to its end, and she started it over again, for maybe the hundredth time: *Her name was Hula Lou, the kind of gal who never could be true.* The room spun into focus. Beulah stopped dancing. Harry—Moo—was still on the floor. The trickle of blood from his back had grown to a pool that now threatened to consume him, like a sinkhole after a spring deluge. It was nearly five o'clock.

Why, you're nothing but a dirty goddam jailbird!

Yes, she'd said that. She remembered saying it now. That was when everything changed. Men didn't like to be reminded of who they were. She'd looked up, right into the hatred burning out from him. It sucked the breath out of her. She couldn't be blamed for what happened next. She just wanted him to treat her right. Nobody ever did. Nobody who mattered. She picked up the phone again. This time she called her husband at the garage where he worked.

"Come home, I've shot a man," she cried when Al came on the line. "He's been trying to make love to me."

ɔɹɔ

"Where is the gun?" the officer asked when the door opened.

Al Annan offered up the revolver. The policeman gave Beulah the once-over. She hadn't put on a wrap or anything, though she knew the police were coming. You could see the full outline of her body through the slight fabric of her camisole; the sling of her thigh wavered into view like a dream. "Hula Lou" was still playing on the Victrola.

Al didn't have any choice but to let the man look. Nothing was private now. He hadn't really heard what his wife said on the phone; he'd only registered the fear and panic in her voice and rushed out. He started to think about the possibilities during the mad dash home in the taxi. When he came in the door, the first thing he saw was another man's coat and hat on the chair. He knocked them to the floor with the back of his hand. He wanted to do the same to his wife next. Then he saw the body crumpled on the bedroom floor—and his wife, sobbing, hysterical. She told her story again, quickly, between dried-out retches. This man had come in and tried to make love to her. She'd fought him off and shot him with the gun. She'd then waited for a while, hoping he'd get up and leave, before calling the garage. Al looked into his wife's eyes and wobbled. He believed her. Why else would a man be lying dead in their apartment? Al rang up the police. Beulah clawed at him, begging him to put down the phone. When a voice tweeted over the line—Sergeant John O'Grady sitting behind the front desk at the Wabash Avenue station—Beulah heaved the receiver away from Al and shrieked, "I've just killed my husband!"

The patrolman kneeled beside the dead body. More officers arrived at the small apartment at 817 East Forty-sixth Street, just five blocks north of the Washington Park bridle path that had been Belva Gaertner's favorite. To the residents of Beulah and Al's South Side neighborhood, known as Grand Boulevard, the city's elite didn't seem a mere half-dozen blocks away. The nearness of wealthy Hyde Park and Kenwood was a geographic reality but an abstract one; the park system provided an excellent barrier. Instead of being insulated by greenery, as Hyde Park was, the Grand

Boulevard neighborhood was crisscrossed by streetcars and intersected by an elevated line that made the Stockyards seem closer. Rickety wooden houses and chunky three-story brick apartment buildings populated the neighborhood, and they were filled with workers from the Michigan Southern Railroad yards to the west. Grand Boulevard had been a Catholic community for years, with St. Elizabeth's parish accommodating hundreds at its peak, before the area began turning Jewish in the early 1900s. The Sinai Temple, Chicago's first reform synagogue, stood at Forty-sixth and Grand, a short walk from Al and Beulah's apartment.

Beulah didn't think anything of the Catholic exodus; she'd grown up in the Baptist faith and didn't bother with church anymore. The growing numbers of blacks, however, worried everyone. Memories and stories of the 1919 race riots percolated thickly in every South Sider's mind. Mass violence had broken out that summer following news that a Negro boy drowned after sunbathers wouldn't allow him to come ashore on the white area of a beach. Fighting raged for days on the South Side, with white gangs sweeping through black neighborhoods, setting houses on fire, and beating anyone who was on the street. The newspapers pecked away at the story from the periphery, fearful of sending reporters directly into the black areas that had become a war zone. After a couple of days, the *Herald and Examiner,* whose editors believed they'd given the Negro a fair shake in their pages, decided to get a firsthand account. One of the paper's circulation enforcers mounted a motorcycle while a reporter climbed into the sidecar. The driver jammed a *Herald and Examiner* placard in the windscreen. "This will get us by," he said. "The paper's been giving the jigaboos all the best of it. They won't pop off at us." The two men made it less than a block into "Darkie Town" before explosions crackled in the sky. There were men with rifles on the roofs of the buildings. The driver pulled out a revolver and fired off a few rounds as he tried to steer the motorcycle around the corner and back out of the neighborhood. The papers stayed out. After more than two dozen people had been killed and hundreds injured—mostly blacks—Governor Frank Lowden sent six thousand National Guard soldiers to calm everyone down.

Despite the whupping, the "jigaboos" didn't go away. South State Street had become the "Mecca for Pleasure" for the black community, with hot jazz pouring out of nightclubs every night. "Midnight was like day," the writer Langston Hughes recalled after visiting the entertainment strip. "The street was full of workers and gamblers, prostitutes and pimps, church folk and sinners." The black Ebenezer Baptist Church had taken root at Forty-fifth and Vincennes, which loomed in Beulah's walk home from the streetcar each day. She was sure the Negro boys looked at her with the same baleful lust as the white boys, and everyone knew the blacks had less capacity for restraint. That was a good enough reason to keep a revolver in the house—the revolver that now resided in a policeman's pocket.

Officers worked their way through the apartment, noting the position of furniture and rooms, surveying the placement of the body from every angle. One of the officers, Sergeant Malachi Murphy, asked Al where the gun was kept. Al told him the bureau drawer. Beulah's husband looked down at the dead man, at all that blood soaked into his floor, and he began to believe *he* had done it. "I came home and found this guy going after her," he said, as much to himself as to the sergeant. "It was me that shot him." When another policeman turned to him, Al started to tell more, stumbling, falling over himself, saving his darling Beulah. She hadn't stopped crying since the police arrived; he couldn't take it. He looked at her. She was helpless, the tears squirting out of her in a fury.

"No!" Beulah said. The police now swiveled to her. She said it again: No. Harry belonged to her, not to Al. He was all hers. She wouldn't give Harry up for anything. "I am going to quit you," Harry had said to her, and she couldn't have that. No way. Then she'd only have Al.

"I told him I would shoot," she said in a whisper. "He kept coming toward me anyway, so there was nothing else for me to do but shoot him."

"In the back?" one of the officers asked.

Beulah didn't seem to hear him. She stood still, a tuning fork whanging in her head. Then she bent slightly at the knees, and her head tipped back, as if she were taking a drink after a long trek through the desert. She dropped—a dead-away faint. No one caught her.

☙❧

Conscious thought—perception of the world—began to return. There were men in her apartment—she could hear them talking. Some seemed to be talking to her. Beulah looked through a doorway and saw shoes—polished shoes, gleaming in the light from the kitchen.

Assistant State's Attorney Roy Woods introduced himself. "Don't you know me?" he asked, hovering over her.

Beulah realized she looked a mess: her cheeks splotchy from crying, her nose red, breasts like crashed dirigibles. "No," she said.

"I am Roy C. Woods." He added that he knew Mr. Wilcox and was a customer of Tennant's Laundry.

Mr. Wilcox? This man knew Harry's brother-in-law? Had he come into the laundry when she was cashiering? Her confusion must have shown on her face, for Woods told her not to be afraid. You shot a man, an intruder, he said. Was that correct?

Beulah liked the sound of that. It was no crime to shoot a trespasser in your own home. She peered up at Mr. Woods. He was still wearing his coat and hat. Could they "frame it" to look like an accident? she asked.

Woods took a step back, shocked. The woman was hysterical. That was obvious. Still. "You don't 'frame' anything with me," he told her.

Albert Allen, the stenographer there to record what was said by witnesses and possible suspects, asked her why she had done it. Beulah turned to him, her eyes pleading. Her body shook, tears dripped down her face again. She said she didn't know why.

She put her face in her hands and, for the first time in her life, wished all the men would go away.

7

A Modern Salome

Al Annan couldn't keep control of his emotions anymore. "I've been a sucker, that's all! Simply a meal ticket!" He held his head, clutched at it. What had happened that afternoon, and what it meant, had finally sunk in. He was distraught. "I've worked ten, twelve, fourteen hours a day and took home every cent of my money," he raged in the Hyde Park police station. "We'd bought our furniture for the little apartment on time and it was all paid off but a hundred dollars. I thought she was happy. I didn't know . . ."

Maurine Watkins, there at the station with a handful of other reporters, wrote down what Al said to the police officers, to the walls, to himself, but she apparently didn't approach him for an interview. Such naked emotion from a man may have unnerved or embarrassed her. The *Daily Journal*'s reporter stepped up to Al and asked a question. Al turned to him suddenly, as if jerking awake. "I guess I was too slow for her," he replied. "I don't get any kick out of cabarets, dancing and rotten liquor. I like quiet home life. Beulah wanted excitement all the time."

At some point, the hacks left Al and walked down the corridor to the small matron's room where women suspects were held. Beulah sat alone, a guard near the door. The reporters introduced themselves to Chicago's latest girl gunner.

This one wasn't at all like Belva Gaertner, or even Kitty Malm—Maurine could tell that right away. The young, slender woman, with "wide blue eyes and a halo of auburn curls, freshly marcelled," wore an open, light-colored coat over a low-cut nightdress, the curve of a nearly naked breast heaving tantalizingly in full view. Beulah sat before the reporters without shame, seemingly oblivious to her disrobement. She tilted her head slightly, and a wan, buttery smile spread over her lips.*

She launched into her story. "He came into my apartment this afternoon and made himself at home," she said. "Although I scarcely knew him, he tried to make me love him. I told him I would shoot. He kept coming anyway, and I—I did shoot him." Beulah looked longingly at her audience, tears stippling the corners of her eyes. "I didn't know—I didn't realize—I—I . . ." She stopped, collected herself. *I had to do it,* she finally said. *I didn't have a choice.*

The reporters didn't believe the woman's story any more than her husband did. Neither did the police, but getting her to break wasn't as easy as they'd expected. She said the same thing over and over: Harry Kalstedt was advancing on her, and when he wouldn't stop, she shot to "save her honor." Finally, late in the evening, after most of the reporters had called in their stories, Captain Edward Murname, along with assistant state's attorneys Bert Cronson and William McLaughlin, took her back to the apartment so she could change clothes. Then they walked her through the events of the afternoon again, step-by-step. They pounded her with questions, made her look at the blood pooled in the corner, where Harry had lain for hours, and asked her to point out what had happened where.

Why, they asked, were there wine bottles and empty glasses if she didn't know Harry Kalstedt or invite him in? Why was he shot in the back if he had rushed at her? Why had she waited for hours after the shooting before calling police?

Beulah couldn't stand it. Reliving it again, right there in the apartment where it happened, was too much. She began to sob as it all came back to her. Harry's voice hung in the air: "My God, you've shot me!" he'd called out when she pulled the trigger. It wasn't the grunt of pain that was so horrifying. It was the shock in his voice at the realization that she would do such a thing, that she would actually shoot him. Because he loved her. He really loved her. Beulah had realized that as soon as she'd shot, and

---

*Photographs of the suspect in her revealing attire had to be cropped at the collarbone to run in Friday's newspapers.

she tried to take it back. "No, you're all right—you're not shot," she said, as Harry twisted, reached out for nothing, and fell against the wall.

"You are right, I haven't been telling the truth," Beulah told the three men, not even trying to control the sobbing anymore. "I'd been fooling around with Harry for two months. This morning, as soon as my husband left for work, Harry called me up. I told him I wouldn't be home, but he came over anyway. We sat in the flat for quite a time, drinking. Then I said in a joking way that I was going to quit him. He said he was through with me and began to put on his coat. When I saw he meant what he said, my mind went into a whirl and I shot him. Then I started playing the record. I was nervous, you see."

Beulah said she sat next to Harry on the floor and washed his face and kissed him. After the shooting, she became "distracted and started to cry. I was afraid the neighbors would hear me. So I put on the record and took Harry in my arms, and cried and cried." In time she was cried out, which led her back to the phonograph. "I went to it and started it over again. I couldn't stand the quiet." She danced mindlessly and tried not to cry and didn't look at Harry anymore. After a couple of hours, she realized she had to do something about him, so she decided to call her husband. "I kept calling numbers but I couldn't seem to remember his," she said. A voice over the line, unbidden, told her to try directory assistance. She finally got Al on the phone and told him to come home.

Beulah was worn out. They took a break, and then the prosecutors and the police captain made her go over it again, as if for the first time. She had calmed down by this late hour; she seemed to have settled something in her mind.

"How much did you drink?" they asked her.

"Half a gallon."

"The two of you?"

"Yes. We had an argument."

"What about?"

Al wasn't at the apartment with them—Beulah had no idea where he was—so she told the men everything about Harry. They'd been intimate, she and Harry Kalstedt. She loved him, but she had begun to realize that he didn't deserve it, that he didn't really care for her. She said she had tried to make Harry jealous by pretending there was another man she was running around with.

"Did he say anything to you about your having done things that you shouldn't?" her inquisitors asked.

"Oh, yes, and I said to him: 'Well, you're nothing!'"

"Did you call him anything?"

"Yes." Beulah told them what she'd said, seemingly unembarrassed to admit to the use of coarse language.

"What did he say then?"

"He jumped up." He was angry, Beulah said. She could tell that. She and Harry both looked toward the bedroom. He saw Al's gun in there. Al usually kept it under the pillow, but it was in plain sight now.

"Then you say he jumped up?" Murname prompted her.

"I was ahead of him," Beulah said. "I grabbed for the gun."

"And what did he grab for?"

"For what was left—nothing."

"Did he get his coat and hat?"

"No, he didn't get that far."

"Why didn't he get that far?"

"Darned good reason."

"What was it?"

"I shot him."

Murname, Cronson, and McLaughlin seemed content all at once, and Beulah clearly didn't know why. It wasn't because she was giving them "come-on eyes," though she was, just out of habit. It was because she had all but put a noose around her neck. Beulah sighed. She probably wouldn't have cared even if she'd understood their smiles. There was some kind of protective shield around her. The anger was gone; so was the fear. For the moment she was at peace.

The four of them headed back to the station, the three men quietly exuberant. They had her. Sabella Nitti and Katherine Malm had proved that women, finally, weren't safe in front of juries anymore, and now they had a pretty one to go along with the society lady, Belva Gaertner. Cronson and McLaughlin were going to bust the idea that you couldn't convict a beautiful woman in Cook County. Back at the station, flush with pride at securing a confession, they told the *Daily News* reporter that Beulah Annan was a "modern Salome."

By this point, Beulah could barely keep her eyes open, but still she wanted to talk. The late-night interview at the apartment, which would come to be known as the Midnight Confession, had somehow freed her. Now she had a lot to say. She wanted to tell everybody about what she'd been through with Harry Kalstedt.

"Harry was my greatest love, and rather than see him leave me, I killed him," she told the police matron looking after her at the station. A tear rolled down her cheek as the matron led her to a holding cell. She looked at her jailers, a marked woman but defiant.

"I am glad I did it," she said. "It ended an affair that was wrecking my life."

༺∾༻

The next day, Friday, all of the newspapers hit hard.

"Mrs. Beulah Annan, termed by her questioners 'a modern Salome,' sat quietly this morning in the matron's room at the South Clark Street police station," wrote the *Daily News*. She "greeted visitors with an imperturbable glance from under long lashes drooping over half-closed eyes. . . . Out of her eyes had gone every trace of the fire that must have illuminated them yesterday, when, she told Roy Woods, assistant state's attorney, she danced to the tune of jazz records a passionate death dance with the body of the man she had shot and killed."

Now there was a gruesome image. A beautiful young vixen, swaying to a jazz beat with her dead lover in her arms, "raising the head of the victim and implanting kisses on his cold lips."

It wasn't quite true, but it was too good to pass up. The *Journal* and the *Post* offered similar "death dance" scenes, with Beulah lost in a traumatized "whirl." In the *Tribune*, Maurine wrote that the popular ditty "Hula Lou" was "the death song of Harry Kolstedt [*sic*], 29 years old, of 808 East 49th street, whom Mrs. Annan shot because he had terminated their little wine party by announcing that he was through with her." She added mischievously that after playing the Hawaiian song over and over, Beulah then "began to wonder about her husband. What would he say when he came home and found a dead man lying in his bedroom?"

The *American*, however, topped them all by moving beyond the jazz theme. It borrowed from Edgar Allan Poe for an operatic re-creation of the guilt-filled hours that passed between the shooting and Beulah calling her husband:

> Laughter—a woman's laughter from the apartment across the way—mocked her. The clock, ticking steadily—stolidly—sternly, took on a voice that said:
>
> *"Mur-der, mur-der, mur-der, mur-der, mur . . ."*
>
> The phonograph had run down. The woman rose. Anything—anything but that clock. Ah! —*

The story that went out on the Universal Press wire—and got picked up by newspapers across the country—was just as compelling, if not quite as fanciful.

> CHICAGO—A grotesque dance over the body of the man she killed was described by Mrs. Beulah Annan, pretty 24-year-old slayer of Harry Kalstedt, of Minneapolis. Mrs. Annan admitted shooting Kalstedt Thursday night when, piqued by her attempt to rouse his jealousy, he threatened to leave her.
>
> "I tantalized him with a story of an imaginary lover, to see what he would do," said Mrs. Annan. "When he reached for his overcoat to leave, I shot him. I was in a mad ecstasy, after I saw him drop to the floor. I was glad that I had killed him."

In the afternoon, Beulah met her attorneys and prepared to go before a coroner's jury. William Scott Stewart and his partner, W. W. O'Brien, had

---

*The story inspired a leering cartoon strip in the next edition. "Harry has bought some booze—some red wine—prophetically red, like blood. Al is forgotten—shoved into the discard," a caption read, under a drawing of a giddy, tipsy Harry and Beulah in the midst of undressing.

come on the case that morning, with some reluctance. The two lawyers always fretted about getting stiffed for the bill. Sometimes it seemed that running down payment from clients took as much time as trying cases. Stewart, at the age of thirty-four, and O'Brien, a decade older, demanded cash up front, though for the right client, they still accepted partial payment, along with an acceptable explanation for how the rest would be raised. Al Annan didn't have an acceptable explanation—no wealthy family members, no significant assets he could liquidate. But after seeing Beulah Annan's picture in the morning papers, Stewart and O'Brien decided to make an exception. They took the case.

Like many criminal defense attorneys, Stewart and O'Brien initially made their reputations as prosecutors. Stewart's name was better. He was so successful with murder cases during his time as an assistant state's attorney that he became known as the hanging prosecutor. The first high-profile prosecution he handled was the Carl Wanderer case in 1920. Wanderer was a veteran of the World War and an upstanding citizen. He worked hard and never smoked, drank, or gambled. Then a "raggedy stranger" jumped him and his pregnant wife, Ruth, when they were coming home one night. The man shot Ruth, and he would have shot Wanderer, but the former soldier knew how to handle himself. The raggedy stranger ended up dead. "I got him, honey. I got him," the newspapers quoted Wanderer as saying while his wife lay dying in his arms. Except he likely said no such thing. He was too busy making sure his wife was dead. In the days that followed, as the papers hailed him as a gallant and tragic hero, the police tracked the gun the stranger had used, an army-issue Colt .45, to Wanderer's cousin. Soon the hero cracked, admitting he'd grown tired of his wife and had enlisted the help of a bum in a scheme to kill her. "I didn't want her anymore," Wanderer said of his wife. "I killed her so no one else would have her." The papers understandably turned on him and elevated Stewart as a replacement hero. The prosecution earned banner headlines. So did the hanging, when Wanderer, goaded by a reporter who said he enjoyed the condemned man's singing voice, eased into the chorus of his favorite song, "Old Pal," just before the trap door was hatched.

Stewart may have been expert at gaining convictions, but he had no trouble making the switch to defense work; in fact, he felt more comfortable with it. Lanky, with a long, rawboned face, the lawyer looked like a man you could trust, a valuable attribute when representing men (and women) accused of heinous crimes. His commitment to professionalism, as he defined it, was absolute. Devotedly married and the father of a young son, he prided himself on being a reliable man on the darkest of days, believing he was saving lives, like a doctor. He prepared for each court appearance, no matter how trifling, as if his career depended on it. The graduate of Chicago's undistinguished John Marshall Law School viewed his success as a lawyer, and his growing acceptance as an intellectual force in the community, as inevitable. "I am a great believer in original construction," he liked to say. "We are born with bones and muscles, a certain physical equipment, plus a mental power which might be called the motor, with a fairly fixed horsepower. This horsepower is called intelligence. It may be improved a little by mental exercise, but no school or study can give brains."

Stewart's partner in private practice would never have the standing—or perhaps the mental horsepower—that Stewart did. W. W. O'Brien graduated from the University of Notre Dame's law school in 1900, but he didn't feel called to the bar. Instead, he worked as a theatrical promoter for twelve years, "making three or four hundred dollars a week." He eventually came back to the law through politics. He proved to be an effective campaigner for Democratic mayor Carter Harrison Jr., which led to a patronage job in the city's Corporation Counsel's office. After a brief stint with the state's attorney, he felt confident in setting up his own defense practice.

Unlike Stewart, who loved the law and his own intellect above all else, O'Brien's paramount interest was women. He married a performer, Louise Dolly, in 1905 and divorced her twelve years later after cheating on her with numerous women. As soon as the divorce was finalized, he married a woman named Margaret Meehan, but that union was annulled within a year. In 1922, he married a third time—a beautiful nurse, Zoe Patrick. O'Brien succeeded in court for the same reason he succeeded with women. He was fun. He loved the theatricality of trial work. He aspired to be the next Charles Erbstein, the flamboyant Chicago defense attorney who had defended twenty-two women accused of murder and saw each one acquitted. (The same Charles Erbstein who represented Belva Gaertner in her 1920 divorce.) Erbstein's legal career was winding down by the early 1920s, and in many ways the always entertaining O'Brien was the ideal successor. There was just one problem: a strong scent of corruption trailed him. In 1922, two assistant state's attorneys accused him of trying to bribe them on behalf of a client, the pickpocket "Lucky Chubby" Lardner. O'Brien faced disbarment hearings but held on to his license. A year later, he stared down another bribery accusation.

These weren't the only signs of trouble. O'Brien also had a knack for getting shot. In 1921, he caught his first bullet while drinking in a saloon frequented by gangsters. He refused to cooperate with the police investigation. Two years later, it happened again. He was standing on the corner of Fifty-ninth and Halsted when some fifteen shots were fired. O'Brien didn't know if it was a machine gun or multiple gunners, but the police had no doubt that he was the target. If so, he was amazingly lucky: Only one shot hit him, catching him high up on the leg, perilously close to the groin. He again refused to answer police questions about the shooting.

❧❧❧

Al Annan quickly got over feeling sorry for himself. He was a practical man. He loved Beulah—that was what mattered. "I haven't much money," he told reporters when he came downtown in the morning to secure Stewart and O'Brien's services, "but I'll spend my last dime in helping Beulah. I'll stick to the finish."

Al had begun frantically searching for loans. About the time Beulah was confessing to Murname, Cronson, and McLaughlin Thursday night, Al placed a call to Beulah's native Kentucky, rousting her father, John Sheriff, from bed. But he would get no help from Sheriff, a prosperous farmer in the Ohio River Valley. Beulah's father would not go to Chicago to see his daughter, and he would not send money. Both his former wife, Beulah's mother, and his present wife beseeched him to change his mind, but he wouldn't. Beulah had gotten herself in trouble before, and she would get in trouble again. "Beulah wanted a gay life, and she's had it," he said. "I don't think my wife and I should die in the poorhouse to pay for her folly." John Sheriff was a hard man.

Beulah may have been estranged from her father, but she still took after him. The distraught young woman they'd brought into the Hyde Park police station after the shooting, the woman who'd broken down and confessed at length, was gone by Friday afternoon. In her place stood a placid, steely doppelgänger. Before the inquest at Boydston's undertaking parlor started, Beulah posed for photographers in the entrance hall. She had washed up and changed clothes again. She looked ravishing, the expression on her face somehow both stoic and melancholic. She wore a light brown dress, a darker brown coat, black shoes, and, wrote Maurine, a "brown georgette hat that turned back with a youthful flare." Al held his hand over his face whenever the lens was pointed toward him. From the next room could be heard strains of "Nearer, My God to Thee," played for the funeral of a former soldier.

Inside the room where the inquest would be held, Maurine sat down next to Beulah. She asked her how she felt.

"I wish they'd let me see him," Beulah said. Picturing Harry Kalstedt laid out in a coffin, she offered Maurine a frown. "Still," she added, "it would only make me feel worse."

Maurine asked Beulah where she was from; she no doubt recognized the accent. Beulah told her she'd grown up in Kentucky, near Owensboro. The two women likely bonded over their shared bluegrass roots. Beulah said she'd been married to Al for four years and had been married once before. She had a seven-year-old son still in Kentucky, living with "his father's people." She hadn't seen the boy since he was an infant. She had married that first time when she was sixteen, she said.

Other reporters moved in to get their time with the accused. Beulah accommodated them with patience and good humor. "I didn't love Harry so much—but he brought me wine and made a fuss over me and thought I was pretty," she said, her husband just a few seats away. "I don't think I ever loved anybody very much. You know how it is—you keep looking and looking all the time for someone you can really love." She gazed longingly at the reporter, a look that suggested maybe he was the one. She was beginning to make an impact, as she knew she would. The male reporters and sob sisters, seeing her calmed down and dressed up, felt the gravitational pull of Beulah May Annan—that soft Southern accent, lilting and plangent, coming out of that perfect face. Maurine, writing another page-one story, the first that would carry her byline, also recognized the reaction Beulah provoked: "They say she's the prettiest woman ever accused of murder in Chicago—young, slender, with bobbed auburn hair; wide-set, appealing blue eyes; tip-tilted nose; translucent skin, faintly, very faintly rouged; an ingenuous smile; refined features, intelligent expression—an 'awfully nice girl' and more than usually pretty."

Would the fact that she was more than usually pretty be enough to set her free? Probably not at the inquest, where the state only had to show there was evidence—any evidence—to hold her over for a grand jury. Assistant State's Attorney Roy Woods laid out the events of the previous day before the coroner. Mr. Harry Kalstedt, he said, told Mrs. Annan he was through with her, but she didn't let him walk out. She grabbed up a revolver that her husband kept in the bedroom and fired at her boyfriend, hitting him in the back.

"Both went for the gun!" W. W. O'Brien called out. "Both sprang for it." He and Stewart, sitting with Beulah at the front of the room, had already established the outlines of their defense. They would present their client as a "virtuous working girl" caught up in a crazy age. They had already discovered that Harry Kalstedt had a criminal record; the dead man had spent five years in a Minnesota prison for assault before moving to Chicago to work for his brother-in-law at the laundry.

Whether Kalstedt and Beulah both sprang for the gun or not, there was no question about what had happened after Beulah fired the fatal bullet: nothing. The inquest established that almost three hours passed from the time of the shooting until Beulah called her husband at five in the afternoon. Dr. Clifford Oliver testified that he arrived at the apartment at 6:20; he said Kalstedt had been dead only about a half hour. Woods made clear what that meant: Beulah had watched her boyfriend succumb to a slow, agonizing death and had done nothing to help him.

The inquest dragged on, and Beulah grew bored. She stared off into space and occasionally turned and smiled at reporters. Finally, late in the afternoon, the jury reached a decision. They concluded that Beulah Annan was responsible for Harry Kalstedt's death, having fired the gun "by her own hand." The case would now go to the grand jury and then certainly to trial. Beulah rose, traded a few words with O'Brien, and headed toward the door with her police escort. Al, who'd sat a row behind Beulah, wringing his hands throughout the proceeding, leaped up and stepped into the aisle to intercept her.

The *Daily Journal* found Al's undiminished love for his wife, less than twenty-four hours after learning she'd been unfaithful, moving. The paper wrote:

> He pressed a $5 bill into her hand as they took her away, and those near him knew he had borrowed that from a friend who sat near him during the inquest.
>
> "I'll see you Sunday, honey," he said as they parted. He did not know that no visitors are allowed at the jail on Sunday.

❧❧❧

After the inquest, the police moved Beulah to the Cook County Jail, where she would share a section of the women's block with about a half-dozen inmates, including Katherine Malm, Sabella Nitti, and Belva Gaertner. ("Murderesses have such lovely names," Maurine mused.) Beulah was still wearing the clothes she had on for the coroner's jury, her "smart fawn gown," naked hose, and georgette hat. She stayed in her cell all evening, while the other inmates did their daily chores, ate in the dining hall, and played cards.

In the morning, Sabella clomped past the cell. She stopped at the sound of weeping. There was a lot of crying in the women's quarters of the jail, a lot of screaming and rending of hair, but this soft sob seemed to get to the Italian woman. It was so poignant. She squatted on her thick calves and squinted into the poorly lit cell. She could make out Beulah's profile. Sabella had begun to understand some words and phrases in English. The other inmates were right: The new girl was beautiful. Sabella shifted her weight, put a hand against the bars. "You pretty-pretty," she croaked. "You speak English. They won't kill you—why you cry?" Beulah swiveled her head slightly, but at the sight of Sabella grimacing at her, she turned away.

Sabella saw that the new girl wasn't alone in the cell. Beulah had turned back to a reporter. She was giving an interview. "Poor thing," Beulah told the reporter, as Sabella, chastened, moved away. "She's a lost soul—nobody cares about her."

It was easy to reach that conclusion if you read the *Tribune*, as Beulah did every morning. The paper had set Genevieve Forbes loose on Sabella Nitti the previous summer, with horrifically memorable results. Forbes mocked Sabella throughout her trial, denigrating her appearance, her background, and her confusion at proceedings conducted entirely in English. When the Italian immigrant was convicted, Forbes capped a frenzied week of vitriol toward her subject, writing, "Twelve jurors branded Mrs. Sabelle [sic] Nitti 'husband killer' and established a precedent for the state of Illinois at 3 o'clock yesterday afternoon by giving the death penalty to the dumb, crouching, animal-like Italian peasant, found guilty of the murder of Frank Nitti. . . . Prosecutor Smith in urging the death penalty had challenged them to forget that Sabelle Nitti was a woman. But as they filed out it was, perhaps, hard not to remember that she was a woman—a cruel, dirty, repulsive woman."

Beulah Annan would not get the same treatment, from Genevieve Forbes or anyone else. She was not repulsive, no matter what she may have done. The city's newspapers, which on principle agreed with each other as infrequently as possible, were unanimous in declaring Beulah "the prettiest girl" ever on Murderess Row. Reporters, watching as Sabella peered into Beulah's cell, even conscripted the condemned woman into helping make the case. The *American*, in a page-one headline sweeping across the width of the paper, declared:

MRS. NITTI CONSOLES BEULAH

"LADY SLAYER" TOLD NOT TO WORRY FOR "BEAUTY WILL WIN"

8

Her Mind Works Vagrantly

Beulah had caught up on her reading by the time she spoke with reporters again.

"Twenty-three, not twenty-nine," she scolded a *Daily Journal* scribe on Saturday afternoon. "Oh, don't accuse me of such a thing. Murder is bad enough." She repeated the correction of her age to every reporter she saw.

Her years on earth established, Beulah got down to even more pressing business. Now that she had met with her lawyers, key elements of her story changed. Harry Kalstedt wasn't walking out on her anymore. And the gun wasn't kept in the bureau drawer, no matter what Al said. Harry was, however, still angry with her for calling him a jailbird. "Harry said, 'You won't call me a name like that,' and he started toward the bedroom," she told a group of reporters gathered at her cell. "There was only one thing he could have been going for. The gun was there—in plain sight. It had been kept under the pillow, where it was always kept, but the pillow was turned back and it showed. I ran, and as he reached out to pick the gun up off the bed, I reached around him and grabbed it. Then I shot. They say I shot him in the back, but it must have been sort of under the arm."

Like Sabella before her, Belva Gaertner lingered outside Beulah's cell. The "divorcee of page one notoriety" was drawn to the commotion, the herd of reporters, not to any weeping. It had been just three weeks since Belva hit the city's front pages, and her trial was still a couple of weeks off, but she was suddenly old news and knew it. She had introduced herself to

Beulah before the hacks arrived. She suggested they have a picture taken together, but Beulah put her off. The newcomer said she was too distraught. Beulah had read every article she could find about Belva and believed she had learned from the older woman's mistakes and successes with the press. She now sat before reporters, hunched forward, long arms wrapped around herself. Somebody, maybe Belva, brought her a plate of food, but she waved it away. "No, no, no. It would choke me." The thought of what she'd done to her husband made her want to die, she said. It "must have been a blow for him to discover what had been going on behind his back." Her eyes filled with tears. She said she felt very ashamed: "My husband says he'll see me through. I wouldn't blame him if he didn't."

Reporters pressed Beulah about her relationship with Harry Kalstedt and why she had stepped out on her husband. She listened to the questions while staring at her hands and sighing. She struggled to answer them, trying to remember her lawyers' instructions.

"I suppose it is true that a man may drift into any woman's life at some time and overpower one with his personality," she said. "Before you know it, without any intention to misstep, you find yourself completely engulfed. That was the way it was with Harry." She said she'd hoped that somehow her illicit romance would "turn out like in the story books. But I guess it never does."

Al wasn't sure what role he was supposed to be playing in his wife's storybook. He had refused to talk to reporters at the inquest on Friday—"just shook his head sadly to all questions," Maurine wrote. But while Beulah held court in her cell, Sonia Lee, one of the *American's* sob sisters, tracked Al down at the garage on Baltimore Avenue where he worked as a mechanic. Lee had decided that this loyal husband deserved as much attention as his wayward wife.

Al was still wary of reporters, but when asked direct questions by a well-dressed young woman gazing intently into his face, he could only do the polite thing and answer. "I can't believe it, I can't," he said. "When I met her, it was in Louisville. She was all that I thought a woman could be. Shortly after she came to Chicago. I followed two weeks later. Then we were married. I gave her every cent I made and she worked too. Our income was sufficient to provide a very comfortable home, and I believe she made the best of our union until this"—he clenched the wrench that he held in his hand—"until *he* came along."

Next up was Al's boss, R. M. Love. Albert Annan, the man told Lee, was quiet and decent. He worked hard and never complained: "He puts in overtime and Sundays and never offers a murmur. Just for her." The garage manager, his answers obviously guided and shaped by the reporter, said that "Annan rushed up to me at about 4:30 Thursday afternoon. 'My wife just phoned me and said she shot a man!' he gasped. 'My God, she must not— I'll take the blame!' That's the kind of four-square man that he is. Every boy here in the garage is willing to give his last cent to help him out."

～～～

Beulah noticed the saint treatment the *American* and other papers gave Al, and it bothered her. She couldn't help feeling this whole thing was his fault. A part of her believed Al had made her cheat. He never wanted to take her out dancing or on romantic walks. He never wanted to take her anywhere. He just slumped in his chair in the evening, whimpering about how hard he worked. Beulah had felt this disaster coming on for months and months. She could flip back through her diary, if she'd had it with her, and see the proof. It had started more than six months back, right after she met Harry. She'd written it all down in looping cursive, day after day:

> Sun. Oct. 7: Daddy and I had an argument. He told me to go to hell and I went out—didn't come home.
> Mon. Oct. 8: Al called me at the office. Said we would be friends until next Sat. I got "stewed" before coming home.

Daddy. It wasn't a reference to her husband. Al was never Daddy. Harry was Daddy. Was he ever! Al, maybe, could be Mommy. She sometimes felt he was as weak as a woman. What would he say if he knew how Harry had made her feel, if she'd spelled it out for him, what they did right there in their apartment, on their bed, for months?

Beulah could come up with a long list of reasons to think poorly of her husband. Two years ago, she and Al had taken a trip to Michigan, and a burglar had come right into their room and grabbed the watch and chain she'd given him for Christmas. He also took her engagement ring and a pretty cameo ring with diamonds set at the top and bottom. Al did nothing. Just slept. The burglar snuck off into the night without a worry in the world. Yeah, Al bought a gun after that and kept it in the bedroom, but Beulah didn't believe he could use it, even to protect her. She was the one who used it.

A day after Sonia Lee had camped out at the garage to get her exclusive with Al, Beulah strayed from her rote story. She explained to the *Journal* that her infidelity was, in a way, for her husband's sake. "I didn't want to hurt Albert," she said. "He works often until 8 or 9 o'clock at night, when it is too late for us to go out anywhere, because he always had to go to work early in the morning." She "never led a gay life," she said, insistent on dispelling that notion, but she had to go out sometimes, for her own sanity. So when Harry Kalstedt came along, she took advantage of his kindness and interest. She should have known nothing good could have come of it. Sitting in her cell, she added, "When my present husband and I were not altogether happy, I said little, and I thought I loved Harry and could keep things going smoothly. That's largely the trouble that brings most of the women in here. They fall in love with the wrong man."

❦

The wrong man. Beulah had thought it many times as Harry dozed beside her late in the afternoon, after work or on her day off. She'd get out of bed, go over to the window without getting dressed, and look for Al coming down the sidewalk—hoping to see him, longing to hear his footsteps on the stairs, with Harry there in the bed. She wanted everything to be revealed; she wanted to force Harry to declare himself for her. It was terrible not knowing how he felt about her. It was like physical torture—the skin breaking and peeling away, the blood just about to bubble to the surface. It was more awful still to be unable to tell anyone how *she* felt. To not even be able to tell Harry that she loved him, she truly loved him.

Before Harry Kalstedt, it had always been the other way around. Boys loved her; she didn't love them. They stared at her, followed her, told stupid jokes to make her laugh. Perry Stephens was one of those boys. They grew up together in the fields of rural Kentucky, outside Owensboro. He wasn't afraid to talk to Beulah, like so many of the boys were. She liked it when he walked alongside her after school, chatting and trying to impress her. She and Perry were just teenagers when they slipped over the border into Indiana and got married. Perry had a good job as an apprentice Linotype operator at the *Owensboro Inquirer,* and he worshipped her, so why not? On her marriage certificate, dated February 11, 1915, she listed her age as nineteen. A year and a half later, she gave birth to a boy. They named the baby after the father.

The joy of new parenthood didn't last long. The baby seemed to ratchet up Beulah's need for attention, and whenever she could, she went out without her son or husband. She dived into an affair, possibly more than one. It didn't take Perry long to figure out what was going on. Beulah kept his last letter to her. "You have never showed that you are capable of resisting temptation," he wrote. He told Beulah she should leave Owensboro, for the sake of their son. "There will always be temptations. . . . I love you. We would have been very happy. I don't think you would make a good mother."

Beulah thought about that letter now, all these years later. With tears rolling down her cheeks, she insisted that at heart she was a decent person and a good wife. She should have stayed in the home, she told Ione Quinby, who sat with Beulah in her cell. "If I hadn't been working, I'd never have met Harry. We were trying, I mean my husband Albert and I, to get ahead. We paid $75 a month rent on our apartment and $75 a month on our furniture. We planned to get a car. Albert makes only $65 a week and we needed money. I love to cook and keep house and go marketing . . ." She stopped and suddenly looked at her questioner in desperation. "Oh, why did I ever take that job? They lie when they say I tried to kiss Harry after . . . after . . . I *didn't*. All I did was wash his face."

Quinby found Beulah's demeanor odd. The woman was dreamy and scattered, laughing one moment and then bursting into tears. "She does not seem to completely realize what she has done. Her mind works vagrantly," the *Post* reporter observed. Quinby had waited an hour with other reporters that morning while Beulah talked with W. W. O'Brien, who Quinby quipped was "doing his best to engender a touch of cheer" in his client. She knew the lawyer was drilling into Beulah the story she was supposed to give to the press.

Trying to get back on track after her interview with the *Post,* Beulah focused on a key theme with the next reporter. "Well, thinking it all over, I think I would rather have been shot myself," she told the *Daily News.* "Of course, it all happened so quickly I didn't have time to think then. Harry had been drinking before he came to the flat, bringing the wine, and he was in a bad temper. I didn't say anything to him to start a quarrel. He got angry and sprang for the bed. There was a revolver under the pillow. I got it first. If he'd got it he'd have shot me. But I'm sorry now; I think I'd rather it had been me that was killed."

To another reporter she said she was ending things with Harry, and that had provoked the fight. "I am just a fool," she said. "I'd been married to Albert four years. I haven't any excuse except that Harry came into the Tennant laundry, where I worked as a bookkeeper, and I fell in love with him. I met him last October. He seemed fairly to worship me. Then I found out he had served a term in the penitentiary and all my dreams were broken. He knew I was through and that I had found out he wasn't worth the cost. I was ashamed of the way I had fooled myself. He knew I was going to quit him and words led to words. We both ran to the bedroom, where a revolver was kept. I got there first."

"I had never shot a gun but once, on New Year's," she told still another reporter. "Every day I'd pick it up so carefully. I was afraid of it. I don't know how I happened to hit him. I don't know." Apropos of nothing, she sobbed: "It's Spring today!"

࿆

W. W. O'Brien showed up in the city's newsrooms shortly before deadline on Saturday, repeating over and over that Beulah would be pleading self-defense and that Harry Kalstedt had spent five years in prison for assaulting a woman. It wasn't necessary. Beulah may not have always stuck with the rehearsed story, but she'd proven to be a sympathetic interviewee nonetheless. The shame showed on her: It lit her up, coloring her cheeks a deep, invigorating pink, flushing away her guilt. Of course, it could simply have been her flame-colored hair. Redheads held a special place in the typical American male's fantasies. "Will Her Red Head Vamp the Jury?" the *Daily News* wondered. To the eyes of many reporters, her gorgeous locks painted everything about and around her a rosy hue.

"Forty hours of questioning and cogitation has burned the red-hot coals of remorse and repentance into the soul of Beulah May Annan, red-haired beauty who shot and killed Harry Kolstedt [*sic*], 'the man whose love was wrecking her life,'" the *Evening Post* blared on its front page. It continued:

> Behind the bars of the county jail, her eyes ringed with deep purple shadows, her hands clasping and unlocking, Mrs. Annan today turned her face to the once whitewashed ceiling and prayed.
> Then:
> "I'd rather be in Harry's place," she said. "Rather be dead."

Hearst's *American* went further still. It made an epic tragedy of the killing—not the tragedy that had befallen Harry Kalstedt and his family, but that of Beulah and her husband. The *American*'s editors knew what made compelling drama for their working-class readers. This sordid killing was part of a heartrending modern love story. "Beautiful Beulah," lured into the world of jazz and liquor, had broken her marriage vows, like so many young married women forced by financial necessity to work outside the home. But she was repentant, and she and her husband's love was battered but not broken. "Stunned—almost to the point of desperation—Albert Annan has experienced the shattering of his finest ideal, the pretty girl from the Blue Grass country that he took for his bride four years ago," the *American* wrote. That ideal was now gone, but still Al clung "tenaciously to a certain faith and belief in the vision of the woman whom he had once thought above all others to be deserving of his confidence."

Beulah remained a fallen woman in the *American*'s pages, but now she was a fallen woman who could be saved. "A noose around that white neck with Venus lines—that was the shadow on the white cell wall," the paper wrote. Such a threat would cure any woman of immoral living—and for a woman as beautiful as Beulah, it seemed to be working after just one night behind bars. "It was morning when the numbness became prickly pain in her fingers. And Beulah Annan, the fifteenth woman held in the jail for killing, slowly began to realize that the mad swirl had brought more than dust in her eyes." Already she had forsworn alcohol and the jazz lifestyle, the *American* insisted.

Maurine Watkins, for her part, was having none of it. She had figured out Beulah Annan right away. Alone among the city's papers, her inquest story didn't include any of Beulah's excuses, sobbing regret, or meandering explanations of self-defense. Alone among the reporters, she wrote that Beulah calmly "played with a piece of paper and softly whistled through it" during damning testimony before the coroner's jury. "She played again with the paper as the state's attorney read her confession of intimacy with Kolstedt [*sic*] on three occasions and laughed lightly as the lawyers quarreled over the questioning." Maurine also fit in Al's embittered tirade at the police station Thursday night—"Simply a meal ticket!"—which the other reporters, all male, kept out of print.

The *Tribune*'s editors might have expected that Maurine's refusal to embrace Beulah's proffered story line would hurt their sales, especially with Hearst's newspapers pushing the love-triangle melodrama so aggressively. But from the very first day, the Beulah Annan story was so huge it didn't matter. It was bigger than Kitty Malm and Sabella Nitti combined. It was bigger than Belva Gaertner. It was bigger than any of the gangster shootings that usually dominated page one. With Beulah's dewy, snapped-open eyes staring out from the front page, newspapers sold out from newsstands across the city on Friday and again on Saturday. Men "gazed at photographs of her lovely, wistful face" and reached down into their pockets for coins. Newsboys came back to the loading bays for extra bundles over and over.

Beulah didn't seem to notice Maurine's cynicism. She was too busy reveling in the clamoring attention. It came in wave upon wave. She needed to do nothing but get out of her bunk in the morning and invite the reporters and photographers into her cell. That first day behind bars she received a beautiful red rose from an anonymous admirer. The next day, somebody sent her "a juicy steak, French fried potatoes and cucumber salad." Letters began to show up at the jail, dozens of them, from men around the country proclaiming their love for her. The story had gone out on the wires and appeared in newspapers everywhere. Belva Gaertner's trial was scheduled for April 21, just two weeks away, but Thomas Nash, her lead attorney, recognized that the public fascination and sympathy they'd counted on had swung over to the new girl. Nash pushed the trial date back.

Beulah didn't worry about provoking any jealousy on the cellblock. She believed she deserved the attention. Hopped up on the press's and the public's unwavering interest, Beulah, on her third day in jail, posed with dramatic flair for a news photographer. She clutched the cell's bars with her little fists, her head tilted back as if awaiting a kiss, wide-open eyes gazing rhapsodically toward the heavens. She'd seen a cinema actress pose like that once.

9

Jail School

The *Evening Post* announced that April 21, the day after Easter, was "ladies day" in the Criminal Courts Building. The reason: Beulah Annan, Belva Gaertner, and Sabella Nitti were making an appearance before Judge William Lindsay.

The courts building, two blocks north of the Chicago River, wasn't anything special. It sulked at the corner of Dearborn and Austin like an emptied fireplug, square and uninspired, with the exception of an understated arched entrance at street level. But the three women didn't get to come through that lovely entrance like everyone else; they walked across the "bridge of sighs"—an enclosed span facetiously named after the canal crossing in Venice that Byron made famous in *Childe Harold's Pilgrimage*. This bridge connected the courthouse to the jail behind it, allowing for the safe, stress-free transport of prisoners to court. Judge Lindsay's courtroom was usually sparsely populated with defendants' family members, but this Monday morning found it packed with reporters and other observers, filling up the benches and spilling out into the marble-floored hall. There hadn't been this kind of crowd since Kitty Malm's trial in February.

Surrounded by deputies, Beulah and Belva swept into the courtroom like exiled royals being returned to power. They knew what to expect. They'd read every line of copy about themselves and seemed to have internalized the coverage. The *real* reality—the hard jail beds, the daily chores, the skittering vermin, the threat of execution—had been replaced by the newspapers' reality: the romance of their struggle. They now believed, like the newspapers, in innocent womanhood. They believed that modern life degraded values and that bootlegging was evil.

Beulah, as expected, received the most attention. The reporters still wanted to know about "Hula Lou." Had she really danced with her dead lover to her favorite song, holding his heavy, cold head in her hands? The question was insulting, stupid, inevitable. She did love "Hula Lou," though. The song got in your bones and stayed there. You couldn't help but smile and move to it. The Broadway star Mae West had been hired to pose for the song's cover in 1923, and for good reason. West's signature dance was the shimmy, which she'd picked up during her time in Chicago before the war. She'd discovered the clubs in the black neighborhoods of the South Side, just a few blocks from where Beulah and Al now lived. West had never seen anyone move like those black couples moved. "They got up from the tables, got out to the dance floor, and stood in one spot with hardly any movement of the feet, just shook their shoulders, torsos, breasts and pelvises," she said after witnessing the dance for the first time and falling in love with its "naked, aching, sensual agony." Was it the shimmy that Beulah Annan had danced over the dying body of her boyfriend eighteen days before? She wasn't saying.

Beulah, Belva, and Sabella, who'd trailed behind, sat on benches and wooden chairs in the courtroom, looking around for recognizable faces, reporters' faces. Spectators stood in clusters near them and at the back of the room, hoping to get a good look at Beulah's pleasing ankles when she stepped up in front of the judge. The scene was something new and strange. Mae West wasn't a Broadway star anymore. She'd been relegated to a minor-league vaudeville circuit after a string of rapid-fire setbacks and right now was in Texas, appearing fourth on the bill, one slot below "Marcel and his Trained Seal." Beulah Annan, a complete unknown just three weeks ago, an assistant bookkeeper at a laundry, was a bigger star. Love and understanding shone down on her. "I think in most cases where a man is shot by a woman, he has it coming to him," one fan told a reporter. Many like-minded men were in the courtroom supporting the beautiful young woman whose lover had it coming. No one seemed to blame Beulah for her predicament. "A woman has to be pretty bad to be as bad as the best men," a café owner said. Maurine Watkins, witnessing this response to Beulah, decided that, for women, Chicago was "the ideal locale for getting away with murder." She would floridly reference Beulah's looks over and over in her articles as a snide dig at the limitations of the male mind and predominant mores.

As the three women waited, a dour family, the Montanas, stepped before the judge. Five people—three generations of the family—stood accused of killing a policeman during a liquor raid on their home. Normally, a cop killing was page-one news, but the reporters paid little attention to the clan. Photographers surrounded Beulah, Belva, and Sabella and asked them to pose together. They were directed to sit behind a long wooden table, next to each other but fanned out just so—Belva, then Beulah, and finally Sabella.

The women had come prepared. Belva wore a black Easter bonnet with blue chinstrap ribbons streaming down her back, a blue suit, and a summer fur around her neck. A small smile wormed across her lips as the camera caught her. Beulah, in the center, was as composed as President Coolidge, the famously stoic "Silent Cal" who'd replaced the late Warren Harding last fall. She wore a more modern hat than Belva, which certainly pleased her (though she didn't let her pleasure show). She was decked out in a fawn-colored suit and, like Belva, had a light fur lying over her shoulder like a napping pet, its snout nuzzling happily in her collar. While Belva and Beulah attempted to strike dignified poses—the poses of proper women rudely detained against their will—Sabella, the third wheel, beamed like a child. She couldn't help herself. It was a good day. She wasn't going to be hanged today. A week after standing before the state Supreme Court, she was now seeking bail.

Men and women had stared as Sabella Nitti entered the courtroom right behind Belva and Beulah. There was no way to know if it was in admiration of the company she was keeping or in disgust that a convicted murderess might soon be set free. Belva and Beulah were in court to ask that their cases be held on call. Their respective lawyers had other cases to complete. But Sabella had already had her day in court. Chicagoans, fed a diet of news stories over the past nine months that characterized Sabella as "dirty," "repulsive," and "animal-like," found themselves conflicted about the Italian woman's fate. Sabella had never received the kind of coverage her two companions enjoyed. Even when indicating their likely guilt, reporters lauded Beulah and Belva for their beauty and bearing, attributes that opened the door to the possibility of innocence. Not so Sabella. No reporter ever entertained the thought that she might be innocent. After a four-day trial in the summer of 1923, she was convicted by a jury of twelve respectable men and sentenced to die.

Yet "ladies day" at the court belonged to Sabella Nitti anyway. "Beulah has been told she's beautiful. Belva knows she's stylish," pointed out the *Tribune.* "Sabelle is neither—and she's happy."*

It was so unlikely, and yet it was true. Sabella Nitti walked into the courthouse with her two more glamorous cellmates, and she felt as if she were walking on clouds. Her joy expressed itself in her dress as well as her attitude. During her trial, she went to court in the rags she'd been wearing when arrested, the makeshift clothing of a poor farm woman. She looked worn, old, pathetic. Today, following Belva and Beulah, Sabella stepped before Judge Lindsay in a tailored black dress, her hair professionally curled, and with a small gray hat fixed to the top of her head. The transformation was amazing—and completely unexpected. It may have saved her life.

୨୧୨୧

The person most responsible for Sabella Nitti's makeover was a twenty-three-year-old attorney who had recently set up her own practice because no law firm would hire her. Nine months before Sabella made her bravura Easter Monday court appearance, Helen Cirese had walked into the women's section of the Cook County Jail for the first time to meet her new client. The steel door closed behind her, and the wheel handle turned and then caught with an echoing *thuck.* She stared, mesmerized, at the two

---

*Her given name was Isabella and her nickname Sabella, yet most of the papers insisted on calling her Sabelle.

rows of cramped, ill-lit cells, one on each side of her, and at the cracked cement floor that rolled into a shimmering nothingness. Before "stylish" Belva Gaertner, before "beautiful" Beulah Annan, Cirese made an impression on the reporters who trawled the downtown jail for news. Tall and slender, she wore a white blouse under a long, thin vest that was pinned to her hips by a belt. A large feathered cloche sat low against her brow, giving her face a childlike cast. She was a dear sight standing there, nervous, holding her bag in front of her. Her photo appeared in the *Tribune* the next day, and she cut it out and saved it.

It was late summer of 1923, and Cirese had every reason to believe that powerful men were arrayed against her. She and five other young Italian lawyers had just taken on Sabella Nitti's appeal, pro bono. The state's attorney and the police were determined to make sure the new defense team failed. It embarrassed them that some 90 percent of the women ever tried for murder in the jurisdiction had walked free. And none—until Sabella—had ever been sentenced to death. Chicago's police chief declared that when women "kill wantonly, no effort should be spared in the interest of justice."

The lawyers who'd volunteered for Sabella's case had decided that Cirese, the lone woman among them, would be the best emissary to the scared, bereft inmate, who spoke barely any English. Sabella, who was somewhere in her forties, had been convicted of helping Peter Crudelle, a farmhand and possibly her lover at the time, murder her husband. In early July of 1922, Sabella had reported Frank Nitti missing to the police in Stickney, a town on the edge of Cook County. The next day, when the police told her they could not find her husband, "she wept and pulled her hair and scratched her face." The father of children ranging in age from three to twenty-five never returned to his little farm. In March 1923, Sabella married Crudelle, but they would not live happily together for long. Two months after the marriage, police found a badly decomposed body in a sewer catch basin and identified it as Frank Nitti. Sabella and her fifteen-year-old son, Charlie, were brought in for questioning. After a long inquisition, Charlie told police that Crudelle had murdered his father on Sabella's orders and that he and Crudelle had disposed of the body. Sabella, not understanding what her son was saying in English, said that whatever Charlie told them was true. On May 25, 1923, the state indicted Sabella Nitti, Peter Crudelle, and Charlie Nitti for murder. Sabella and Peter Crudelle were convicted. (After Charlie testified, charges against him were dropped.) Sabella didn't comprehend the verdict when it was read. The next day, when an interpreter informed her that she had been condemned to hang, she cried out in terror and fainted.

Then a strange thing happened. People throughout the country became interested in Sabella. The *Los Angeles Times* put her on the front page:

> For the first time in the history of Illinois, a woman has been given the death penalty for murder. More than thirty women have been tried for slaying their husbands or lovers and some have been convicted—three rare cases in which the defendants were unattractive and one a negress.* In every case where the murderess was young and pretty, she was acquitted. The death penalty in Illinois is carried out by hanging.

For months Sabella had been reviled in Chicago as a dirty, vicious killer. Now, almost overnight, the death sentence had made her a national cause célèbre. Those in favor of the sentence argued it was past time for Illinois to treat its women criminals in the same manner as its men, and who better than this grotesque foreigner to be the first to swing? New York, they pointed out, had executed a woman more than twenty years before, in 1899. But humanitarians used the sentence as a rallying cry. The wife of one of the jurors soon announced she would "go home to mother" if the Italian woman was hanged. Religious leaders made impassioned pleas for mercy. After weeks of being ignored by her fellow inmates, Sabella suddenly was "a woman of importance in the jail," wrote Genevieve Forbes. "All those others who were waiting trial for robbery with a gun, for accessory to burglary and other more or less pallid charges, became, almost unconsciously, willing handmaidens ministering to this nationally famous woman."

*The *Los Angeles Times* dramatically undercounted Chicago's murderesses. One hundred two husband-killers alone were tried in Cook County between 1875 and 1920. Sixteen were convicted, nine of them African American.

Sabella didn't realize any of this. Twice she tried to commit suicide, first by choking herself, and then, when that failed, by ramming her head repeatedly into a cell wall, leaving spatters of blood on the wall and red rivers coursing down her face.

For days after the verdict, Sabella sobbed and moaned and tore at her hair, until finally she managed to calm herself and come to terms with her terrible fate. "Me choke," she told anyone who'd listen, a doleful look on her face. With her limited English she got it just right. Hanging made it past the "cruel and unusual punishment" restriction in the Constitution in part because the neck was supposed to be broken by the body's drop from the trapdoor. As often as not, though, the noose didn't catch just right, and instead the condemned prisoner choked to death—a ghastly, protracted, dry-drowning spectacle. "This takes from eight to fourteen minutes," pointed out *Daily News* reporter Ben Hecht, who'd witnessed a fair number of hangings in Chicago.

> While he hangs choking, the white-covered body begins to spin slowly. The white-hooded head tilts to one side and a stretch of purpled neck becomes visible. Then the rope begins to vibrate and hum like a hive of bees. After this the white robe begins to expand and deflate as if it were being blown up by a leaky bicycle pump. Following the turning, spinning, humming, and pumping up of the white robe comes the climax of the hanging. This is the throat of the hanging man letting out a last strangled cry or moan of life.

Hecht referred to the hanging *man* not simply out of linguistic convention; he did so because when he wrote the passage, it was almost inconceivable that a responsible prosecutor would seek the ultimate penalty for a woman or that a civilized jury would impose it. There had been more than a hundred executions in Cook County since 1840, when records began being kept. Leaders in the Italian community did not think it a coincidence that the first woman so condemned would be a poor, unattractive, non-English-speaking Italian immigrant. Faced with one of their own being put to death, Cirese and the other five lawyers (an attorney named Rocco de Stefano would serve as lead counsel) stepped forward.

The court agreed to hear a motion to set aside the verdict. Judge Joseph B. David postponed the execution, which had been scheduled for October 12, 1923—Columbus Day. But Judge David didn't put much stock in Sabella's chances. "This is a grave matter," he said. "I will consent to hear you, but there is not one chance in one hundred that the sentence will be vacated and a new trial granted."

The defense team's argument before the state Supreme Court wasn't going to be original. The lawyers planned to prove that Sabella's trial attorney, Eugene Moran, had been incompetent. They insisted that Sabella, whose court request for new counsel was signed with an X, "could not understand Mr. Moran, he could not understand her, and they had great difficulty in making themselves understood even through interpreters." They also planned to show that the evidence the prosecution used to convict was suspect. The lawyers believed the identification of the body had been a sham—there was good reason to doubt that the corpse found in the catch basin was Frank Nitti. They planned to argue that the testimony of Charlie Nitti, Sabella's son, had been coerced, and that the motive put forward by the prosecution, namely the subsequent marriage of Sabella and Peter Crudelle, hardly constituted proof of anything.

Sabella's conviction, her defense team believed, had been assured by the ethnic and class biases commonplace in the country. Much of the reporting on the case, especially Forbes's coverage in the *Tribune*, had been offensive, showing the kind of vicious stereotyping that had led to U.S. immigration laws being changed to limit the numbers of southern Europeans coming into the country. Sabella's poverty, illiteracy, and inability to speak English had fatally wounded her case. Who she was, in the eyes of your typical Cook County juror, showed in her face and dress and posture. Sabella herself understood this, having watched two pretty blonde sisters—Mrs. Anna McGinnis and Mrs. Myna Pioch—walk out the jail door a month before she was convicted. "Nice face—swell clothes—shoot man—go home," she said in despair to her fellow inmates. "Me do nothing—me choke."

The fact of one's gender was a valuable piece of "evidence" for any woman charged with a violent crime in Illinois. But Sabella Nitti, derided by Forbes as a "repulsive animal," was barely granted even that qualification. Sabella had sat in court during her trial, quietly moaning, utterly uncomprehending. In the eyes of decent society in general and of Forbes in particular, she was like a demon in physical form: different, alien, dangerous. "Her cheap, faded blouse hikes up from her sagging black skirt, in spite of the sturdy safety pin," Forbes wrote during the trial. "Her hair, lots of it, is matted into a festoon of snails, hairpins and side combs."

Forbes's coverage of the trial shocked Cirese, who read the *Tribune* every day. Even Sabella's fellow prisoners were outraged. A group of them wrote a letter to the *Tribune* in defense of Sabella, signing it "Comrades of Mrs. Nitti." They took exception to descriptions of Sabella as a "dirty, disheveled woman," insisting that she was in fact "one of the cleanest women in the department, in her cell and her personal appearance. Therefore, Mrs. Nitti cannot be classed as a 'dirty, repulsive woman.' She is the mother of two small girls and has shown her motherly spirit here with the girls always."

A motherly spirit, of course, mattered not a whit if you were viewed as little better than an animal. Helen Cirese knew what she had to do. She knew what meant the most to Illinois' all-male juries—everyone did. "A jury isn't blind, and a pretty woman's never been convicted in Cook County," one of the women inmates told Maurine Watkins at the jail. ("Gallant old Cook County!" Maurine responded in print.) It was easy to mock the typical jury's predilection for pretty women, but it would be unwise—and poor lawyering—to ignore it. Cirese's most important job on Sabella's case would have nothing to do with writing briefs or making courtroom arguments. It was to make sure Sabella Nitti was as pretty and demure as she could be.

Cirese came to the jail every week, sat with Sabella, gained her trust, and slowly began to turn her into a new person. By March 1924, Ione Quinby noticed the transformation under way. "If Mrs. Sabella Nitti-Crudelle ever gets out of prison, she will go forth a wonderfully improved woman," the *Post* reporter wrote. "Hers is probably one of the few cases on record where it has been established beyond all doubt that long confinement behind bars did the prisoner any good." Sabella had never had store-bought shoes before going to jail. She'd never had a mirror or a pillow. If she could have her two youngest children with her, Sabella told Quinby in halting English, she'd never want to leave.

"We simply reconditioned her," Cirese later said. "I got a hairdresser to fix her up every day. We bought her a blue suit and a flesh colored silk blouse. We taught her to speak English, and when she walked into that courtroom she was beautiful—beautiful and innocent. I'll never forget how she looked. You wouldn't have known her."

After a year behind bars, Sabella Nitti looked and felt great, better than ever in her whole life. And the one chance in a hundred came through. Early in April, six months after Sabella was supposed to have swung from the gallows, the Illinois Supreme Court reversed the trial verdict and remanded the case to the Cook County court, insisting on "a further investigation with competent counsel representing the accused. Safety and justice require that this cause be submitted to another jury." Many court observers believed this decision had more than a little to do with Sabella's new look. "When she came to the county jail, she appeared to be fully capable of murder," observed Quinby. "But she doesn't now."

✸✸✸

With the Sabella Nitti case, Helen Cirese began building a unique law practice—a woman criminal-defense attorney, a rare enough thing, specializing in women clients. In the spring of 1924, as she waited for Sabella's retrial to be scheduled, she took up another, even more hopeless case, this one without the assistance of a team of lawyers. In December, Mrs. Lela Foster had been arrested and charged with the murder of her husband. Just before the victim died, the man told police his wife had done it. Lela, in an account that mirrored Beulah Annan's, said her husband had threatened her with a revolver and that she shot him after they struggled for possession of the gun. She said that he regularly beat her up and that she had the bruises to prove it. Still, Lela couldn't expect to get much sympathy from jurors or the newspapers. (The press almost entirely ignored the case.) This was because Lela, who was white, had married a Negro. Maybe the dead man got what he deserved, went the popular thinking, but so did she.

What did she expect from marrying a "coon"? The fear of miscegenation was so great that the state could boast of witnesses who claimed Mrs. Foster "chewed the end of lead bullets to make the wounds bigger." Up to this point, the only mention of the case in the papers was a brief item stating that it was "believed to be the first time that an alleged murderess has been represented by a woman attorney."

The prospect of women attorneys representing women murder suspects before all-male juries was almost as terrifying as interracial coupling. One Virginia newspaper, commenting on the situation in Chicago after the state Supreme Court's ruling on Sabella's case, wrote that "now that fair women attorneys, full of feminine wiles, have been added to the equation, conviction of pretty lady killers is hardly even hoped for."

That was fine with Cirese. She would take all the help she could get. She was young and unconsciously graceful, with an imperious Roman nose and preternaturally full lips. If that counted as feminine wiles, she'd happily use them to help get clients out of jail. After all, nothing had come easily in her young professional life so far, which was no reflection on her skills. Too many lawyers and judges simply didn't believe women belonged in the courtroom in any official capacity. Most female lawyers could, at best, land jobs as court stenographers. "Women make good law students. . . . They can pass the examinations, including the Bar examinations, with honors and flying colors," opined William Scott Stewart, Beulah's attorney. "But conditions are such that they do not seem to me equipped for the actual knock-down and drag-out fight required in the actual trial of lawsuits." Stewart's opinion was entirely ordinary and uncontroversial in the legal community.

Cirese, less than three years out of DePaul University's law school, was determined to prove Stewart wrong. Sabella's retrial would be soon, likely in May, before Lela Foster's trial. Of course, Sabella, in a very real way, already could be counted a success. Now that she could communicate to a fair degree with her fellow inmates, she was noticeably happier. Of the women on the cellblock, Kitty Malm was the nicest to the Italian woman; she always made an effort to get a smile out of her. One of the girls dubbed Kitty the Girl with the Big Heart. Elizabeth Unkafer, who had shot down her boyfriend in February, would also smile at Sabella, but Elizabeth would smile at the wall and her big toe. She scrubbed the jail floor day after day, her matted mop of red hair in her eyes, flabby cheeks flapping, mumbling to herself, having a conversation. Her attorneys planned to have the forty-six-year-old woman plead insanity at her trial. She had, after all, said she'd killed her beau "because it was in the Bible that I had to." Belva Gaertner, meanwhile, gave Sabella coins for making up her bed every morning and doing other chores for her. She seemed to genuinely like Sabella. When the good news came down about the Italian woman winning a retrial, Kitty and Belva were the first to meet her when she returned to the jail. Belva organized a celebratory party and led the festivities.

Best of all, Sabella Nitti wasn't just innocent—that was how the women of the jail interpreted the higher court decision—she was also beautiful now, or at least presentable. If it helped sway Supreme Court justices, it would surely make the difference in a new trial. After the *American* photographer took a "ladies day" portrait with the three women inmates, he positioned Sabella for her own picture. Her changed appearance was dramatic enough to warrant it. The inmate the *American* had derided as a "bent old woman, with a face like sandpaper," is sitting erect and smiling in the photograph. She looks like a respectable suburban housewife on a pleasant spring outing. In the background, in the corner of the frame, Beulah gazes blandly off into the distance.

꧁꧂

Genevieve Forbes, for one, didn't like the precedent Sabella Nitti and Helen Cirese had established. Sabella had learned how to dress with style, how to apply makeup, how to give herself a manicure. She had also begun to learn how to speak English. This hardly should have been considered ground-breaking trial preparation, but it helped change the atmosphere at the jail. It changed the whole point of the inmates being there. Many of the women at Cook County Jail didn't really have lawyers. Judges assigned private defense attorneys to cases with indigent defendants. It wasn't unusual for a lawyer, if unable to extract a fee from the defendant's relatives, to put up a token defense at best or persuade his client to plead guilty. But now the inmates in the women's quarters realized that they didn't have to just helplessly wait around for a sentence to be imposed on them. They could do something. They could *learn.* They could go to what Forbes derisively labeled jail school. If Sabella could do it, any of them could. "A horrible looking creature she was," Forbes wrote with her typical sensitivity, "with skin like elephant hide, nails split to the quick and the dirt ingrained deep in the cracks of her hands. Her hair was matted; her skirt sagged to a big safety pin." Then, Forbes wrote, "Sabelle went to the jail school. She learned to understand English, then to speak it, presently to write it." She learned beauty tips, the reporter went on, such as "the value of lemon juice to whiten skin."

Influenced by Sabella's success before the Supreme Court and the wave of press attention bestowed on Belva and Beulah, the other women prisoners enrolled in jail school, too. They cut each other's hair in the latest style. They discussed how to wear cosmetics. They gave themselves and each other manicures. Friends and lawyers brought in new outfits for the inmates, and the women conducted impromptu fashion shows on the block to choose the best clothing for their trials. "They study every effect, turn, and change," Maurine Watkins noted, "and who can say it's time wasted?" Maurine certainly didn't think it was. In court, even more than in life, clothes made the woman, especially the woman murder defendant. "Colorful clothes would mark her as a brazen hussy flaunting herself in the public eye and black would be interpreted as a hypocritical pose," Maurine later wrote. "Yes, there's need for an Emily Post on murder etiquette."

Maurine was joking—but she was also right. For just that reason, a spirit of sisterhood now prevailed among the inmates. The women, "all mankillers," wrote one New York newspaper, had become "Chicago's most picturesque group." Belva offered fashion tips and gave comportment lessons to girls who were about to go before judge and jury. She was "a good stage manager," Forbes wrote. "When the girl in cell No. 4 was informed that her trial would be the following Tuesday, Belva gave her some really good ideas on costuming, coiffure and general chic. It helped the girl in No. 4, and it whiled away otherwise lonely hours for Belva, with the 'clothes sense.'"

It was too good to last, of course. Three days after Sabella, Belva, and

Beulah walked over to the courthouse together, the *Evening Post* splashed a headline in massive 96-point type across its front page:

LOVE-FOILED GIRL SEEKS MAN'S LIFE; KILLS CARETAKER

BEAUTIFUL EX–DEPUTY DISTRICT ATTORNEY SLAYS AN OUTSIDER IN DEATH STALK FOR AD MAN

All of the city's newspapers had similar front-page headlines that Thursday afternoon. Unwilling to be trumped on a guaranteed newsstand seller, the morning papers cranked out special evening bulletins about this latest "beautiful girl slayer," a young Polish lawyer named Wanda Stopa. Only an hour after the unfortunate caretaker fell, with the girl still on the loose, "bankers, professional and laboring men, and even housewives were reading descriptions of the murderess," Ione Quinby recalled. The story was an instant sensation, the excitement heightened by the fact that the drama was ongoing, with a massive police search that "for morbid interest and mystery held the attention of the public as no other murder hunt had done in years."

The mood at the jail changed at once. The recent camaraderie in the women's quarters had surprised the guards, who were accustomed to frequent arguments and even physical fights among their charges. The atmosphere had been remarkably placid and supportive for weeks, but there was an unmistakable pecking order underpinning it, with Belva and Beulah at the top and Sabella in her own special category. Now the leading ladies suddenly felt threatened. On April 24, the newspapers only had one subject, page after page, photograph after photograph: the breathtaking love-foiled girl. The jail matrons weren't at all sure that cellblock harmony could withstand a new beautiful woman on Murderess Row.

Part II

❧

THE GIRLS OF MURDER CITY

"And that hat—ah, that hat!" rhapsodized Maurine Watkins in the
Chicago Tribune. *Belva Gaertner, the "most stylish" of Murderess
Row, appears in court for all the world to see. (Her white-maned
attorney, Thomas D. Nash, sits beside her.)*

10

❧

The Love-Foiled Girl

Thursday, April 24, 1924

The smoke pulsed like a bleeding sore. It oozed slowly over rooftops and dripped from trees, squeezing out the morning light and leaving only a suffocating gloom. Visitors to the city described it as "a dense atmosphere," a "sinister power." They spoke of its aggressive nature, how it swept "across and about them in gusts and swirls, now dropping and now lifting again its grimy curtain."

Chicagoans called the problem the "smoke horror." It was the result of more than fifty years of unfettered industrial development that had put mammoth factories and small manufacturing concerns on almost every block, each belching a vicious cloud of toxins into the air. Everybody complained about it. Chicago had become too cultured and prosperous, civic leaders said, for "this stew of steel and smoke" hanging over everything. Each election season, the mayor and the city council promised to act on the issue. Yet even now, the smoke did still have its purposes. For twenty-three-year-old Wanda Elaine Stopa, the sooty miasma was the perfect attendant for her return to the city. At about seven on Thursday morning, Wanda decamped from a train at the Illinois Central depot on Twelfth Street, stepping back onto Chicago soil for the first time in four months. Carrying only a shoulder bag, she materialized out of the mist and headed for the curb, looking for a taxi. She wore a blue serge suit, a light scarf, and a dark hat. Despite the smoke and her conservative dress, she failed to go completely unnoticed. This was inevitable: She was a striking girl, just an inch over five feet tall, with pronounced Slavic cheekbones and glowing blue eyes, eyes the color of the sky, way up above the city's black shroud.

A line of cars idled at the taxi stand out front. Ignoring etiquette, Wanda bypassed the cab at the front and approached one near the back of the queue. It was an old Cadillac without license plates—a rogue cab, someone just trying to make a few extra dollars. She asked the car's driver, an older man wearing a black cap and a long black coat, if he would drive her to Palos Park. The man, Ernest Woods, said he imagined he could find the way. After some haggling, Wanda agreed to pay $4 an hour, then climbed into the back. Woods eased out of the taxi line and pulled onto Fifty-fifth Street. At Western Avenue, he turned south, and then at 111th he swung west and headed out of the city. The car picked up speed. It rumbled along on the new slab for mile after mile, the tires moaning like an old woman. From time to time, Woods would glance in the rearview mirror. His client seemed to find the drive soothing: She stared as if being pulled toward sleep, her head bobbing on a long, graceful neck, hair swinging like a curtain. She kept her eyes cast down at her knees. After nearly twenty miles, the car turned into bucolic Palos Park. The road narrowed to a single lane. Mature oaks soared into the sky, interlaced at their bases by rustic fences.

Wanda had sat in silence the entire way from the train station, the window shade fastened in the back, but she did not find the drive soothing. The last time she had been in Chicago, life was unbearable, a constant black agony. The memories swirled like ghosts. "Got up in a cold, lonely room, dressed at seven, went over to breakfast. Alone, all alone with a dreadful sinking in the center," she had written to her man. ". . . Grandest, dearest, are you coming back this week? Come if you can. Don't leave your babe too long." But it had been too long. Months had passed with barely a word from the man Wanda Stopa loved.

With his passenger lost in thought, Woods stopped the car so he could find a telephone book and look up the address for the name she'd given him. Wanda didn't respond when the driver told her why he was stopping. Minutes later, the cab jolted down Palos Park's main street and then pulled in at the little post office. Woods got out of the car and walked over to Harriet Scoffield, who lived next to the post office. The elderly woman was raking leaves and had kneeled on the lawn to check on some flowers. Woods bent down to her. He whispered, "Do you know where the Y. Kenley Smiths live?" The woman pointed down the street and told him to go around the corner. Eighty-ninth Avenue and 123rd Street. As Woods disappeared back into the car, Scoffield climbed to her feet, dusted herself off, and ambled toward the post office. This being a small town, she had to pass along any new information. "There's company come to your house," she told Henry Manning, the Smith's live-in handyman, who happened to be at the mail slot in front of the building. Manning's eyes popped. He jerked his head around to scan the road just as the Cadillac disappeared from sight. He bolted from the post office, bounding across the neighboring lawn toward the Smith cottage.

At 8:30, the taxi approached the house, which was set far back from the street in a small alcove cut out of the surrounding woods. Wanda told the driver to stop the car near the end of the driveway. He must turn the machine around and be ready to go, she said, because she had to catch a train and time was short. She gave Woods a $10 bill and told him she'd be right back.

Wanda, pretty and demure in her blue serge suit, walked up the long, winding drive and knocked on the front door. When it opened, she asked politely for Mr. Smith. The maid said he was not at home, causing Wanda's eyes to narrow into slits. She bulled past the maid and into the house. She found Mrs. Smith—Vieva Dawley Smith, known to friends as Doodles—in bed, where she was recovering from the flu. Mrs. Smith didn't seem surprised to see Wanda.

That was when Manning arrived, panting furiously. The handyman was sixty-eight years old and unaccustomed to running. Catching his breath, he tried to position himself in the bedroom doorway, between Smith and the younger woman. He told Wanda that Mrs. Smith was ill and asked her to go into the kitchen. Wanda shook her head slowly. "Right here is good enough for me," she said. Manning continued to try to coax her out of the bedroom, but she ignored him.

"Are you going to divorce your husband so I can have him?" she screamed at Kenley Smith's wife, tears bubbling at the corners of her eyes.

"Of course not," Mrs. Smith replied.

Wanda couldn't believe what she was hearing. "How am I going to live?" she bellowed. "Who's going to take care of me?"

Doodles had never had much patience for Wanda Stopa, not nearly as much as her husband. "You're a lawyer," she snapped. "Why don't you go to work?"

Wanda *was* a lawyer, but that wasn't the answer she wanted to hear. She pulled out a .38 caliber revolver and aimed it at the haughty woman propped up in bed. Manning, trying to stutter out a word, backed toward Smith and stretched out his arms. He urged Wanda to calm down, but it was too late for that. Wanda believed she could thread the needle—or more likely she only saw Kenley's wife, her tormenter, even with Henry Manning standing right in front of her. Wanda pulled the trigger and the gun issued a massive bang. Smith ducked under the sheets, an instinctive response unbecoming a woman of her intelligence, but when she heard Manning's body hit the floor, her brain kicked in. She heaved herself up, sprinted for the open window, and—with two more explosions rocking the bedroom—leaped headfirst into the yard. Rolling, she realized Wanda had missed with both shots. She got up, the broken window screen around her neck, and ran.

A moment later, Wanda appeared at the front door and charged down the path. She looked around for Smith but couldn't locate her. "I'll get you yet," she shouted, "and I'm going downtown now to get your husband."

Wanda walked down the drive, climbed into the backseat of the Cadillac, and told Woods to take her back to the train station. Woods started the car. He didn't notice anything to alarm him; the girl didn't seem nervous or agitated. He would claim later he was partially deaf and so heard no shots and suspected nothing. The car pulled out onto the road and headed back toward Chicago.

Once again, they drove in silence, but Wanda's mind roiled. She needed to calm down; she didn't want to have a seizure. Wanda had had epileptic fits ever since she was a child. She and her family kept the seizures quiet, for such attacks were widely believed to be a sign of insanity. The stress of the secret weighed on her constantly. She never told anyone, not even her closest friends. Not even Kenley. A mile or so before the station, she insisted Woods pull the cab over. Her train wasn't leaving for another hour, she told the driver. She would get out here and visit friends in the neighborhood.

<center>~~~</center>

"Live your own life!"

Wanda Stopa, having just marched into the room on unstable legs, barely got the words out. The party roared on.

"Are you listening?" she asked. She rose up on her toes. Wanda—her new friends called her by her "more sophisticated" middle name, Elaine— waited. The party stuttered. Dancers slowed up, expelling air. The intellectuals, huddled together on the couch, squinted over their cigarettes. Wanda leaned in, confiding now. "Tomorrow, I'm leaving here for Chicago and when I arrive I'm going to kill a woman—perhaps a man. But anyhow a woman. I'm going to kill her, do you hear?"

They heard. By now the neckers had disengaged and wiped their mouths, the girls adjusting themselves on their boyfriends' laps. Wine was quietly swallowed and glasses put down. The music from the phonograph scratched abruptly to nothing. The best party all year in Greenwich Village had taken an unexpected turn.

Wanda clenched her fists at her sides and pivoted on tiny feet. She had made the decision: She was going back to Chicago, for the first time in four months, to face him. Her white skin tingled. She had been a perfect hostess until now. After all, these were the friends who excited her, the kind of smart, challenging, *free* people who for most of her twenty-three years she couldn't imagine really existed. She could be her own person here, utterly removed from the suffocating expectations forced on women in Chicago's Little Poland. Wanda had been busy during her short time in New York, meeting fellow bohemians, attracting attention at every stop on her exploration of the Village, an enchanted world so much truer, better, than the "sham Bohemia" she'd left in Chicago.

Wanda was a natural in Greenwich Village. For starters, she looked exquisite in artists' rags, somehow both hungry and ripe as she scuffed down slick, dirty streets, going nowhere in particular. She luxuriated in the area's damp, nonelectrified ateliers, never bothered by old-fashioned plumbing or cockroaches or the lumps of candle wax that congealed on the floor. Her only flaw—and make no mistake, it was a doozy—was her determined refusal of all sexual advances. She was hung up on a man.

It didn't seem to matter that the man, Mr. Yeremya Kenley Smith of Chicago and Palos Park, Illinois, a thirty-seven-year-old advertising executive and self-described patron of the arts, didn't return her ardor. Encouraging Kenley to leave his wife, Wanda had written to him that, when he did, "Once a week I will go to your little house, put it in order, bring your laundry, which I will have sent, look over your clothes and mend as may be necessary, and replace them in their proper drawers. . . . At no time during the week except on Saturday, when I shall change your linen and clean house for you, will I intrude on you. I promise, however, to hold myself in readiness to come to you whenever you may wish me, outside of working hours. You may have me when you want me."

That letter would have disappointed her new friends if they'd known about it. They were all "Feminists" in New York City. They believed in equality, in free love, in the destruction of all traditions. They believed that marriage was "just a scrap of paper." Wanda had to write desperate letters to Kenley; she couldn't help it. But the groveling disappointed her, too. It was exactly how a lovesick girl from Little Poland was expected to act. So she sent her man a box of poisoned candy. He didn't eat it, though, and neither did his wife. And still she couldn't stop writing to him. "When I get you back I am never going to leave you go," she wrote. And: "Your absence is so looming and dark that it takes all my interest in other things away."

None of this—this quivering, childish dependence—made sense, not coming from Wanda. Any girl except Wanda. This was the girl that friends in Chicago called "The Light" and "The Fire," and those names weren't a joke—not to her group of admirers. Wanda Elaine Stopa was that brilliant. Boy, could she talk! About cubism and Freud and sex—and the future, the beautiful future. In conversational flight, Wanda's whole body practically vibrated with excitement. Her eyes jumped, her right hand slapped the arm of the chair or the top of the table. She smiled—suddenly, brilliantly—at the apex of a peroration, her whole being blooming when she saw she'd made an impact on her audience. She'd even reach out and squeeze your knee, encouraging you, physically guiding you over to her point of view. This "pleasing little wisp of a girl" surely would have made a great lawyer, a groundbreaker for her sex, if she'd stuck with it. She'd been the first "girl lawyer" ever to work for the state's attorney and the U.S. district attorney in Chicago. One of her law professors said he'd never had a student of greater promise. Her career, for a woman, was limitless.

But those were just words now. Her family regretted ever sending her to law school and out into the world. The last time Wanda was back home, on Augusta Street in Little Poland, her widowed mother noticed how pale and thin she had become, how her hand shook when she held a fork. Mrs. Stopa knew what was going on. Even on Augusta Street they had heard about narcotics. Wanda didn't deny it, didn't even want to. "Oh, mother, it's such a good feeling," she said.

Besides, dope helped her survive without Kenley; it helped her plot how to get him for her very own. She knew she wasn't supposed to care about such things, about trapping a man and tending to his every need. Wanda hated Augusta Street, the squat women in boudoir caps sitting on the stoops, trudging to market and back, always with mewling babies in their arms. The men who looked at their wives with dead stares every evening, exhausted by their lives, completely unthinking and uncommunicative. Wanda shivered at the thought of them. It was an instinctive hatred, a restlessness that she had no ability to control. That was why she had studied so hard—to avoid the same fate as all those girls she grew up with. That was why she went to law school, time and again the only girl in a classroom full of boys. That was why Kenley Smith's exhortations for the unconventional life, *real* life, resonated. That was why she went to bed with him.

She never recovered. Their night together blasted the precepts of free love to pieces, right there. Wanda's bohemian attitudes, to her own horror, had been exposed as a hoax. She had never truly felt free among the artists of Chicago's North Side, she realized. The discovery sent her into a hopeless spiral. At first Kenley responded to her constant letters seeking reassurance and love. "I looked in the shop windows today for something you would like but I didn't see anything," he wrote in one missive. "One hat was possible, but how could I confirm it without the little Polish bean to check up by? Polka, I hope you have been a little easier these last few days. I pray that I may yet be the springboard from which you dive into the lake of song, laughter and happiness." But soon Kenley was backpedaling, then running for the hills. "Oh, Toots, I love you, I love you, I love you," Wanda wrote to him. "I know you dislike to have me write things on paper, but I do not seem to be able to discuss things with you any more without becoming excessively emotional. . . . I feel that my attachment for you is becoming a sort of millstone around your neck; that you never intended it to reach the hectic stage it has. But I am intensely romantic and you are Romance to me!"

Romance. Wanda actually used that word—and meant it. Even though bohemia had no room for such sentiment. Free booze and food and sex were enough for this lot. She gazed at a girl in green who just moments before had been flinging herself about in a fevered dance, large metallic earrings swinging in rhythm with her body. Wanda turned and stared down a hulking young man, the same one who had climbed onto her kitchen table earlier and belted out a song. It all seemed so stupid now, these people, bohemia, art, New York City.

"I'm going to kill her, do you hear?" Wanda shouted. "Shoot her because she refused to give up the man I love." She felt herself sweating, a stinging prickle along her brow and under her arms. But it felt good to say it out loud. To acknowledge that she was in love and that there was no hope.

"You talk about life, about freedom," she continued, her voice hoarse. "You make me tired with your synthetic emotions and your words. God, you're naïve! You think you're sophisticated, but you're just shallow children . . ."

Wanda stopped. She glared at these men and women she'd invited to her apartment. She wasn't getting through to them. They thought she was giving a performance; that was what you did in the Village. She looked down at herself, as if surprised by her body. She was wearing the best gown she owned, a sleek semibackless dress that teased out the delightful curves in her frame. Her bronze hair shimmered under the light. She had a gorgeous orange shawl wrapped around her shoulders and waist and thighs, setting her alight, a beautiful girl on a pyre. She didn't know it, but just the day before, Easter Monday, three women accused of killing their men—Belva Gaertner, Beulah Annan, and Sabella Nitti—had appeared in court together in her hometown. They'd created a bit of a happening. If Wanda had stayed in Chicago, if she'd still been working as a court stenographer for the state's attorney, she'd have witnessed the scene up close. She could have told her brothers and mother about it, enthralled them the way she used to do after spending the day at the library gathering knowledge. Instead she was in a strange city, surrounded by strangers, people whom, just an hour before, she'd been desperate to have like her. Wanda yanked a bracelet off her arm. Then another. "Here," she called out, "take these to remember me by."

Her arms were packed with bracelets, her own unique style, and she slid them off one by one and threw them at her guests. Next came her necklaces, tossed to the ceiling. They clinked on the floor, where scrabbling hands quickly scooped them up. Finally she tore off her rings and flicked them away. She stood there in the center of it all, jewel-less and barefoot amid silence. Her guests stared at her, waiting for more.

The moment was broken, inevitably, by a drunkard. The man lurched forward, wrapped Wanda in his arms. "Atta girl, that's the way to talk," he said. The two of them swooned, and everything hung there for a few seconds, right on the edge, the grinning lout and the grim-faced hostess staring at each other. Then the room burst into laughter and cheers, and the party jerked haltingly back into motion. A dancer swung past them. The drunk continued to hold Wanda. "But listen, kid," he said, leaning in close. "When you shoot, shoot straight, because dead ones don't tell tales."

Wanda filed the advice away. She stepped from him and walked out of the room. She didn't return. The party cranked up to full volume again.

Some hours later, alone at last, Wanda took stock. There were overturned chairs, empty bottles, sandwich detritus. Wine blotched the carpet. Wanda slipped her gown off her shoulders and let it drop to the floor. She used to enjoy being naked. It was a sign of her freedom, her maturity. She picked up the phone and put through a long-distance call. When her man came on the line, Wanda said, "I am coming to see you for a final show-down." He hung up on her. Wanda went into the back of the apartment. She washed, climbed into a clean skirt and blouse, added rouge to her cheeks so she wouldn't scare any children. She eased a revolver into her bag. Hefting on a coat, she headed out to buy a train ticket to Chicago.

⁂

The city was in a panic. News from Palos Park, picked up by radio sta-tions, had spread with surprising rapidity. Reports warned that Wanda Stopa, gun in hand, "had disappeared as quickly and completely as though the earth had opened up and swallowed her." Towertown, the North Side bohemian enclave near the old water tower, flooded with policemen, both uniformed and plainclothes, all on the lookout for the woman. Police wired descriptions of Wanda and the man driving the cab to authorities across the country. The initial assumption was that the driver was Vladimir "Ted" Glaskoff, who, police had learned, was Wanda's estranged husband. Wanda had married him two years ago because he promised to take her into the heart of bohemian life, but within weeks, he had left her and skipped town. Glaskoff, who claimed to be a Russian count displaced by the Bolshevik Revolution, got married frequently; it was the easiest way to get the naive girls into bed.

"Spurned Portia Forgets Law," a *Chicago American* teaser announced just hours after Wanda had fled Palos Park. The banner headline across the front page read: "Girl Lawyer Shoots at Wife of 'Friend,' Kills Old Man." The paper breathlessly related that "Police squads were sent in pursuit of the Stopa girl's taxicab and a special detail was sent to guard the offices of the John H. Dunham & Co. advertising agency, room 1916, Wrigley Building, where [Y. Kenley] Smith is employed."

"What were her thoughts as she strode up the gravel path to his home?" the *American* wondered. "What drove her there, she, a woman with a law training, who would not be expected to take justice in her hands?"

Less than an hour after the shooting, Kenley Smith walked into the state's attorney's office in the Loop and asked for protection. He had been at a dentist's office when his wife called and warned him that Wanda Stopa was headed his way. "That woman has been after me for two years," Smith told the prosecutors. "She was disillusioned about my physical attractions. She wanted me to divorce my wife and marry her, and I refused. I was her warm friend."

Prosecutors quizzed him about the nature of their relationship. Smith said that he had been taken by Wanda's "amazing intelligence." He admitted to giving her money and sending her to New York City, adding that he wanted to help "get her away from the ne'er-do-well husband she had married, emotionally." A year before, Wanda had needed a place to live, and the Smiths' apartment in the city was available, so he and his wife rented it to her. The Smiths had a history of giving shelter to young artists, including Ernest Hemingway, who was a friend of Kenley's younger siblings. (Hemingway claimed that Doodles, whom he found repulsive, made sexual advances toward him during his stay at the apartment in 1920.) Grudgingly, as the questions continued, Kenley Smith confessed that, even after Wanda had moved in, he would still sleep at the flat on nights when he had to stay late at the office. "But," he insisted, "it was all very platonic." The prosecutors, who knew Wanda from her days as an assistant in the office, expressed surprise, which got Smith's back up. "Now, get this straight," he huffed. "I'll draw you a diagram to show you the living room that separated my room from Miss Stopa's studio."

Smith, the papers reported that afternoon, liked to prowl the North Side's "Bohemia" and had set himself up as Wanda Stopa's "mentor." Smith understood the connotations. He continued to deny that he'd had an affair or done anything improper with the girl. "I'm not a bohemian," he said. "I'm an advertising man." Wanda was the bohemian, and she was also a "demented girl," averred Smith. Being an advertising man, he could be convincing. "Miss Stopa, we have learned," Assistant State's Attorney Robert McMillan told reporters later in the day, "was a neurotic."

She was a neurotic with a gun—the best kind for the newspapers. Dozens of reporters, including Maurine Watkins, Genevieve Forbes, and Ione Quinby, fanned out to Wanda's known haunts to hunt down stories about this latest girl gunner. An *Evening American* reporter targeted the lawyers and clerks at the Federal Building. The hack found plenty who remembered the young woman from her days as an assistant for the district attorney. One described Wanda as a "wild little woman."

"She liked to be bohemian," the man said, "and she didn't care who knew it."

Another man added: "She often would smoke cigarettes while she was taking dictation and seemed to be proud of it."

Over in Towertown, Wanda's artist friends appeared to be impressed by their gunslinging comrade's actions. It was as if Wanda had struck a blow for them against the status quo—a blow Maurine would describe as "a moth singed in the fires of 'freedom.'" Maurine was hardly alone in her derisive tone.

The shooting gave reporters an opportunity to castigate the dilettantes of Chicago's North Side artists' community, which modeled itself on the well-known youth subculture in Greenwich Village that had grown up in opposition to the mainstream ethos. Newspaper staffs were predominantly made up of bootstrappers from working-class families; most reporters never had the means to go to college. They viewed the responsibility-free attitudes of the bohemians, often college dropouts financed by indulgent, well-to-do parents, as beneath contempt. The *American,* under a series of graduation photos of a sweet-looking Wanda, her blue eyes as bright as starbursts even in black-and-white newsprint, pointed out how the pictures "show the Wanda Stopa that was the sincere, ambitious girl student," before she fell into a rebellious lifestyle. The paper added: "Watch for the pictures of Wanda Stopa—the killer—after she is apprehended and see what 'dope' and 'Bohemia' have done to this frank, pretty face."

Every hack covering the story took a dig at Towertown's young lay-abouts. "They scoffed at convention and talked about inhibitions," Quinby said of the community. "They spoke loftily of living their own lives, and phrases of self-conscious daring tumbled from the lips of young flappers asking advice about free love and birth control." Genevieve Forbes mocked the notion that bohemians were artists, writing, "Anybody could be an artist or poet" in Towertown. "And pretty nearly anybody was." She added that bohemians "live in tiny rooms, sharing kitchens and baths with other 'artistic' tenants. Nobody locks doors, it's so unfriendly. And trailing kimonos add to the picture."

❧

Chicago's police and reporters would have no luck searching for Wanda Stopa among the trailing kimonos of Towertown. Despite walking away from Ernest Woods's cab before reaching the train station, she did get on a train. As Chicagoans read shocking details about the murder in special editions rushed to press, Wanda was checking into the Hotel Statler in downtown Detroit. She registered as "Mrs. Theodore Glaskow of New York."

It wasn't until the next day, Friday, that she was spotted, by a businessman named Eugene Chloupak. The man, in town from Indianapolis, saw Wanda standing at the mail desk in the hotel's lobby at about noon. He noticed her for the same reason most men did—she was beautiful. But there was also another reason: He'd seen her face in his morning paper. He approached and surreptitiously glanced at the letter in her hand. It was addressed to "Mrs. Inez Stopa"—Harriet Stopa, Wanda's mother. Folded up in the envelope was about $100 in cash, a Polish government bond, and a $200 insurance policy made out to Harriet Stopa. The letter, in Polish, ended simply, *"Matka, droga matka"*—Mother, dear mother—in a scratchy scrawl.

Chloupak, of course, only saw the address on the envelope, and that wasn't quite enough to push him into action. He didn't know what to do. This petite young woman with the sharply cut cheekbones was a wanted woman. He stood there in the lobby, paralyzed. It must have been hard for him to believe that his newspaper had come to life and was standing right next to him. Finally, Chloupak managed to convince himself she was for real, and he told the hotel's assistant manager about his find. By then, though, Wanda had posted her letter and walked away.

The police, when they arrived at the hotel, assumed Wanda Stopa—or whomever the man saw—had disappeared into the midday crowds out on the sidewalks. In fact, she went upstairs to Room 1156. There, in her room, she collected her few personal items into an orderly pile on the bed: a dressing gown, cold cream, a comb, her diary. The only accessory she left on her person was a gold band with a sapphire set in a red Buddha. She fetched a glass of water from the bathroom and sat down. She added sugar to the water and mixed it in. She then carefully poured another substance into the glass. She closed her eyes and threw the liquid down her throat before she could change her mind.

At 1:30 Wanda placed a call to the house physician. "I am feeling very sick," she said quietly. That was all. The doctor could tell from the caller's voice that the situation was urgent. He arrived at her room just moments later. As the door swung open, Wanda was falling backward onto the bed, unconscious.

11

It's Terrible, but It's Better

On Friday afternoon, a coroner's jury at the city morgue in Chicago announced that Wanda Elaine Stopa had fired a revolver at Henry Manning "with murderous intent." Kenley Smith stood up slowly as the jurors filed out of the room. Smith had sat in the back during the inquest, pale and nervous, keeping his head down and his eyes peeled. The time and place for the inquest had been publicly announced, and he was convinced that Wanda planned to barge into the room, shoot him, and, in a grand final gesture, shoot herself over his lifeless body. Her failure to appear may have been a blow to his ego, but as he stepped from the room, relief replaced disappointment when a reporter pulled him aside. Wanda Stopa, the hack said, had been found dead in Detroit.

"So Wanda has committed suicide?" the distinguished-looking ad man replied. He ran a hand over the top of his slicked-back hair, to press down any stray strands. "I knew it would come," he said. "It was her ultimate step. Given that psychopathic temperament, it was inevitable that some emotional crisis would cause her to end her life. It happened to be this one. If not this, it would have been some other."

The news may not have surprised Smith, but it shocked the rest of the city. Everyone had expected Wanda to take her place among the murderesses of the Cook County Jail. Her crime was the most sensational—and the most heartbreaking—of them all. On top of that, she was so beautiful, maybe even more beautiful than Beulah Annan. This was cause for mourning among the newspaper corps. Now police reporters would never get to crowd around Wanda's cell for daily interviews. Now they wouldn't get to fight for seats to her trial. In the *Tribune* on Saturday, April 26, just two days after Wanda had burst onto the city's front pages, Genevieve Forbes wrote:

> Wanda Stopa, the Polish girl who wanted to "live her own life," ended everything by taking her own life yesterday afternoon at 1:30 when she swallowed cyanide of potassium in room 1156 at the Hotel Statler, Detroit.

By now news of Wanda's epilepsy had broken, and that seemed to explain everything. Epilepsy, the *Tribune* wrote, "is a manifestation of the old motor nerve system, in contrast to the new motor system which obtains in all normal human beings. The old motor system, according to the newest theory, is atavistic and a throw-back in a few individuals to the animal kingdom. On this basis, an epileptic fit is as atavistic a performance, and as far from the human norm, as the Thursday morning murder was atavistic and out of the orbit of the healthy minded individual."

So that was that. Wanda may have been beautiful and intelligent, but she was also fatally flawed. Her actions were inevitable, predictable. The *American*—followed by the city's other newspapers—brought this conclusion home by publishing excerpts from unaddressed letters that police found in the Smiths' Chicago studio. Wanda's words were deeply emotional, obsessive, hypnotizing:

"You are the one I need. Oh, Bummy dearest, I miss you so! . . . I am nothing without him, only a lonely, tired soul groping in the world. . . . I do not believe I can bear it much longer. . . . Life for most people is lament. . . . How I would love to throw off all this care and go peacefully to sleep."

The letters went on and on, with metronomic force, a gold mine for the newspapers, which stretched them out over multiple days. The *American* published a selection of the excerpts on their own across the top of the front page, over portraits of Wanda Stopa looking young and gay and unbearably innocent. Kenley Smith, now that he no longer had to worry about Wanda leaping out at him from the bushes, talked openly and frequently

"Beautiful Beulah" Annan strikes a pensive pose shortly after being arrested for killing her boyfriend. "It's so little we get out of cheating," she told reporters. "But the pleasure looks big, for the moment, doesn't it?"

Belva "Belle" Brown was the "queen of Chicago's cabarets." She traded it all in to become the queen of Hyde Park as Mrs. William Gaertner.

Belva transformed herself into a sophisticated member of respectable South Side society. But she didn't give up the party life. Below, Belva, decked out in one of her favorite dance-hall outfits, sits on her husband's knee during an elaborate costume revel at the Gaertner mansion.

Maurine Watkins studied the classics at Transylvania University, with plans to get a Ph.D. But her desire to discover "real life" took her in a different direction.

W. W. O'Brien, man of action.

William Scott Stewart, Beulah, and her husband Al get their story straight before going into court. As the trial began, Beulah "smiled and pouted, sighed and turned r.s.v.p. eyes on the jury."

Maurine Watkins's beauty proved so distracting to her colleagues that the *Tribune*'s managing editor considered banning women from the newsroom.

Ione Quinby, the *Evening Post*'s diminutive dynamo, at about the time she began her newspaper career.

Katherine Malm, the "Tiger Girl."

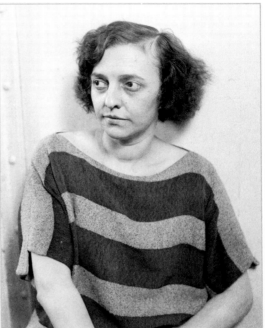

Belva in jail, without her powder puff or diamond rings. She still managed to project an aura of wealth and style.

The flirtatious Beulah expertly manipulated reporters while awaiting trial. But the newspapers—and public sentiment—eventually turned against her.

Sabella Nitti, in Cook County Jail after being condemned to hang, receives a visit from her youngest child.

Helen Cirese decided to take up Sabella's appeal after reading the *Tribune*'s biased coverage of the trial. The twenty-three-year-old lawyer's beauty and comportment tips for her client caught on with the other inmates.

Katherine Malm checks out what the morning papers have to say about her. Reporters didn't treat her as kindly as they did Beulah Annan and Belva Gaertner.

Ione Quinby gave a sensationalized account of Chicago's own Wanda Stopa, brilliant law student and gun-wielding bohemian, in *Master Detective* magazine.

MURDERESS!
This woman was guilty of one of the most cold-blooded crimes in the history of Chicago. One of the most unusual criminals who ever lived, you'll meet her in the pages of next month's issue of THE MASTER DETECTIVE

The *Chicago American* aggressively fueled the "Wanda sensation." Coverage of the love-triangle shooting was so popular it pushed Beulah and Belva entirely out of the papers.

A *New York Times* reporter, on meeting Maurine Watkins, noted that it was easier to believe she was "the author of poetry such as that penned by Edna St. Vincent Millay, than of a play like *Chicago*."

Beulah Annan signs divorce papers with the press watching. Asked why she was leaving her husband, she said, "I want lights, music and good times . . . and I'm going to have them."

to reporters. "I feel sure Wanda was morally and emotionally insane, but that intellectually she was sane as it is possible to be," he said. Later, he insisted that Wanda's decision to shoot at his wife "was conceived under the influence of narcotics. I feel sure of that, and I feel sure that she wanted and needed money with which to buy more dope."

With Wanda's life splayed so awkwardly before the public, the Stopas felt they had no choice but to respond. "My daughter often begged to be allowed to bring Mr. Smith to our home so she could introduce him to us," said Wanda's mother, Harriet Stopa. "But I always refused her. I told her this home was sacred and that she could not bring bums in it, for a gray-haired man who makes love to a little girl when he has a wife at home is nothing but a bum. She used to cry and say she wished she could stop thinking about him. She said he was so brilliant, so well educated, he knew so much about the fine side of living, and that he had taught her so much. She used to tell me everything."

Wanda's twenty-two-year-old brother, Henry, his face blasted into a stony mask, tried to find something positive in his sister's decision to take her own life. He loved her deeply, and so he'd rather see her dead than have her become one of those women on Murderess Row being paraded out for the public's titillation. "Yes, it's better to be dead than to be added to that list of women held for murder over at the county jail," he said. "It's terrible, but it's better. The thing had to end tragically, and this was the best of the ways."

❧❧

The train station was cloaked in low fog and a persistent rain when Wanda Stopa's body arrived in Chicago early on Sunday morning. Ione Quinby and Maurine Watkins stood in a group with other reporters, waiting for something to happen as the casket, encased in a pine box, was lowered onto the platform. But nothing did. The Stopas apparently had misunderstood the arrangements and expected the body to be delivered to the family home, not just to the station. Men and women climbed down from the passenger cars, popped open umbrellas, and quickly departed. The conductor hustled from the train to the station house and back again. The platform emptied out—except for the reporters. It was a sad sight, the cheap pine box sitting out in the elements, slowly being soaked by rain, no one going near it. Finally, the train screeched back into motion and pulled away as the reporters continued to wait. When it became clear no one was coming to claim the body, railroad staff carried the box to the street and loaded it onto a wagon, bound for a holding pen somewhere, but the reporters flagged down the driver before he could pull the wagon out into the street. They pooled their money to have the casket delivered to its proper destination.

As the reporters were haggling with the wagon driver, people began to arrive at the Stopa family's third-floor walk-up at 1505 Augusta Street. It was mostly people from the neighborhood: old men who'd known her father; Wanda's childhood friends, some of them toting children; her brothers' work colleagues and schoolmates. Once the casket arrived at the flat and was properly arranged in the front parlor, mourners and reporters lined up before it. They offered condolences to the family and peered down at the dead girl, whose face glowed under two huge candles that flickered at the head and foot of the casket. The apartment was filled with flowers, including a floral basket from the Kent College of Law—even though Kent wasn't Wanda's alma mater*—and one from "the boys at the district attorney's office." The somber scene moved Maurine. She was more understanding of Wanda, so much like Maurine in her love for home and her need to leave it, than she ever could be of Belva or Beulah. The reporter remained impassive as she watched, but later in the day she would carve out a carefully composed report, elegiac without being sentimental:

> And Wanda came home at last.
> "Bohemian freedom," morphine and love, murder, suicide, and then—back in the Little Poland she had deserted for Chicago's Bohemia; back with the mother and brothers she had left for a glamorous "count" who married her, and for a business man who didn't; back with the friends "a thousand years behind the times" she had forsaken for others "who speak my language and understand."

*Wanda, like William Scott Stewart before her, graduated from the John Marshall Law School.

Maurine, pinned in by a long, meandering queue that filled the stairway to the apartment, had to wait for hours before filing her story. The family expected the mourners to be gone by early afternoon, but at noon the line stretched down the block like a picket of soldiers. Wanda's mother and two brothers expressed surprise at seeing unfamiliar faces coming up the stairs, but they accepted that Wanda had known many people they'd never met. Some hours later, though, the line outside, inexplicably, had grown longer still. The small parlor filled beyond capacity, until the carpet was soaked and pictures on the walls knocked askew. The family realized these were not Wanda's friends. The viewing had become something that had nothing to do with mourning the death of a young woman. The newspapers, with their breathless coverage of Wanda and the shooting, had brought out hundreds of thrill seekers. "All day they came in steady streams; strangers, laughing and chewing gum, curious to see Chicago's latest, youngest, 'brainiest' murderess," Quinby observed. She, Maurine, and other reporters worked the line just inside the parlor, taking notes, asking for reactions. Looking down on the dead girl, Quinby noted "an expression of supreme triumph on her beautifully molded face. Knowing the legal penalty for murder, which she had woven in the emotional pattern of her brief explorative life, she had made her exit with a finesse that made her appear more a figure of fiction than fact."

The procession of Chicagoans outside the Stopa home seemed to be in agreement with the reporter's sentiment. They had come to see the denouement of a cinema story. Inching up the stairs and through the parlor, the citizens of the city debated the life they had fervently read about over the past four days, feeling as if they were intimates of the young woman they'd never met. "The true story," one said, "will never be known. Smith made love to her, promised to marry her, grew tired and cast her off; her heart didn't mend in four months and she came back—"

Someone interrupted. "Not to kill Smith but to shoot herself in his presence."

She was "naive as a child," offered another.

Hour after hour, people came through the apartment and gazed down on Wanda smiling in death in her mother's parlor, the murky room lighted only by the holy candles. The church had refused to provide services, some-one from the neighborhood whispered. "Wanda would not mind," came the reply, in tempered disapproval, "for she gave up the church, too, in her quest for 'freedom.'"

Late in the day, Maurine worked up the nerve to approach Harriet Stopa. "She wanted to spare us the agony of a long trial, the disgrace of a sentence and perhaps years of suffering," Mrs. Stopa told Maurine quietly as they stood next to the body. "When she realized what she had done—that she had committed murder—when she came to her senses—"

Harriet Stopa, stoic through the gum snappers and the gigglers and the old women who looked at her with despairing righteousness, at last could stand no more. Maurine had nudged her over the edge. Mrs. Stopa sat, put her head to her lap and sobbed: "My poor little girl! My poor little girl!"

And still, the line outside grew. It seemed to be self-replicating, a sin-gle, inexhaustible organism marching forward. Here and there, the crowd broke off into individuals who, impatient, rushed around the building and up the back staircase, only to find the rear door locked. They put their shoulders into the door—*bang!*—in case it was just stuck, startling family members on the other side. Around the front, tempers began to flare. The banister on the tight stairway leading to the apartment rocked against the pressure of dozens of hands and arms. Policemen walking their beat in the afternoon recognized the potential for trouble and called in for help. "At 8 o'clock," wrote Maurine, "5,000 persons swarmed in front of the build-ing at 1505 Augusta Street, and squads of policemen were sweating in the business of maintaining order. Ten abreast, the 'mourners' were packed in a line that was two blocks long."

Two hours later, the Stopas called the police in desperation. They feared the officers on the scene were being overwhelmed by the mob. Central Sta-tion told them reinforcements already had been dispatched. Soon, thirty fresh policemen arrived and rushed forward as a human wall, swinging their clubs. The crowd gasped and fell back. "There were screams, laughter, a few curses," Maurine related. "Two women were clubbed by the police. For a time it seemed that the crowd would win out, and a call was sent in to the fire department. The [fire wagon] arrived just as the throng began to disperse."

≈≈≈

The Stopas wouldn't get much of a respite. The funeral was two days later, and it would be even worse than the viewing. The curious began showing up shortly after dawn on Tuesday. The newspapers, with their lurid descriptions of Little Poland disintegrating into chaos over the weekend, convinced thousands more people to make the trek out to the Northwest Side to see what all the excitement was about. Men and women settled in for a siege—or for a picnic. They wouldn't be disappointed.

"Battle Crowds at Wanda Rites!" screamed the front page of the *American,* in huge type that dwarfed the newspaper's nameplate. The battle was still raging when the edition rolled off the presses that afternoon. In the morning, Maurine had headed back out to the Stopa residence for another round of interviews, but this time it wouldn't be so easy to get in. She found her progress blocked by more than "10,000 morbid sensation seekers" who had congregated on and around Augusta Street to see Wanda's body taken to Bohemian National Cemetery.

Maurine wasn't exaggerating: There were thousands of people pressing in on the small apartment building. This was group madness, a sight so incredible, it stayed with the reporter for years. The crowd rolled and bucked outside the building, spilling out of Augusta Street into Ashland Avenue. A phalanx of policemen and firemen walled off some of the adjacent streets in a vain effort to keep the throng contained. Peanut vendors skirted the periphery of the crowd, quickly selling off their product and squeezing out of the crush to race off and restock. Maurine was thunderstruck at how, in death, everybody seemed to love Wanda Stopa. It no longer mattered that the woman had shot and killed an innocent man; it mattered only that her beautiful face and mournful words appeared above the fold of every newspaper in the city. The problem wasn't so much public attitudes toward crime, she decided, "but in the fact that no one considers the crime." She recognized the same moral blindness coloring public opinion toward Beulah Annan and Belva Gaertner, two murderesses who remained very much alive.

Ione Quinby, also back for another day of exhaustive Wanda coverage, found it impossible to fight her way through the mob. Everyone wanted to be right in front of the building when the body was brought out, keeping the *Post* reporter from getting near the entrance. "The only path I found was through the alley at the back, and entrance from this passage to the house was to be effected only by scaling a brick wall five feet high," she later remembered.

Getting around the crowd and over the wall—not an easy climb in a tight ankle-length skirt—was only the first challenge Quinby faced. She now had to bring out her acting skills. After the sick voyeurism on display at the viewing, the Stopas weren't letting anyone in but family and close friends; they placed their largest men at the doors to block anyone else from entering. The men had been given instructions to turn back, preferably with a thump to the head, any artist from Towertown or other interloper who dared make an appearance. Thinking on her feet, Quinby hid her notebook and insisted to the door-minder that she was a friend of Wanda's from law school. The man hesitated just long enough for Quinby to duck inside and run up the stairs to the apartment. Her hopes for an exclusive were short-lived, though, for when Quinby stepped into the Stopa parlor again, she found that Maurine Watkins also had somehow managed to get in.

The Catholic Church had indeed refused to send a priest, so a Baptist minister, the Reverend John Frydryk, conducted a brief service in the house. Frydryk preached his sermon in Polish, but Maurine, always interested in the word of God, took pains to write some of it down and get it translated. The minister took John 11:21 as his text: "Lord, if Thou hadst been here, my brother had not died!" The small group of mourners did their best to concentrate on the minister's quiet, solemn words and to ignore the "sensation seekers" leaning over balconies and fire escapes in reckless attempts to peer into the Stopa living room.

When Frydryk finished, the pallbearers—six of Wanda's childhood friends—stepped forward. As they began to walk carefully toward the stairs with the coffin, the front door was opened and the tumult outside rushed forward in ear-popping screams and titters. Grasping hands assaulted all of the pallbearers as they stepped down the stairs. The people outside began to shift in response to the casket's arrival, some moving toward it, others trying to inch away to give it room. Bodies ground together like tectonic plates. A grotesque sound burbled up, a collective gasp and squeak, the unnatural expulsions wrought by body upon body slamming together unnaturally, necks twisting and bobbing to the point of muscle breakdown. A detail of policemen pushed through the crowd to the white hearse idling at the curb, clearing a path for the pallbearers. Most of the people fell back, but some resisted, their torsos contorted in their effort to get closer, seemingly on the verge of the kind of fit that Wanda Stopa was now famous for.

Right behind the coffin, Mrs. Stopa and her sons and then the rest of the family marched darkly into the maw. The Reverend Frydryk handed Quinby a wreath of flowers with instructions to take it to the hearse. "I did," the reporter later said, "forcing my way along the front of the house, but on the way two women snatched several of the roses, mementoes, I suppose, to be pressed in their scrapbooks. Another tried to rip off one of the tulle ribbons and gave me an angry shove when I tore it out of her grasp." The reporter was relieved when she reached the hearse, her responsibility fulfilled. "It was a funeral that would have interested Wanda; an Augusta Street rid of its inhibitions," she said.

With great effort, the hearse pulled away from the curb and left behind the crowds and the peanut vendors and the police cordon. The family undoubtedly thought the worst of it was finally over, but at the cemetery they discovered another five thousand Chicagoans waiting. Mrs. Stopa and her sons, Henry and Walter, gaped at the sight of still more people blocking their way. Standing at the gravesite, they tried to disregard the crowds through extreme concentration on their grief. They kept their heads down and held on to one another, just trying to get through the day. Henry was the first to break. Wanda's brother, just a year younger than his dead sister, had expressed rage in the past four days but produced no tears. Now the tears came, violently, uncontrollably. He collapsed onto the coffin and pushed away everyone who tried to help him back on his feet.

Edward T. Lee, dean of the John Marshall Law School and Wanda's mentor before she disappeared into bohemia, offered some last words before the coffin was lowered into the earth. He had come to testify, he said, "to her lovely character, her brilliant mind, her eager pursuit of her studies, her lofty and noble ambition."

Sobbing punctuated this expression of Wanda Stopa's lost potential. Dean Lee described the murder as a "great misfortune" but added that Wanda was now relieved of the burden of what she'd done. "The law has been fulfilled: it cannot follow the dead," he said. "The moral guilt is beyond our power to judge—Christ only could speak on such occasion and he would say: 'Let him that is without sin cast the first stone.'" Maurine wrote down the professor's heavenly invocation, obviously concerned with Wanda's journey ahead in the afterlife.

After Lee had finished, there was nothing left to say. The only sounds now were "Nearer, My God, to Thee" being played quietly from somewhere behind the family and the soft clop of dirt being dropped down onto the casket—until a child interrupted the somber moment, exclaiming something to his mother. That was when Walter Stopa broke. Harriet Stopa's seventeen-year-old son slapped the child, suddenly and ruthlessly. The boy's mother, a woman named Anna Konpke, objected. "Mrs. Stopa's nerves gave way" then, Maurine related, "and she promptly gave the mother three blows, breaking her eyeglasses."

The woman and her child were rushed away from the gravesite to a nearby open area, where reporters descended on them. Mrs. Konpke didn't know who the Stopas were or anything about Wanda Stopa, she said. She had come to the cemetery to visit her son's grave and noticed the teeming mob rolling like a wave across the grounds. Curiosity, she said, got the best of her—"just like all the rest of them."

12

What Fooled Everybody

William Gaertner came to see his Belva almost every day at the jail. He assured her everything was going to turn out fine. After all, she had arguably the best defense attorney in Chicago and without question the best connected. Thomas Nash, a former alderman, represented the city's biggest names. Three years ago, he had helped secure acquittals in the "Black Sox" World Series game-fixing trial—and everyone knew those boys were guilty.

By the second week of May, however, even Nash's reputation wasn't enough to make Belva feel better. She'd had the start of her trial postponed back in April when Beulah Annan was taking up all the air. Now her new date loomed, and the mood at the Cook County Jail had only gotten worse. On May 7, a jury convicted Elizabeth Unkafer of killing her lover and sentenced her to life in prison. Lizzie was a loon; she'd said she committed the murder because it was God's will. Still, she continued a distressing trend. Over the past two months, Cook County's all-male juries inexplicably had become unafraid of convicting women. Before Lizzie Unkafer, Mary Wezenak was convicted of manslaughter for serving poisonous whiskey. Before "Moonshine Mary," Kitty Malm was sent "over the road." Before Kitty, Sabella Nitti had started it all last summer.

More distressing still was the similarity between Belva's case and Unkafer's. Maurine Watkins had noticed and, right after Unkafer's conviction, asked about it. Belva told the reporter there was no comparison between the two cases, not that her protestation did any good. She opened the paper the next morning and saw that Maurine had written it up in her own weird little way, as always.

Of the four awaiting trial, the cases of Mrs. Annan and Mrs. Belva Gaertner would seem most similar to Elizabeth Unkafer's; each is accused of shooting a man, not her husband, with whom her relations were at least questioned; each is supposed to be a "woman scorned" who shot the man "rather than lose him." But neither was at all disconcerted by Mrs. Unkafer's sentence.

"I can't see that it's anything at all like my case," said Mrs. Gaertner, the sophisticated divorcee indicted for shooting Law, the young auto salesman, as she twirled about in her red dancing slippers.

"The cases are entirely different," said Mrs. Annan, quite the ingénue in her girlish checked flannel frock.

Had Belva been twirling about while talking to the *Tribune* reporter? Hardly likely. She did wear red slippers, though. William had brought them. They were comfortable. They made the cell feel a little homey.

At least the reporter included Beulah in the comparison game with Belva, rather than Sabella or Lela Foster, the other women with murder trials coming up. It didn't mean, though, that she and Beulah were equals in the eyes of the press, and there'd be no point in pretending otherwise. Belva had understood that from the very first day Beulah stepped through the jail's doors, back at the beginning of April. The pretty, fragile ones had got in Belva's way her whole life. The large eyes, the trembling lip, the wee waist you could almost put your hand all the way around—men could never get enough. Men who might have been her husbands. Men who might have been her boyfriends. The thought of it enraged her. But this time, she had decided she wouldn't fight against the other girl, the prettier girl. She would fight alongside her.

On Beulah's first day in the jail, Belva began scheming to get her picture taken with the new inmate. They would be best pals all the way. She wasn't as attractive or as young as Beulah, but if she played it right, she believed the papers would lump them together: "the prettiest women in Cook County Jail." That was worth something. Here, William's ready cash came in handy. The "forbidden cabinet," the one that held the cosmetics taken from new prisoners when they were processed at the jail, now opened for Belva and only her.* With young, male reporters swaggering around the jail every day, all of the girls wanted access to their beauty products, but only Belva got preferential treatment. "Belva has her powder puff again," the other inmates would say, clucking respectfully, when they caught sight of Belva looking glam on the cellblock. She was an expert with makeup; she could make herself look a decade younger.

After a couple days of jockeying, Belva got her picture with Beulah. Shots of the duo together appeared in most of the city's newspapers. Belva looked good—bemused and sleepy-eyed, her head cocked imperiously like the society doyenne she once was, gazing slightly down on her "dear friend," "Beautiful Beulah" Annan. In every caption she earned equal billing. The *Tribune* labeled its photo "Killers of Men." Maurine, knowing full well that everyone was talking about the two cases, reported that the women, incredible as it might seem, "have not talked over their common interests. A man, a woman, liquor and a gun."

The photos with Beulah had been a significant coup for Belva; they kept her in the headlines. But that was then. Now, a month after those photographs ran, the powder puff wasn't going to be enough for her to stay in the picture. In the wake of the "Wanda sensation," and with Elizabeth Unkafer's conviction playing prominently in all of the papers, Beulah was having her own crisis of confidence. And like Belva, she had decided to do something about it.

≈∘≈

On May 8, the day after Unkafer's conviction, Beulah Annan gathered the press and told them she was pregnant. Harry Kalstedt, she said, had attacked her that fateful day in April after she informed him she was carrying her husband's child.

---

*The inmates were allowed to use makeup only on days they appeared in court.

Reporters thrilled at the unexpected news—a new twist that would tug at hearts and further goose a story that already obsessed readers. They crowded in on Beulah in the corridor of the women's section, shooting questions at her. The mother-to-be scolded Belva for spilling her secret, even though Beulah's announcement was the first that reporters had heard of the pregnancy. Nevertheless, the papers that Thursday afternoon stuck with Beulah's account: "Mrs. Beulah Annan, young and beautiful slayer of her sweetheart, Harry Kalstedt, today bemoaned the publicity given the fact she is expecting a visit from the stork in the Fall," wrote the *American*. The newspaper continued:

> Today, when seen in her cell at the county jail, she blamed Mrs. Belva Gaertner, divorcee, awaiting trial for the killing of her sweetheart, Walter Law, married automobile salesman, for disclosing the secret.
>
> "Belva should not have told," said Mrs. Annan. "But women always tell such things. It was to have been my own little secret, but I just had to confide in someone and I told Belva."
>
> Roy C. Woods and William F. McLaughlin, assistant state's attorneys, declared the fact that Mrs. Annan was awaiting motherhood did not change the fact that a murder had been committed.
>
> Assistant State's Attorney Edward Wilson declared that if Mrs. Annan were convicted and sentenced to death, there was no legal reason why she should not be hanged.

No legal reason? Perhaps that was so, but such a fraught decision hardly would be decided on legal merits. They were talking about an innocent little baby. And with Beulah as its mother, it would certainly be "a most beautiful child," the *Post* stated. The day after she disclosed the pregnancy, Beulah announced through her lawyers that she "wants no postponement of her trial on account of her approaching motherhood." The state responded in kind, bravely insisting, "We are ready to go to trial today."

The pregnancy revelation surprised Maurine. During the immediate excitement of it all, she hung back, took stock. She decided to chat with some of the other inmates while a group of reporters interviewed Beulah.

It seemed that, among the hacks covering the development, Maurine alone was suspicious. In the next day's *Tribune,* she hinted that the whole thing was a ruse, hitting with the kind of lacerating sarcasm that was beginning to earn her a following.

What counts with a jury when a woman is on trial for murder?

Youth? Beauty? And if to these she adds approaching motherhood—?

For pretty Mrs. Beulah Annan, who shot her lover, Harry Kohlstedt [*sic*],* to the tune of her husband's phonograph, is expecting a visit from the stork early this fall. This 23 year old murderess, now waiting trial, is making this the basis for a further appeal to clemency.

Maurine went on to suggest that Unkafer's verdict on Wednesday had prompted Beulah's announcement, "for the conviction of one of their number broke the monotony of their life and startled them into a worried analysis," she wrote of the seven inmates remaining on "Murderess Row." The official line from William Scott Stewart, she added, was that Beulah's "condition has no bearing upon the legality of the case." But, prompted by Maurine, he had agreed that "it might affect the jury." Maurine was also alone among the reporting corps in bringing up the "four-term rule," which Beulah's attorneys could invoke to prevent the case from being held over for more than four terms of court—meaning Stewart and O'Brien could ensure Beulah went to trial well before the baby was due to arrive. "Will a jury give death—will a jury send to prison—a mother-to-be?" Maurine asked.

She clearly thought Cook County jurymen wouldn't be able to do so, especially to a mother-to-be as lovely as Beulah May Annan. For weeks, Maurine had reminded readers that Beulah's story about the Kalstedt shooting—that is, her latest story—didn't add up. The criticism hadn't dented the suspected murderess's popularity at all, and now the reporter was questioning Beulah's veracity about that most sacred and mysterious

*Maurine could be rather careless with names. It took her more than a month to spell Harry Kalstedt's name correctly. She also initially flubbed Belva Gaertner's and Walter Law's names.

of womanly things: pregnancy. People—especially men—wanted to believe Beulah. They were conditioned to believe her.

Maurine's derisive articles stayed true to the *Tribune*'s niche in the market—the hanging paper, the paper that didn't write sob stories—but she also made a good case. It was an unlikely coincidence, after all, that the pregnancy announcement came just days after the massive Wanda Stopa coverage. For a thrilling, salacious week, Wanda had blotted out all of the women of Cook County Jail, even "Beautiful Beulah" Annan. The Polish girl gunner pushed Beulah not just off the front page but out of the papers entirely. The story became so big that twenty-four-year-old Ernest Hemingway, a foreign correspondent for the *Toronto Star,* picked up a Marseille newspaper in southern France one day and, to his surprise, found himself reading about his childhood friends' older brother, Y. Kenley Smith. At his request, his family sent him all of the *Tribune*'s articles about Wanda Stopa, which they annotated with "suitable moral comments." Hemingway became caught up in the coverage. "Pity the female Polak lawyer couldn't shoot when she pulled a gun on Doodles," he wrote to a friend, still disgusted by the thought of Kenley's wife eyeing him. The Palos Park shooting and its circumstances were so scandalous that it's believed they inspired Hemingway to write a short story, "Summer People," in which a Hemingway-like protagonist engages in anal intercourse with a wild young woman named Kate. Surely that was the kind of "perversion" bohemians undertook, especially the ones who went mad like Wanda Stopa. ("I love it. I love it. I love it," Kate calls out during the sex act, which of course occurs not in a bed but out in the woods.)

Beulah's trial had been scheduled to start the Monday after Wanda burst into the news, before her lawyers managed at the last minute to push it back to late May. That original timing must have terrified Beulah. How could she go to trial if all anyone was talking about was Wanda Stopa? But her instincts, as always in seeking press coverage, were pitch-perfect. She later said, "What fooled everybody when I told them in jail that I was going to become a mother was this: We had kept it a secret that the reason I shot Kalstedt was because he would not let me alone when I told him I was going to have a baby."

No reporter bothered to ask why she would keep such a compelling reason for her violent act a secret. Maurine, for one, had come to believe that her colleagues simply preferred Beulah's revisionist account of what happened on the night of April 3. There wasn't much they could do with a hard-hearted confession, but her desperate fight against a brute—that was perfect. There certainly was no denying that Beulah Annan knew how to play pathos for all it was worth. "Albert probably won't want me back—my life's ruined anyway; I can never live it down," she told any reporter who would listen, the tears coming easily. "Even if I went away where nobody knew, you can't get away from yourself. And I'd always remember that I'd killed him."

Men riding into work on the streetcar shook their heads and winced at such plangent words, then gazed at the latest picture of the dear murder suspect, who, Maurine noted, "posed prettily for the photographers" every day. Their wives at home snuffled at reading the same words, the tears coming almost as easily as they did to Beulah. Despite Maurine's caustic commentary and Belva Gaertner's attempts to regain the spotlight, the Beulah juggernaut could not be stopped. Even William Gaertner's millions couldn't help his ex-wife stand out against such exceptional competition. Beulah Annan was simply a natural. A rumor floated around the city's newsrooms that if Beulah won acquittal, one of the Hollywood movie studios was prepared to offer her a contract. (This surely infuriated Belva, who actually had been a professional performer.) The rumor wasn't true; there had been no discussions with Hollywood representatives. But Beulah assumed some kind of life in entertainment would be open to her. At the very least, she knew she could be a vaudeville freak act, a term that referred not to mustachioed women but to performers who had box-office drawing power for some reason other than talent. The boxing champion Jack Dempsey was a top-drawer freak act, once making $10,000 in a week. So was Evelyn Nesbit, the infamous object of desire who'd sparked the murder of the noted architect Stanford White. Freak acts cracked bad jokes, talked through songs, told supposedly true stories from their lives, or did a simple soft shoe. Beulah Annan surely could manage that.

13

A Modest Little Housewife

On Thursday, May 22, the bailiff in Judge William Lindsay's courtroom said the words everyone had been waiting to hear: "Beulah Annan."

The defendant, her head bare, hands interlaced at her waist, rose and walked toward the bar. She progressed as if at the head of a funeral procession, her head cast slightly downward, steps slow and deliberate. Reporters took up most of the first handful of rows in the packed courtroom, and Beulah exchanged smiles with them as she approached. She passed her husband in the first row. Al leaned forward in his seat, twisting his cap in his hand, a worried gaze fixed on her. She did not meet his eyes.

Beulah knew everyone would be looking at her, the comely expectant mother of Cook County Jail. She didn't disappoint. Her freshly marcelled hair arced with precision across her forehead. The lace collar of her new blouse suggested innocent modesty but at the breastbone dipped tantalizingly into shadow. "The courtroom was full of appreciative smiles directed toward the lovely girl beside the prisoner's table," noted a reporter from out of state. "There were flashes of consideration. The sheiks of the town crowded the spectators' chairs. The pretty, bob-haired maid assuredly was the fairest thing that had ever graced a murder trial in Chicago."

The *Daily Journal*'s hack appeared equally impressed. He described in detail Beulah's expertly tailored suit, even her black satin slippers.

Slightly pale from her recent illness but blossoming with the comeliness of face and figure which has spread her name broadcast, Mrs. Annan looked more like a boarding school girl tripping up to the principal's "carpet" than a defendant in one of Chicago's most sensational murder trials.

Perhaps there was "method in the madness" that prompted her to enter the courtroom bareheaded. With her flaming red hair showing at its best with a fresh trim and marcel, she made a picture which would rival paintings of the famous Titian.

The *Journal*'s reporter was right: There was a method to Beulah's appearance. Her lawyers, Stewart and O'Brien, with the help of a "fashion expert" they'd hired, had carefully thought everything out, including the bare head. A beautiful woman who went bareheaded in public could only be a whore or a goddess. Beulah managed to be both. The "boarding-school girl" look played into a popular male sexual fantasy while also visually showcasing Beulah's innocence. She looked sweetly childlike and at the same time delectably ripe. The fashion expert earned the fee—Beulah's outfits would receive as much comment as the evidence presented in court—but the defendant's beauty alone was undoubtedly enough to do the job. It confirmed a woman's nature, her innate moral place in the world. Time and again Beulah Annan was described as if she were a work of art: her hair was not simply red but "Titian," her coy smile that of a "Sphinx" withholding a thrilling riddle.

The male reporters covering her case had long ago come over to her side. The pregnancy announcement simply sealed it. The *Post* alluded to a metaphor by Alexander Pope, describing Beulah as "a butterfly on a wheel, the center of many curious eyes, some friendly, some hostile. She wore a neat brown dress, with a soft fur piece about her neck." Her lawyers couldn't have asked for a better image than that of a helpless, fluttering Beulah, in her neat brown dress, being tortured on a wheel to achieve something as unimportant as a conviction.

※※※

It seemed to Maurine Watkins that she was the only one who remembered the ugliness of the killing. While the *Journal* and the *Post* remained officially neutral on Beulah, and the Hearst papers sometimes bordered on fawning, Maurine worked herself into a righteous fury. What any decent defense attorney in Chicago wanted in a jury, she believed, was "twelve good morons"—and she was convinced, and horrified, that W. W. O'Brien and William Scott Stewart were going to get them.

Maurine had seen enough of Beulah's attorneys to know that Beulah was lucky to have them. Stewart and O'Brien had been in partnership together less than two years, but they had proved an excellent team from the start. So far they'd never lost a case—a record rapidly approaching two dozen acquittals in a row. They'd had such success that they were about to set themselves up in the swank new Temple Building in the heart of the Loop. Their rent would be a whopping $350 a month.*

On the face of it, the partners made an unusual pair. O'Brien exuded tough-guy charm; he didn't so much smile at you as ease his lips into a kind of swagger. He was impressive in a quintessentially Chicago way, decked out in colorful shirts, always making a show, the kind of man who kept his hat pulled low over his eyes, winked at attractive young ladies on the street, and dangled a cigarette from his lip as he talked. He had a propensity for going on weeklong benders, surfacing just in time to walk into court.

Stewart wasn't a teetotaler, but in contrast to his partner, no one ever saw him drunk. A journalist labeled the always well-dressed Stewart "the Beau Brummel of the courtroom." He was low-key, fastidious, a perfectionist. "There is an atmosphere around every law office," he would say years later, speaking to young lawyers getting their start. "It is either businesslike or it is not. Avoid those offices which look like hangouts, where those about the office play cards in plain view, smoke cigarettes and keep their hats on. . . . Your client cannot have a very good impression when he walks into such an office. Such people are apt to appear discourteous and not handle messages properly." He was likely speaking from direct experience.

But in spite of their differing styles, the law partners trusted each other implicitly—and no one else. Stewart's theory on hiring a secretary for the office was "somewhat like that often given concerning marriage. . . . Get them young and tell them nothing." He insisted that he and his partner

---

*The $350 rent they paid when they moved into the Temple Building in 1925 is comparable to more than $4,000 eighty years later.

not only tell their girl nothing but also that they should "give her not the slightest responsibility, and drum into her by constant repetition that she should not give out any information."

Stewart and O'Brien didn't seem to need any help, from a secretary or anyone else. They were smart, efficient lawyers. They were each making at least $20,000 annually by 1924, an impressive haul. They didn't take any case for the publicity—unless they were sure they could win it. Stewart liked to say that "it is difficult to catch a good lawyer on the wrong side of a case." Innocence was not necessarily the right side, though he never ruled it out. "When your client claims to be innocent, do not despair, even when things look black," he said. "He may in fact be innocent."

There was no obvious reason for the two lawyers to be so confident that they were on the right side of the Beulah Annan case. Sure, she was beautiful, and O'Brien and Stewart were getting a lot of publicity with her, especially after her pregnancy announcement. But this was a woman who had admitted to cuckolding her husband and shooting her lover when the man attempted to walk out on her. In the past year, Sabella Nitti, Kitty Malm, and now Elizabeth Unkafer had been convicted of murder, a sudden and dramatic reversal of tradition. On top of that, O'Brien and Stewart were essentially a two-man band, whereas, "In Chicago," Stewart pointed out, "the prosecutor has about sixty assistants, in addition to clerks, stenographers, investigators and police." Roy Woods and William McLaughlin, the assistant state's attorneys trying Beulah's case, were considered to be among the best in the office.

Despite such challenges, the two men showed only confidence in public and in their meetings with Beulah. O'Brien, in particular, seemed enthusiastic about defending the case. He liked Beulah—he liked women as a rule—and killer women were becoming a specialty. (He would represent thirteen female murder suspects in his career.) Stewart would do the heavy lifting on the case; he'd deal with the actual evidence. But O'Brien was going to throw the gut punch. He planned to argue that Beulah was a "virtuous working girl . . . a modest little housewife" who'd been lured astray by booze. He may have even believed it. Beulah, her choice in a husband notwithstanding, seemed to get to tough guys the most. That little smile of hers, her gaze direct but unfocused, inevitably turned them to jelly. O'Brien needed some tough guys on the jury. He could talk to them man to man.

⋙⋘

The prospective jurors filed into the room and took their seats right after Beulah. They sat up straight in their best suits, their eyes moving between Beulah at the defendant's table and whichever lawyer was asking them questions. The crackpots in the jury pool were weeded out first, those with blatant bloodlust, or simply lust, for the defendant. "Too damned many women gettin' away with murder," said one man who was dismissed by the defense. Another man exclaimed, "Kalstedt got what was coming to him—the fool! In a married woman's apartment!" He was sent home by the state.

Maurine seemed amused by the cynical attempt at jury packing by both sides, noting that the selection process had nothing to do with producing justice. The reporter watched Beulah as Stewart quizzed the prospective jurors. The defendant nodded her head when she liked a juror and offered a "pouting 'no'" when she found one off-putting. Maurine imagined Stewart consulting with his client on the selection of jurors through surreptitious glances over to the defendant's table. The men accepted by the defense, Maurine wrote, were "a good looking lot, comparatively young, and not too 'hard boiled'—for Beulah herself passed on them. And she's a connoisseur in men!"

The jury selection moved along slowly, ultimately taking the entire day. Beulah grew bored. She "leaned wearily on one white hand—with Raphaelite profile turned toward the jury—and pensively sighed now and then." But she perked up when the prosecution indicated its plan of attack for the trial. "Would the fact that the defendant and the deceased had been drinking wine together before the murder influence your judgment?" each juror was asked, eliciting a gasp from Beulah's mother, Mary Neel, who sat "mopping her eyes" in the front row, next to her son-in-law. Woods and McLaughlin wanted to present Beulah as a wild, drunken woman. They recognized the potential payoff of linking Harry Kalstedt's death to the loosening of moral standards in the country.

It was a logical approach, considering widespread perceptions about the state of the city. Three days earlier, federal agents had raided a factory on the West Side. They confiscated hundreds of barrels of beer, taking into custody two of Chicago's highest-profile bootleggers, Johnny Torrio and Dean O'Banion. The operation scored heavy newspaper coverage, but no one had illusions about either of the gangsters ever standing trial—at least not a trial that had any possibility of conviction. In a follow-up raid, this one at the Stock Yards Inn, officers were forced to level their rifles at dozens of saloon patrons who had become incensed when they realized the feds were emptying the place of all its booze. The enraged drinkers rocked the police wagon, almost overturning it before being forced back. Worse yet, as jury selection for Beulah's trial got under way that Thursday morning, news about the kidnapping of a fourteen-year-old prep-school student flashed through the city's newsrooms. The boy, Bobby Franks, was from a wealthy South Side family, which had received a ransom letter. This was followed within the hour by news of the discovery of a boy's body. The *Tribune* immediately offered $5,000 for exclusive information about the crime. As Beulah's jury selection continued, the story of the kidnapping hit the front page of the city's afternoon papers.

Stories like these terrified the average, law-abiding citizen, the type of man who proudly made the time to serve on a jury when called. He read the newspaper every day and could only conclude from its pages that the men around him, on the streetcar and sidewalk, in the office and factory, increasingly were out of control. Anything—literally anything—could happen. And anything, the state insisted, meant it wasn't just men who were dangerous. Even beautiful young women now committed heinous crimes. They would prove, the prosecutors told the newly impaneled jury at the end of the day, that Beulah Annan was responsible for "a cold-blooded, dastardly murder" as horrible as the one inflicted on little Bobby Franks.

੨੨੨

The twelve men who would get to pass judgment on Beulah reported for duty on Friday. The newspapers printed the names and addresses of all of them. They included a bank clerk, a mechanical adjuster, two accountants, a tool inspector, and a real estate broker. Maurine pointed out in the *Tribune* that the defense "favored bachelors, to a count of five," but Stewart and O'Brien took offense at the implication. "We are not relying on the beauty of this woman to prove her guiltless," they told reporters before heading into the courtroom. "We will prove she shot this intruder in self-defense."

Right off, Beulah was called to the stand, but without the jury in the room. Before the trial could get under way, Judge Lindsay had a decision to make: Could the confessions Beulah gave the day of the shooting—especially the most damaging one, the one the newspapers called the Midnight Confession—be used against her? O'Brien and Stewart argued that the confessions were legally worthless because they had been obtained by coercion—by "third-degree methods"—while Beulah was drunk. Assistant State's Attorney William McLaughlin responded that the statements had been validly obtained and should be used in court, despite the fact that, at least with the initial confession, "she was palpably 'ginned up.'"

Patricia Dougherty, writing as Princess Pat in the *American,* noted that the "portion of Mrs. Annan's confession which the defense fought hardest to keep from the jury was her admission of close friendship with Kalstedt, just prior to the quarrel which she settled with a revolver." In William Randolph Hearst's newspapers, sob sisters spared no bloody detail in describing a brutal killing, but they mentioned a murderous wife's alleged unfaithfulness with delicacy, if at all. O'Brien and Stewart would have expected nothing less of a responsible reporter. Murder happened every day, but a woman running around on her husband was a scandal. The very idea of it cut deep into the heart of every married man who headed to work in the morning, leaving his wife with the whole day rolling out before her. A jury, made up only of men, would have little sympathy for a wanton woman, and the defense knew it. "We're not trying a case of adultery, judge," O'Brien said.

On the stand, Beulah now had a chance to frame the case herself. Gazing out at the rows of spectators, at the men standing shoulder to shoulder in the back of the room, she appeared "radiant in her titian-red hair, which chimed with a fur piece that hugged her neck," wrote the *Evening Post.* But even with the jury absent, she was nervous. She smiled at the lawyers, and at the reporters in the front row, but she was trembling. Her bottom lip heaved as she tried to maintain composure. She touched her face, caressing herself, fingertips fluttering along her jawline and then flying away to pet at her hair. She paused frequently to take small gulps of air as she spoke. Responding to a question from Stewart, Beulah said that Assistant State's Attorney Roy Woods had stood in her kitchen after the shooting and told her that he "wanted her to make a complete statement because she had nothing to fear, since she had shot a man in her own home."

"Who was the first person to arrive at your apartment after the shooting?" Stewart asked.

"Officer Torpy."

"What was said?"

"Well, he said, 'Where is the gun?' And my husband handed him the gun. I don't remember much else."

"Whom did you see next?"

"State's Attorney Woods."

"You fainted in the meantime?"

"Yes."

"What did Mr. Woods say?"

"Well, we went into the kitchen and he said, 'Don't you know me?' I replied: 'No.' He told me not to be afraid, that I had shot a man in my own house and had nothing to fear."

Maurine Watkins, sitting near the front with her colleagues, wrote that the testimony "was uncontradicted by the state, since Mr. Woods, as prosecutor in the case, could not take the stand." But the lack of a rebuttal seemed like a very small victory for the defense. Beulah had said the right things but in the wrong way: breathless, distracted, almost giddy. Stewart continued to press the argument for the exclusion of the confessions, but Beulah, settled back at the defendant's table after the questioning, appeared to have recognized that she'd been shaky when she needed to be firm. "The luck," the *Evening Post* wrote, "seemed to be going against Beulah, who was not any too sure of herself and who, during the palaver, dabbed at her eyes occasionally with a perfumed lace handkerchief and leaned her pretty head on the shoulder of her defender, Mr. O'Brien."

The *Post* was right: The luck went against her. "Her statements are entirely too vague," Judge Lindsay declared. "Moreover, it is peculiar that she was so intoxicated that she didn't know what had happened a few hours after the crime, and today has a perfect recollection of minute details." The judge made his ruling: "I believe the statements are competent and admissible and that it is a matter for the defense to rebut them during the trial."

This was a serious blow to Beulah's defense. If the confessions had been excluded, O'Brien and Stewart would have started with a blank canvas. They could have taken control of the story line through a moving opening statement and, with chutzpah and momentum, carried it through to the end, presenting the defendant as an unsophisticated country girl and Kalstedt as a dangerous man. Now, however, they would have to play defense—an aggressive, risky defense. The confessions allowed the state to make the case about adultery, as well as murder. McLaughlin and Woods now had damning evidence—Beulah's own words—that she shot Kalstedt because he told her he was through with her. The defense would be forced to depend thoroughly on Beulah's ability to refute her previous statements when she took the stand. It would be a high-wire act, with all of Chicago watching.

It wasn't a complete sweep for the prosecution, however. Woods's conversation with Beulah in her kitchen was certain to come up again. And because Beulah had now given, under oath, a different version of what was said than the state's, Woods withdrew from the case so that he could testify, if necessary. This removed from the prosecution the lawyer who probably knew the facts and details of the case better than anyone else in the state's attorney's office. Stewart viewed it as a victory, if only because it was an "embarrassing situation" for Woods. He also believed that if he and O'Brien played it right, it could be "psychologically contributory to the verdict."

❧❧

The admissibility of the confessions decided, the jury was brought into the courtroom. The lawyers started right in with opening statements. O'Brien got to his feet. The more emotional, theatrical member of the team would handle the opening for the defense; the cooler, more paternal Stewart would then take on much of the key questioning and share the closing with his partner.

"It is true that a jazz record was being played at maddening tempo as Beulah Annan shot Harry Kalstedt, but only to drown out the tumult caused by this drink-crazed fiend who invaded her apartment, and so save herself from scandal," said O'Brien, launching into his statement with melodramatic brio. The lawyer had a habit of slapping his fist into an open palm to help him punctuate key words and phrases. He now started punching at his hand viciously. "Kalstedt forced his way into her apartment," he said, the fist coming down with a smack. "He came there at eight in the morning, badly intoxicated. She pleaded with him to go away and avoid a scandal. He cursed her and demanded money, mentioning six dollars. Finally, to get rid of him, she gave him a dollar."

By the end of each speech, O'Brien's left hand must have been bruised and numb from the beating it took, but he always succeeded in keeping his juries leaning forward. Maurine noted that "Tears slowly came to Beulah's eyes as O'Brien told how Kalstedt, a regular 'bum,' had come to her apartment early the morning of the shooting, and had tried to borrow a few dollars to get booze."

"At three in the afternoon," O'Brien continued, "he again forced an entrance. He had a bottle of wine under his arm. They had a drink." The lawyer, confident that he had this jury in his hands, gave them an empathetic look. He wasn't trying to fool anyone, the look said; he was telling it like it was. As proof, he was about to admit that his client made a terrible error in judgment that night. "She foolishly took a drink," he said, "just to humor him and get him to go, and played the Victrola to drown his loud talking. But he started to make love to her, improper advances—and then they took another little drink."

Every man there, every man on the jury, knew how one little drink led to another. Many lives had been ruined this way. Everyone had a brother or cousin or friend whose life had unraveled or was unraveling because of drink. It was the scourge of the age, made even worse by Prohibition. Drink made decent people do bad things, and it made bad people do unspeakable things. Innocent women were victimized by it every day. O'Brien sketched a dark but vivid tableau. Harry Kalstedt, he insisted, was one of the bad people turned even worse by booze. He was a bully, a pervert, a convict. An out-of-control drunk. "Fascinated, the jury followed him down the path of 'another little drink,'" wrote Maurine, "until Kalstedt threatened to attack her, boasting that he had served time for 'having his way with a woman'—'that's the kind of man he was!' Then, according to her attorney, Beulah, in a frenzy, started—O no, not for the gun, but the telephone, to tell her husband the danger she was in! And it was then Kalstedt went for the gun—conveniently parked on the bed—but she had the inside track! And in the struggle she turned around and that's how he was shot in the back! (Attorney Stewart posed to show just how it was done.)"

Maurine, with the promiscuous exclamation points and melodramatic phrasing, wasn't trying to play the sob sister. She was mocking O'Brien for laying out such an implausible series of events: Beulah agreeing to drink with Kalstedt after the drunken "fiend" had forced his way into her flat, Al's gun left out in plain sight on the bed, Kalstedt breaking for the gun first but Beulah still getting to it, Kalstedt ending up shot in the back because he and Beulah had spun like dancers while fighting for the weapon. There's no way to know if Maurine's readers picked up on her ridicule. The real sob sisters, after all, pounded out their accounts with the same outsize enthusiasm, just without the irony. Over at the *American,* O'Brien's speech was related as simple fact: "He put on a jazz record and made advances to her. She pleaded with him: 'If nothing else will stop you, maybe this will,' she said, and told him she was an expectant mother. He ignored her pleas, told her he had served a penitentiary sentence for attacking one woman. There was a struggle. Both reached for the gun."

O'Brien paused when he said this, and then reiterated that vital piece of information. "Both reached for the gun," he said, making clear that it was in plain sight on the bed in the next room. "But he was ahead of her. She fought for her life and in the struggle shot him in the back." The silence that followed this statement was complete. The lawyer was done. With a nod, he turned from the jury and sat heavily at the defense table. The jurymen sat back, thoroughly wrung out. William W. O'Brien was convincing. He believed in Beulah as the virtuous working girl, the good girl gone terribly bad and, because of her beauty and trusting nature, inevitably wrong. Beulah, tears welling in her eyes, her chin quivering slightly, believed too.

The state fought back with eyewitnesses: Policemen laid out what they saw and heard in Beulah's apartment that day; the coroner established a time of death—several hours after the shooting—and mentioned the record she played over and over. "Several witnesses were called," the *Post* wrote, "each describing his impressions of the scene immediately following the death of Kalstedt when Beulah, in order to quiet her nerves, placed the 'Hula Lou' record on her phonograph, and awaited the arrival of the bluecoats."

W. W. Wilcox, Kalstedt's brother-in-law, who worked at Tennant's Laundry and was present in the apartment when Woods questioned Beulah in the kitchen, testified that the defendant had not been coerced to give a statement the night of the shooting. Nor, he said, was she promised immunity. "However, she tried to get it. She asked Woods if he couldn't 'frame' it to look like an accident, and Woods said, 'You don't frame anything with me.'" Wilcox then put the dagger in, insisting that Beulah had frequently smiled and seemed calm and flirtatious while talking to Woods and the police, with Kalstedt still lying in a bloody pool on the floor. (The *American* headlined one of its trial stories in that afternoon's paper, "First Witness in Kalstedt Slaying Says Annan Girl Tried Beauty on Prosecutor.")

On cross-examination, O'Brien returned to the dead man's prison record.

"He was in the St. Cloud reformatory," Wilcox answered.

"For what reason?"

"Wife desertion," Wilcox said.

⤜⤛⤜

O'Brien was doing his best, but the prosecution had come out hard and strong. The evidence continued to pile up against Beulah. Sergeant Malachi Murphy of the Hyde Park station told of arriving outside the Annan's apartment building at eight on the night of the shooting and hearing music—the song "Hula Lou"—blaring from inside the flat. A bloodstained phonograph record was then admitted into evidence. Betty Bergman, Beulah's boss, took the stand and related the phone conversation she'd had with the defendant when Beulah called the Tennant Laundry office on the afternoon of April 3. Beulah had asked for "Moo"—Kalstedt—and sounded "stewed." Bergman told her he wasn't there, and then Beulah asked for "Billy"—W. W. Wilcox, Kalstedt's brother-in-law. When Bergman said he wasn't in the office either, Beulah rang off.

Assistant State's Attorney McLaughlin repeated the time that Bergman said Beulah had called: 4:10 in the afternoon. The jury gaped—McLaughlin made sure they understood that at the time Beulah called Betty Bergman, Kalstedt was spread out on the floor in her apartment, dying.

Court stenographer Albert Allen stepped up to the stand "to read his notes." Allen was present when Beulah explained what happened that afternoon, he testified. He said she had claimed to be surprised when Kalstedt came into the apartment, because she barely knew him. He read Beulah's words from his notes: "'Don't come in,' I warned him, but as he came on I shot. He sank to the floor, crying, 'Oh, Anne, you've killed me.' I must have fainted then, for I don't remember what happened. When I recovered my senses I saw blood stains on my gown." The statement ended with Beulah's denial that she'd shot Kalstedt in the back. Allen said the defendant had made the statements "voluntarily, understanding that they might be used against her in court." He insisted that Woods had never promised her leniency or immunity in exchange for a confession.

Court was still in session when reporters for the evening papers rushed out to file their stories. Large front-page slots were being held for their accounts. As Beulah's trial began, coverage of her shifted, to one degree or another, from romantic melodrama to more straightforward news reporting. The papers laid out the day's events in court and, if generally sympathetic to the defense, left overt opinion to the side.

The *Tribune*, however, continued to lean hard on its unique slant. Maurine recognized that her satirical sense of humor had made her pieces about Beulah stand out from the competition, but that wasn't why she continued to prick the defendant. "In news articles, you are not allowed to write editorials—to my everlasting regret, because I have a preacher's mind," she would tell an interviewer two years after Beulah's trial. It was a nice line, but in practice Maurine never paid attention to such professional dictates. That "preacher's mind" was very much in evidence right from the beginning of her reporting career, and her editors never seemed bothered by it. When writing about Beulah in particular, her articles took on the flavor of indictments. She was convinced of Beulah's guilt and wanted to do whatever she could to effect the right verdict. Her report from the first day of the trial was a case in point: a masterpiece of concise, clearly articulated rhetoric, significantly more powerful than what William McLaughlin had come up with for his opening statement to the jury. "'Beautiful' Beulah Annan's chance for freedom was lessened yesterday," Maurine began, "when Judge Lindsay ruled, after an extended hearing, that the confessions she had made to the police the night following the murder of Harry Kalstedt, April 3, were admissible as evidence."

"I'm the only witness," Beulah has boasted, "Harry's dead and they'll have to believe my story."

But which one?

The confession she made to Assistant State's Attorney Roy C. Woods (with a court reporter present) in her apartment at 9 o'clock the night of the crime, when she said that she shot Kalstedt, whom she barely knew, to save her honor as he approached her in attack?

Or the statement that she made at the Hyde Park police station (also with court reporters present) three hours later? Then she broke down and admitted that she shot him in the back. The man was about to leave her after a jealous quarrel, she said. Will the jury believe that?

Or will the jury credit the story that she'll tell in court, a plea of self-defense: "We both grabbed for the revolver!"—when she takes the stand today?

No one who read the *Tribune* on Saturday morning, no matter how fetching the photograph spread across the front page (and the picture of Beulah was fetching indeed), could have come away with any doubt about which story to believe. The defendant, Maurine Watkins made clear, was guilty as sin.

14

Anne, You Have Killed Me

Beulah Annan, her hands and clothes spattered with blood, spun the record on the phonograph again, moved to the open window, and squinted out at the afternoon sun. The music hopped behind her:

Her name was Hula Lou, the kind of gal who never could be true.
Got a Hula smile, and lots of Hula hair.
She Hula Hulas here and Hula Hulas there.

Beulah's hips twitched. It was an infectious song. Outside, on the sidewalk in front of the building, a group of schoolgirls held hands and twirled each other to the music, their giggles echoing through the adjacent alley. Inside, Beulah did the same on her own.

Except Beulah wasn't giggling. She was thinking about Harry—or to be more accurate, she was forgetting about him. His face was already fading away: the dark eyes becoming an amorphous mass, the slicked-back hair parting on its own and falling away, the snapping white teeth leaching into nothingness. It was as though she'd never known him at all or he was a figment of her imagination. Maybe he was.

"Did you shoot this man, Harry Kalstedt?" William Scott Stewart asked.

Beulah's eyes popped, as if the lawyer had startled her. Settling again into her seat, she glanced at Stewart from under fluttering lashes and took a deep breath. She responded slowly, "in a low, silvery voice," drawing out each syllable. "I did," she said.

"Why?"

"Because he was going to shoot me."

❧❦❧

It had begun. Chicagoans had been waiting for this moment for weeks. Not just Chicagoans, in fact. Reports on Sabella Nitti's and Kitty Malm's trials had gone out on the news wires, but they'd received limited exposure outside the city. Beulah Annan, "the prettiest slayer of Murderess Row," on the other hand, had caught the fancy of editors and readers throughout the country. Her face had become front-page fodder in New York and California and dozens of places in between. Some papers, such as the *Atlanta Constitution,* sent reporters to Chicago for the trial. National newsreel companies had also come to town, setting up their cameras and lights in the back of the courtroom. "The case of Beulah Annan is one of the most remarkable ever to win the interest of an eager public," stated the *Washington Post.*

No city was nearly so obsessed as Chicago, of course. No detail about Beulah—her dress, her facial expressions, what she listened to on the radio in her cell—was too picayune to be put down in print. So her ascension to the stand on Saturday, May 24, the trial's second day, was cause for massive coverage, with large front-page photographs and the opening up of two-page spreads inside for blow-by-blow accounts of Beulah telling her tale to her attorney and then squaring off with the prosecutor. The *American* wrote that "Annan had carefully prepared for her ordeal. She was becomingly gowned in another new dress of blue twill that gave her an extremely girlish appearance, and she wore peach-colored stockings to match her Titian hair."

Beulah looked perfect for the part of innocent victim. Her dress had been chosen only after dozens had been tried on and rejected. It was a conservative dress, but its light fabric softly gripped her chest and hips, giving the jurymen the slightest, but undeniable, suggestion of the sweet hollows that lay beneath, the innocent sexuality that Harry Kalstedt had wanted so badly to corrupt. Assistant State's Attorney McLaughlin may have been heartened by Beulah's nervousness the previous day, when the jury wasn't even in the room, but paradoxically so was Stewart. O'Brien and Stewart had prepped their client well, and now she just had to remember what to say, nothing else. Trembling was allowed, perhaps encouraged. "All you have to do is to tell the truth," was Stewart's advice for any defendant with a naturally sympathetic countenance. "A child can tell the truth about something he knows and the child does not need to know anything about courts or the rules of evidence. . . . So I'm not going to try to explain rules of evidence to you; no use bothering you with them. The jury will understand your lack of knowledge on the subject and they will sympathize with your nervousness."

The value of this advice, needless to say, depended on what the truth was—or what the witness wanted it to be. Maurine Watkins, who had heard all of Beulah's confessions and statements over the weeks, had made up her mind about the truth and Beulah's relationship to it. She knew what to expect. The reporter wrote, "Under the glare of motion picture lights—a news weekly—Beulah took the stand. In another new dress—navy twill tied at the side with a childlike moiré bow—with new necklace of crystal and jet, she made her debut as an actress."

But how could Beulah not have viewed it as a performance? As Maurine noted, she stepped up to the stand with movie cameras grinding. Their lights, dangling from poles in the back of the courtroom, provided a golden spotlight right in the middle of the witness chair. Beulah had observed the setting up of the cameras with frank interest, understanding that it meant her visage would soon flicker in theatrical newsreels across the country. That was an audience of 40 million people each week. But this massive national attention was an abstract concept; the people here right now were very real. Court fans—*Beulah* fans—had begun arriving at the courthouse two hours before the doors opened and rushed for seats as soon as they were allowed inside. A large crowd didn't make it into Judge Lindsay's courtroom; bailiffs had to force the doors shut after the room filled past capacity. The lucky ones who did get in sat on windowsills and stood on benches. Unable to see from the back, young women, throwing propriety aside, asked to be boosted up by strange men. The crowd was so primed that Beulah's appearance in the bright white circle elicited a collective gasp. Necks strained. Men elbowed each other. Was she as beautiful as the papers said? Was she even more beautiful? Beulah, so enamored of attention, for a moment was overwhelmed "and seemed to shrink back in her chair as a [camera] flashlight went off with a bang. Then she clenched her hands and turned her eyes toward her attorney, William Scott Stewart."

Stewart gave his client a good, hard, long look before he said anything. He knew she needed to come back down to earth. They had specific goals for this testimony. The state was trying to convince the jury that Beulah and Kalstedt had been lovers and that Kalstedt had not been a threat to her that terrible day, inferences that McLaughlin insisted were evident by the fact that Kalstedt was shot in the back. Along with knocking down those allegations, Beulah had to successfully deflect the prosecutorial value of her confessions on the night of the shooting: She had to force the prosecutors to face the defense allegation that they had unfairly tormented her while she was in a state of grief and shock.

Stewart opened with some easy questions: He asked her name, her age, where she lived prior to her arrest, whether she lived there with her husband. Maurine, well on her way to becoming a court expert, knew what the defense was doing: "First a series of colorless fact questions—where did you live, what schools did you attend, etc.—that gives the witness confidence in herself, and accustoms the listeners to her simple, straightforward manner. Then a series of questions to establish her general character. And from these we learn—and so do the jury—that she is no butterfly, but an old-fashioned girl who never smokes, seldom dances and drinks but little—her pet diversions, the prosecution would have us believe, being misconduct and murder."

Maurine may have been fashioning flippant comments in her head, but the other spectators massed behind the lawyers' tables treated the beginning of the testimony with due reverence. "Save for the grinding of the cameras, the courtroom was intensely silent," wrote the *Evening Post*. "Beulah's husband, Albert, sat with bowed head near Mrs. Mary Neel, the defendant's mother." The *Daily News* noted that Beulah "hesitated, eyes downcast, her cheeks delicately flushed. There wasn't a breath in the courtroom."

Stewart asked Beulah what had happened that led to the shooting. Beulah focused on her lawyer as he was talking and then lifted her chin to take in the packed room. "Stately and with a calmness that astounded all observers," the *Daily Journal*'s reporter wrote, she began to tell her story in a "clear, firm voice." The voice was soft and sweet, her Southern accent as fluffy as black-seed cotton.

She said that Harry Kalstedt, her coworker at Tennant's Laundry, knocked on the back screen door in the morning. "I opened the inner door and there he stood. He seemed to be intoxicated. He came in and said to me: 'I hate to do this, but I need money. I have to get some wine.' I said to him: 'How much do you need?' He said: 'Six dollars.' I said: 'I can't let you have that much; I haven't got it.' He said: 'How much have you got?' and I went into the bedroom for my pocketbook." Beulah paused to swallow audibly and then added that she gave Kalstedt a dollar and he left.

Stewart asked if she saw him later in the day.

"Yes. At 2 or a quarter after."

As Beulah was answering this simple question, the movie-camera lights suddenly snapped off, returning the defendant to the dull overhead lighting that was for everyone else. "The witness seemed to lose their stimulating effect," an observer noted. Beulah sat there, stunned, as if she'd been insulted. Stewart took a step back, to give his client time to come to terms with what had just happened with the lights. After a moment, he moved in again. He skipped right to the part he knew the jurors wanted to hear most.

"What was said before you jumped off the couch where you were sitting with him in the afternoon?" he asked.

"I had been after him to go, saying, 'Please leave,' and finally I said I was going to call my husband." Beulah was laying on the accent thicker than ever now. "He said, 'No, you are not,' and I said, 'If my husband came in here now he would kill you or both of us.' He said, 'Where is the ------ gun?' [Beulah apparently used an expletive, which was recorded with dashes] and we both moved for the bedroom."

"Had you been in the bedroom before, that afternoon?"

"No."

"Was the bed visible from the hall?"

"Yes."

"Tell what happened."

"We were almost at the bed. He grabbed for the gun, and I jerked the gun away. He said: 'Damn you, I'll kill you,' or something like that."

"Did he make any move then, at the time?"

"He came toward me with his hand up."

"What did you do?"

"I pushed his right shoulder with my left hand"—she said this with deliberate authority, knowing the importance of explaining away the fact that Kalstedt was shot in the back. She continued: "He raised his hand to grab the gun and I shot him."

Stewart asked what his condition was before she shot.

"He was very much intoxicated."

"Did you gather you were in danger of receiving bodily harm?"

Beulah leaned forward, her eyes and voice steady. "Yes."

Stewart nodded at his client, clearly pleased but restraining a smile. He now took a moment, let the mood cool, and then started back in.

"You know this Betty [Bergman], who was a witness here yesterday?" he asked.

"Yes."

"Have you had any trouble with her?"

Beulah's expression and body language remained neutral. "Well, we were not exactly friends," she said.

"What was the trouble?"

"Well, one week before [the shooting], she asked for the key to my apartment."

Stewart, an excellent, understated performer, no doubt gave the jury a look here before turning back to Beulah.

"And you were not good friends after that?"

"No."

With one sentence, Betty Bergman's credibility—not to mention her reputation—had been severely compromised, and Beulah's integrity, with the implication that she had refused her boss's sordid request, enhanced. And it happened so fast—and was apparently so unexpected—that McLaughlin made no objection. Stewart quickly moved on, circling back to when Kalstedt returned to the apartment.

"Tell what was said from the time Kalstedt came in."

"He came to the door and said: 'Are you alone?'" she related with cool precision, a story she knew by heart. "Then he stepped into the reception hall. I had been playing the phonograph and lying on the couch when he came in. He had a package under his arm and said: 'I have brought you some wine,' and he offered me a drink. As he unwrapped the package, I said: 'Don't start anything like that. You have had enough to drink, and my husband is liable to come home.' He said, 'To hell with your husband. What do I care about him?' and took off his hat and overcoat. He said: 'Just one drink and I'll go.'"

Now they came to the part they knew would be hard to sell. Beulah seemed to almost flounce in her seat, as if girding herself for criticism. She said, "I took one drink with him. Then he said: 'Let's have a little jazz.' He walked to the Victrola and put on a record. He said: 'Let's have a little dance.' And then he said, 'Come on into the bedroom,' and I refused and begged him to go. He was intoxicated at the time and went over and sat on the couch. I sat beside him and tried to reason with him, and said: 'Pull yourself together. My husband will be coming home.' He said: 'What the hell do I care about your husband? You know he won't come.' I said: 'Well, then, there's something else. If nothing else will stop you, maybe this will.'"

Beulah suddenly ran out of breath. She appeared on the verge of tears. She turned to face the jury, her eyes pleading.

"Go ahead, Beulah, tell the jury," Stewart instructed her.

Beulah closed her eyes to gather courage and then opened them as if she were easing awake from an afternoon nap. "I told him of my—delicate condition," she said, the words sticking to her tongue like wet paper. "But he refused to believe me—and boasted that another woman had fooled him that way, and that he had done time in the penitentiary for her. And

I said, 'You'll go back to the penitentiary if you don't leave me alone.' He said: 'You'll never send me back there.' And I said, 'I'll call my husband! And he'll shoot us both! There's a gun in there.' And I pointed to the bedroom. 'Where's the gun?' he asked, 'let's see it.' Then we both started for the gun." Beulah then repeated the story she'd started her testimony with: "He reached it first," she said, "but I wrenched it out of his hand. Then he came for me, brandishing his arms. I seized him by the shoulder and spun him around. Then I shot. He sank to the floor and cried, 'Anne, you have killed me.'"

Beulah closed her eyes again, "in horror of the picture," Maurine would mock in the *Tribune* the next morning. With her "face pale under the glare of the movie lights"—which had been turned back on—she continued, her voice now puny. "I must have lost consciousness then. I remember that he was spattered with blood. I tried to see if he was dead. I rubbed his hands and face . . ."

Stewart gave the jury a moment to absorb the emotional trauma on display. Now it was time to challenge the police's assertion that Beulah had danced to loud music after the shooting. "Tell what you did then," he said.

"I heard the needle scratching on the record," Beulah said. There seemed to be no hesitancy in her narrative, no searching for memories or details. She barely needed her lawyer to prompt her. "The record had stopped playing, but the needle was scratching, so I picked it up. I went into the bedroom, and I don't know what I did. I seemed to lose all reason. I went over to where he was lying and sat beside him to see if he was dead. I felt his hand and his face. I don't know how long I sat there. I knew I had to call someone, so I tried to get my husband."

"Did you call Betty?" Stewart asked.

"No," she said. "I got the wrong number all the time but I finally got my husband. I don't remember our conversation."

Stewart quickly established the sequence of events that followed: Beulah's husband and the police arriving at the apartment and then her questioning at the Hyde Park police station. He then asked if she returned home.

"Yes, we went back to the apartment and I was asked to change my clothes," Beulah replied. "Mr. McLaughlin was there and started to ask me how it happened. I said I didn't remember."

"Was anything said in the flat before the stenographer started making notes?"

"Yes."

"Were you questioned after the stenographer started making notes?"

"I don't remember seeing him."

Stewart reminded the jury that McLaughlin wasn't the first assistant state's attorney to question Beulah in the apartment that night. Roy Woods had done so earlier, before she'd been taken to the police station. Stewart asked Beulah to describe the conversation with Woods.

"Well, there was some general conversation, and then Mr. Woods said: 'The mere fact that this man was in your apartment—and that you are married—would indicate that there had been no crime, that is, that it would not have been a crime to have shot him.'"

"Later when you were making a statement, what happened with reference to the stenographer?"

"Well, Mr. Woods would sometimes tell the reporter not to take the answer down, then he would talk to me, and later the answer in a different way would be taken down."

"Had Kalstedt ever been to your home before this day?"

"No."

"Had you been on any parties with him, or to any places of amusement?"

"No, sir."

Stewart thanked her. He was satisfied. Beulah had hit her marks and looked appropriately traumatized and helpless throughout. She'd done everything her lawyers could have hoped for. There had never been a "more dramatic story ever told from the witness stand," the *Daily News*'s reporter declared when he called his story in to an editor. But that was with Stewart asking the questions—questions they'd gone over time and again. Could she hold up under hostile fire?

Assistant State's Attorney William McLaughlin rose and moved toward her. He was a young prosecutor, but premature baldness and a thin, pinched face made him look slightly menacing. He jabbed a finger and launched right in; he wasn't going to give her any time to collect her thoughts. Maurine, from her seat in one of the front rows, observed that Beulah was "a trifle nonplused by the opening attack of the prosecution in cross-questioning, for Mr. McLaughlin tried to establish the fact that her 'story' had been 'framed' by her attorneys."

"How many drinks did you have, Mrs. Annan?" the prosecutor asked, trying to throw her off stride.

Beulah kept her eyes level, half lidded. "Three or four," she said. "Each time he offered me a drink he promised he'd go if I would take just that one more."

"Where were you when your quarrel first began?"

"On the couch."

"Was he in the center?"

"Yes."

"Where were you before then?"

"At the doorway. I asked him to leave. He said, 'I will after you've come across.'"

"How did you come to be with him?"

"He was on the couch and I went over and sat beside him."

"What?" It was like a door suddenly banging shut. McLaughlin said it loud enough, and with enough body English, to startle Beulah—and to focus the jury's attention. He homed in now, his voice as hard and precise as a needle. "You knew what he was trying to accomplish, yet you went and sat on the couch with him?"

Beulah shifted in her seat. She replied in a childlike voice: "Well, he had said something about going to bed."

McLaughlin leaned in, bored in. "I want a more direct answer, Mrs. Annan," he said. "Did you know what he was trying to accomplish?"

"Yes," she said. It was the wrong answer for any proper woman. A lady, a married woman alone in an apartment with a strange man, would never willingly sit on a couch with him if she recognized he had sexual intentions. But Beulah understood her predicament, and understood her way out of it, better than anyone—including McLaughlin—could have guessed. She was risking her reputation as a respectable married woman, but it was the only answer she could give if she hoped to hold on to a workable narrative.

"Then what happened?" McLaughlin asked.

"I told him to pull himself together and go home, and he said he would as soon as I would come across."

"Had you been in the bedroom with him?"

"No."

"Did you tell him your husband might shoot him if he found him there?"

"Yes."

"Then what happened?"

"He jumped up and began yelling, 'Where is the gun?'"

"Where were you when you were having this argument?"

"I was sitting on the couch."

"You say he was sitting near the center of the couch?"

"Yes."

"Where were you sitting?"

"At the end, near the door."

"What was taking place on the couch?"

Beulah knew all too well what McLaughlin was getting at, and she wasn't going to help him. "We were talking about his going," she said, "and I asked him to go, and he said: 'I will later.'"

The prosecutor tried again to get Beulah to admit to passionate grappling on the couch with Kalstedt, but she refused to acknowledge his insinuations. She repeated the same answer over and over. Frustrated, McLaughlin returned to the moment when Kalstedt asked her where the gun was. "Then what occurred?" he asked.

"I got up and started to go to the telephone to call my husband and he started for the bedroom."

"Did you go to the bedroom?"

"Yes."

"Who was first?"

"He was one step ahead of me."

"Why did you go to the bedroom?"

"He was going to shoot me."

"How did he know where the gun was?"

Stewart objected and it was sustained. McLaughlin started right back up, trying to keep the pressure on.

"Did he get to the door first?"

"Yes, one side of it."

"Was the gun in plain sight on the bed?"

"Yes."

"How did you beat him to it?"

"I lunged for it, and I grabbed it."

McLaughlin expressed surprise that Beulah "should be a step behind Kalstedt in the 'get-away' . . . and yet beat him to the gun," but Beulah ignored the snide tone. Her confidence was on the rise. Stewart had worked the nerves out of her.

"What did you do?" McLaughlin continued.

"I grabbed the gun."

"Did he grab your wrist?"

"No."

"What did he do?"

"He put his hand up and said, 'I'll kill you yet!' I put my hand on his right shoulder or arm and pushed him."

"Have you remembered that ever since the day of the shooting?"

"Yes."

McLaughlin smirked at Beulah in disgust. Then, as if suddenly realizing how the cross-examination was going, he started banging at her faster and faster, repeating questions and asking a cascade of similar questions. He was probing for inconsistencies, any contradictory statements he could exploit. But as the rapid-fire questioning continued, an unmistakable desperation—or a lack of strategic thinking—became obvious.

"What time was it when you shot Harry Kalstedt?" he asked for the third time.

"About 2:30 or 3, I think."

"What time was it when you called your husband?"

"I don't know."

"What did you do between the time you shot Kalstedt and the time you called your husband?"

"I don't know how long I sat there. When I came to, I tried to get to the telephone. I knew I had to call somebody."

"Did you try to get rid of the body?"

"No." Beulah gave a surprised, querulous look, as if he'd slapped her.

"Where was the gun usually kept?"

"Under the pillow."

"Did you hear your husband's reply to Sergeant Murphy's question about where the gun was kept—that it was in the bureau drawer?"

"No."

"And did you reply: 'I don't know where it was.'"

"No."

"You had not called Betty Bergman that afternoon?"

"No."

Finally, having exhausted every possible way of asking the same handful of questions, McLaughlin got to the confessions made on the night of the shooting. He went through her statements line by line, and Beulah, still calm, still with that sweet Southern accent, denied practically every word credited to her by the state. She denied that she had said anything to the police about having a romantic relationship with Kalstedt. She denied that she had called him a jailbird and that he had called her foul names in return. She denied telling officers that she shot him because he was walking out on her. "One by one he read her the questions and answers she had made at the Hyde Park police station the night of the murder, in which she confessed killing the man after a jealous quarrel," Maurine wrote. The *Tribune* reporter cataloged the defendant's replies, noting how she varied "the defiance of her 'no' with a childishly petulant, 'I don't remember.'" Maurine marveled at how Beulah shamelessly stared down her inquisitor: "She searched him with her shallow eyes: what was back of it all?" This, in fact, was where the whole thing hung by a breath. Beulah Annan had made herself a sympathetic, put-upon figure during her long testimony, but was she so sympathetic that the jury could accept the notion that the police and prosecutors were brazenly lying?

Despite Beulah's firm denials, McLaughlin would not be deterred from reading every word of each of her confessions. The first statement from the night of the shooting wasn't too far from the story she was telling today. Kalstedt came to her home early in the afternoon, even though she "barely knew him." Against her wishes, he took her in his arms and declared, "Gee, Anne, I'm crazy about you." Scared, she tried to get him to leave and, failing that, retreated to the bedroom. He followed, forcing her to grab up the revolver to protect herself. When, despite her warnings, he continued to approach, "she closed her eyes and shot."

The police then pointed out that Harry Kalstedt had been shot in the back and thus begat the second confession. Beulah Annan, McLaughlin told the jury, now admitted that she'd been fooling around with Kalstedt for two months. As the two lovers sat drinking, she brought up another boyfriend, a Billy or Johnny, who Beulah said had called her that morning for a "date." This infuriated Kalstedt, and he jumped to his feet. He and Beulah ran for the bedroom.

"I was ahead of him," McLaughlin quotes from the confession. "I grabbed for the gun."

"And what did he grab for?" Beulah's interviewer asked.

"For what was left—nothing."

Harry Kalstedt, hardworking laundry deliveryman, never had a chance, McLaughlin told the jury. The prosecutor turned back to the confession. "Did he get his coat and hat?" police asked Beulah that night. "No," she said, "he didn't get that far." He didn't get that far, McLaughlin said, because she had shot him.

Beulah, incredibly, didn't get flustered. She sat with a straight back and her hands clasped in her lap while McLaughlin read her own words to her. She looked indignant at times, sometimes sad, always stoic. There would be no more tears from Beulah Annan. "The witness made a favorable impression, controlling her emotions, except during the dramatic crises of her recital, and keeping her voice up," the *Evening Post* related, as if reviewing a play.

The *Post* understated it. Beulah's was a bravura performance. Obviously well prepared by Stewart and O'Brien, she had a response to all of the testimony and evidence against her, casting doubt on the motives of the state's witnesses and the validity of statements the prosecution attributed to her on the night of the shooting. She also questioned the character of Assistant State's Attorney Woods and the officers at the scene of the killing—and pulled it off. Such accusations were always dicey for a defendant, but they had become increasingly believable to the average Chicagoan. Corruption at all levels of government had exploded since Prohibition, and the public was becoming aware of it, first in slow drips, and now, with the reform-minded Mayor William Dever in office, in a steady stream.

Beulah did all of this while coming across as a small, timid, uncalculating girl—a girl, not a woman, and a remarkably beautiful one at that. It wasn't easy for a married woman who shot her boyfriend in the back to climb to the moral high ground, but Beulah seemed to have done it. McLaughlin tried mightily to trip her up, to get her to admit that she had said any of the things she had in fact said the night of the shooting. But nothing would move her from her story. More than that, she proved in the cross-examination that she understood what she was saying; she clearly knew why she should admit to some things, even if they showed her in a poor light (such as her acknowledgment that she knew Kalstedt was trying to seduce her), while insisting she couldn't remember others, like what time she'd called her husband. She was so good on the stand that, even with the confident, evidence-packed case the state put forward, it was now impossible to guess which way the jury might be leaning.

∽∾∽

Beulah's testimony seemed like the trial's natural denouement, but there was still more to come. The defense called Beulah's mother, Mary Neel. She was questioned only briefly and, it seemed, pointlessly. "Her dark eyes were drawn and mouth set as she answered the few simple questions as to her name, relation to the defendant, etc.," Maurine wrote. Next up was Beulah's husband, Al, who "marched briskly to the stand" as if late for a train. But he would have even less to say than his mother-in-law. Judge Lindsay called the lawyers forward before Al uttered a word. After a brief consultation, he excused Al from the stand. Beulah looked away as Al passed the defendant's table on his way back to his seat.

The proceedings dragged on through the afternoon and into the evening. Finally, McLaughlin called Roy Woods "as a rebuttal witness to refute Mrs. Annan's testimony that he had promised her immunity if she would confess to him." McLaughlin was counting on the authority typically attributed to a prosecutor to win the day for the state. He kept his questioning straightforward.

"Did you tell her it was no crime for her to shoot a man in her own house?"

"Most certainly not," Woods said, leveling his gaze at the jury.

"Did you tell her that she couldn't 'frame' anything with you?"

"I did," he said, again with those eyes hard and steady.

The jury stared at Woods like cows. The recused prosecutor made a good witness—better than good. He was a clear-eyed, straight-backed American. He was completely believable. But the jurymen were tired, and they were having trouble concentrating on the witness. Out of the corner of their eyes, a half-turn to their left, they could see Beulah Annan leaning forward, her limpid gaze fixed dreamily on the men who would decide her fate. McLaughlin moved to obscure their view. He asked Woods to repeat himself.

15

Beautiful—but Not Dumb!

In his closing argument, Assistant State's Attorney William McLaughlin concisely ran through the evidence he had presented over the preceding two days and then turned to the case the defense had put forward. Maurine, sitting in the front row, approved when the prosecutor "pointed out the weak points in [Beulah's] story: that a woman should try to 'soothe' a man who was threatening to attack her by drinking with him; that he knew where the gun was—in a totally strange house; that he was shot in the back."

"No woman living would have stayed in that apartment as long as she did with Kalstedt, constantly repelling his advances, as she says she did," McLaughlin pronounced. "A woman who didn't want him there would have run out of the apartment and yelled for help." The jury, McLaughlin said, knew the truth. "You have seen that face, gentlemen. The defendant is not the kind of woman men would tell to go to hell. She probably had never heard that before and it angered her. That was why she went for the gun."

Beulah, nervous now that her part in the drama was over, sat beside her lawyers during the state's peroration, her head down, eyes closed. She remained calm, the *Daily Journal*'s reporter marveled, "while Assistant State's Attorney McLaughlin trained the guns of the prosecution on her in his argument." Beulah Annan had lied on the stand, McLaughlin kept insisting, working himself from calm summation into controlled anger. He told the jury that if they believed she lied at any point during her testimony, then they should discount everything she'd had to say on the stand.

McLaughlin appeared confident. He believed he had the evidence on his side and that juries had finally hardened to the wiles of women criminals. But he also recognized O'Brien and Stewart's skills—and the power of Beulah's testimony. With his last words to the jury, he attempted to shame them into doing the right thing. "The verdict is in your hands, and you must decide whether you will permit a woman to commit a crime and let her go because she is good-looking. You must decide whether you want to let another pretty woman go out and say 'I got away with it!'" The prosecutor, the *American* noted, asked for no particular penalty.

When McLaughlin finished and turned from the jury, William Scott Stewart expelled a silent breath and rose. He was just thirty-four years old, but he possessed a stern physical dignity that gave him a mature, fatherly mien. There was a touch of John Brown in him, too, a mean, controlled righteousness, though he kept it well hidden, back behind his eyes, until just the moment he needed it. He knew Beulah had done well on the witness stand, better than he had expected, but he and O'Brien remained worried about those confessions admitted into evidence. That was where he immediately leveled his fire. He laid into McLaughlin for using " 'mental third-degree' tactics" on Beulah on the night of the shooting, and he excoriated Roy Woods for withdrawing from the case, not mentioning that it was the defense's challenge of Beulah's statement before Woods that caused the prosecutor to withdraw. "The Supreme Court has censured Cook County officials for tolerating this sort of prosecution," he said, "and these assistant state's attorneys should be ashamed to play these tactics on the defendant and then withdraw from the prosecution in order to be able to testify against her."

Beulah began to sob as Stewart went through just how the police and prosecutors had bullied those confessions out of her, providing an affecting backbeat to Stewart's attack on the state's "third-degree" tactics. When Stewart paused to gather his thoughts, Beulah tried to steady herself but couldn't; her shoulders shook softly, and she dipped her head again. Were the tears a put-on? Maurine Watkins thought so. "Every defense counsel knows the value of tears," the *Tribune* reporter opined later. Maurine couldn't stand it: "She had played the Victrola while the man she murdered lay dying, she had laughed at the inquest, she had sat calm and composed while they read descriptions of the crime, but she broke down when she heard her attorney's impassioned account of the suffering she had undergone at the hands of the police and assistant state's attorneys, who questioned her statements."

W. W. O'Brien took over from his partner to bring home the final message: that Beulah Annan was a virtuous, hardworking girl, a loving and decent wife who had been ruthlessly slandered so that the State's Attorney's Office could rack up a conviction. O'Brien was an expert sentimentalist, and once again it was too much for Beulah. Maurine reported wearily that the defendant was "overcome with emotion when Mr. O'Brien painted the picture of 'this frail little girl, gentlemen, struggling with a drunken brute'—and the jury shook their heads in approbation and chewed their gum more energetically." Stewart and O'Brien made a powerful team, the brain and the heart. McLaughlin, like Maurine Watkins, watched them in sullen silence, his eyes glazed and half-lidded.

❧❧❧

At 8:30, Judge Lindsay sent the jury out to consult and reach a verdict. Many of the reporters in the courtroom headed for the phones, figuring a decision wouldn't come that night. Beulah sat on her own in the building's holding cell, her eyes closed much of the time. She didn't want to talk to her lawyers or the matron watching over her. She remained quiet. At one point her shoulders heaved and she clasped her hands together to keep them from shaking. She took a deep breath and looked up at the concrete wall, her eyes dry. She'd willed away the panic. "Will this woman be convicted, or will her looks save her?" the *Decatur Review,* the voice of central Illinois, asked in its Sunday edition. "The prosecution was careful to ask jurors if they had scruples against convicting a good-looking woman. The twelve accepted answered they are not trembled with the weakness. But it may be that some of the twelve didn't know, and that others of them lied for the woman."

As it turned out, the question was no longer germane even before copies of the *Review* reached its readers' hands. At 10:20 that night, the jury announced it had reached a decision. Usually a quick verdict meant good news for the prosecution, but McLaughlin didn't look confident anymore. The lawyers in the case, McLaughlin and the recused Woods, Stewart and O'Brien, walked back into the courtroom. The seats behind them filled again. Then the jury filed in. The golden circle that had caressed Beulah Annan during her testimony was gone, and the room sat in gloomy half-light, a miasma of ragged emotion. Fear had crept into Beulah's mind. It seemed to take forever for the crowd to settle and the jurymen to find their seats. An observer watched as Beulah "wrung her hands and shifted about uneasily in her chair." She appeared to be holding back tears. The judge read the verdict to himself in silence, then passed the slip of paper to the bailiff. The bailiff read it quickly, loudly, seemingly before comprehending it.

"Not guilty!"

The syllables drifted away like smoke, followed by a gasp—and then a roar. Somebody yelled out something incomprehensible, joyous. Beulah remained expressionless when the verdict was announced, as if stunned, while her lawyers exchanged looks of satisfaction. Beulah's husband, Al, was not nearly so stoical. He wept, his head in his arms.

The defendant climbed to her feet, her head still bare, a smile slipping across her face. The bailiff's words had begun to settle on her: She was a free woman. She beamed at the jurymen and came around the defendant's table. "Oh, I can't thank you!" she exclaimed, reaching out, shaking the hand of the nearest juror. "You don't know, you can't know—but I felt sure that you would—" She moved from man to man, clasping hands with each, making eye contact, exchanging smiles. The handshakes, the words, weren't enough to express what she was feeling. She kissed a juror hard on the cheek, and then another, holding his face with both hands. She didn't care what anyone thought about it.

Al followed along behind his wife, beaming and shaking jurors' hands, blessing them for their forthright work. Reporters rushed into the hall, fighting for the phones again. Photographers took their final shots, the flashbulbs lighting up the room in sudden crackling bursts, and then ran out, well aware that their printing presses across the river were being started up. The remaining spectators, the amateurs, didn't know what to do now that it was over. They wandered in confusion, in ecstasy, in anger. They watched as Beulah agreed to pose for a photograph with the jury. She grasped the jury foreman's hand in a manly shake. The other jurors gathered around, leaning in and smiling. The photograph taken, Beulah broke away from the jurors. The court fans then stepped aside in deference, and Beulah and Al Annan left the courtroom, marching happily into the hallway, arm in arm. They swept out the doors and into the night.

∽∾∽

The *Tribune*'s headline writers, working on deadline, kept it simple. "Jury Finds Beulah Annan Is 'Not Guilty,'" the front page stated on Sunday morning. The subhead added, "Self-Defense Plea Gains Her Freedom; Thanks Each Member After Verdict." Maurine, of course, took a harder-edged approach in the story.

> Beulah Annan, whose pursuit of wine, men, and jazz music was inter-rupted by her glibness with the trigger finger, was given freedom last night by her "beauty-proof" jury. . . .
>
> Mr. Annan, who has stood by her from the very night he found [Harry Kalstedt] lying dead in his bedroom, was almost overcome with joy and gratitude.
>
> "I knew my wife would come through all right!" he said, proudly.
>
> That seemed to be the consensus of opinion.
>
> "Another pretty woman gone free!" was the only comment made by Assistant State's Attorney William F. McLaughlin, who prosecuted the case alone after the withdrawal of Roy C. Woods, who was called as a material witness.
>
> "Beautiful—but not dumb!"
>
> For she had talked incessantly: two different versions of the shooting before she came to trial, and the third one—when she took the stand yesterday—was the charm.

Maurine offered no hedges in stating what she thought of the trial's outcome, writing the story as if it were going into her diary. Beulah's testimony—flat-out lies, as far as Maurine was concerned—particularly rankled: " 'That's my story and I'll stick to it,' was her attitude—and she did, till she stepped down demurely from the witness stand with the settled complacency of a school girl who has said her piece." Maurine pointed out that McLaughlin's closing argument, ultimately in vain, had "hinged on the credibility of the witness, who had made three entirely different statements to the jury." (She was counting the confessions Beulah made to police that were read in court.)

The verdict stung Maurine. She would later decry the softness of all-male juries, the attitudes that made it possible for Beulah to get away with testimony that contradicted compelling physical evidence and her own previous statements: "Men on a jury generously make allowance for a woman's weakness, both physical and moral; she is unduly influenced, led astray by some man, really not responsible—poor little woman!" Maurine believed that "it feeds a juryman's vanity and sex pride to feel that a woman is weaker and less responsible than a man would be in a similar situation." The whole thing left her feeling sick. She was convinced Beulah was a cold-blooded murderer—and a devious, calculating defendant. Her report on the verdict laid bare the raw feelings of a reporter who'd gotten closer to the story than she probably liked to admit.

The *Tribune*—surprisingly, and unlike its competitors—decided not to linger on Beulah Annan. Maurine certainly wanted nothing more to do with the "Titian-haired" beauty and took a pass on the obligatory postacquittal follow-up piece. Her replacement on the Beulah beat for Sunday, perhaps intimidated at the prospect of following Maurine's beautiful, expressive diatribes, kept his unsigned report brief. In its entirety, it read:

> Mrs. Beulah Annan, Chicago's prettiest slayer and latest to join the ranks of the free, is trying to seek seclusion "for a few days." Saturday night, following her acquittal of the murder of her lover, Harry Kalstedt, she packed up her rather extensive wardrobe and moved from the county jail to "address unknown." She was accompanied by her faithful husband, Al.

The junior reporter didn't look very hard for his quarry. "Address unknown" turned out to be Beulah and Al's apartment on East Forty-sixth Street, where she had famously shot down Harry Kalstedt. Al had long ago cleaned up the bloody mess his wife had left behind. Reporters from other papers, local and far afield, found her there on Sunday and met no resistance. Beulah held court for much of the day.

After a night in her own bed for the first time in almost two months, the prettiest woman ever to be tried for murder in Cook County was feeling generous. She didn't take credit for the acquittal. "It was the baby—not me," she told H. H. Robertson, a reporter for the *Atlanta Constitution.* "I knew that no jury ever would convict me, under the circumstances." She wasn't feeling as generous about her dead former boyfriend, however. She restated her assertion that Kalstedt had attacked her when she told him she was pregnant with her husband's child. "Any woman is justified in shooting a man who did what Harry Kalstedt tried to do to me," she said. "The jury realized that." She told another reporter that "I know now better than ever before that a man who goes into the apartment of another man when the husband is away deserves what he gets, no matter what that is, whether he be a man who steals jewels or a man who steals women."

Sitting with thrown-back shoulders in the center of the little apartment, Beulah charmed her journalist callers, as always. "Shaking her Titian hair and relaxing in a dimple smile," wrote Robertson, "Mrs. Annan gazed coyly at her husband and other relatives and said she had learned a lesson." She was a changed woman.

"I'm going to be a devoted wife from now on," she declared. "I am going to forget these terrible things. I am going to prepare for my baby's arrival, and I have sworn an oath that I never again will do anything which might cause reproach to attach itself to my name or to my child's name. The most intense longing which I have is that I prove myself to be a good mother and a true wife. I want to show the whole world what kind of a woman I really am."

❧❧❧

The new, devoted wife made it into the next day's papers, but the fawning headlines looked foolish before the sun set. Beulah and Al must have had a terrible fight after reporters left their apartment Sunday, because on Monday afternoon she appeared in a newspaper office with a divorce lawyer in tow. (Perhaps put off by Maurine's biting reports, she conspicuously chose not to go to the city's leading paper, the *Tribune*.) Sitting with her legs crossed, with reporters and editors gathered around, Beulah announced that she was leaving Al. "He doesn't want me to have a good time," she said. "He never wants to go out anywhere and he doesn't know how to dance. I'm not going to waste the rest of my life with him—he's too slow."

Beulah said she might move to Southern California. The weather there was fine year-round, and the newsreel people had said the camera loved her. Yes, she'd like to be a moving-picture actress, she said. She wanted even more than that: "I want lights, music and good times. I love to dance. I love good food—and I'm going to have them."

Only Beulah and Al knew what transpired between them that turned her professed longing for a quiet life as wife and mother into a desire for the lights of Hollywood. He may have refused to take her out dancing, as she suggested. He may have finally confronted her about her infidelity and wondered aloud who the father of her unborn child was. Or it might simply have been Beulah's internal clock telling her it was time to move on, time to leave Chicago for new opportunities. She had proved to have an excellent sense of timing. She knew when to make an entrance, when to make a surprise revelation—and when to leave the scene for someplace better.

Beulah had gotten out of Kentucky at just the right moment, when the responsibilities of the adult world began to press in on her before she was ready. Now she wanted to get out of Chicago. Something big was happening in the city, bigger than Beulah Annan could ever hope to be. News of Beulah's acquittal received above-the-fold placement on the front page of the *Tribune*, with a photo of the "fair defendant" with the jury that had just set her free. But it wasn't the top story, as she had expected. A banner headline ran above the trial coverage, with type so large that it blared across the entire width of the page: "All City Hunts Kidnappers."

Parents all over Chicago worried that their children could end up like little Bobby Franks, snatched from the streets and viciously killed. The murderous kidnappers, though unknown, were the talk of the town. And that talk was about to get much louder. At about the time Beulah was packing up her "rather extensive wardrobe" and checking out of the Cook County Jail on Saturday night, two brilliant University of Chicago graduate students, Nathan Leopold and Richard Loeb, were in a South Side nightclub not far from the Annan home, double-dating with two pretty girls. When introduced to another reveler, the cocky eighteen-year-old Loeb said, "You've just enjoyed the treat of shaking hands with a murderer."

16

※※※

The Tides of Hell

Maurine Watkins had no time to reflect on what happened in Judge Lindsay's courtroom. While Beulah Annan and her husband celebrated with family members at their little flat on Sunday, the *Tribune* reporter was five blocks away, at the fortress-like house of Jacob and Flora Franks. Maurine may have been within shouting distance of the Annans' brick apartment building on East Forty-sixth Street, but this block in Kenwood, on the other side of Cottage Grove Avenue, was a different world. No mechanics or assistant bookkeepers lived here, except in the servants' quarters.

The mood also was completely different. The wealthy men and women of Chicago's South Side were somber, for they had come to see the Franks bury their son, Bobby. The family held the funeral service in their living room. Jacob, widely known as Jake, had been born a Jew, but he and his wife practiced Christian Science. A large crucifix stood prominently on a table. For much of the morning, as family friends, flowers, and telegrams arrived, Flora remained upstairs, but visitors had no doubt about how she was holding up. Her husband, in the living room with their seventeen-year-old daughter, Josephine, winced noticeably as screams of anguish periodically reverberated through the ceiling.

As she did in her report on Wanda Stopa's funeral, Maurine detailed the scripture readings and religious songs that the other papers glossed over or mentioned only for maudlin effect. The rituals of faith and the promise of the afterlife remained more important to Maurine than the tears of those remaining earthbound. (Maurine was one of the very few reporters to show restraint in her coverage. The *American* even came up with a fictional re-creation of the murder through the eyes of the dead boy himself: "I matched my strength, born of desperation, with that of my fiendish captors, with the tides of hell running like molten lava through their accursed veins.")

Maurine stuck with a straightforward account of the funeral, though she noted the tension in the air caused by the fact that the murder remained unsolved. There was a bubbling dread, some thirty years after a serial killer had roamed the concourse of the World's Fair in Chicago, that the kidnappings were not yet done. "Only relatives, a few close friends, and twenty of Robert's schoolmates from the Harvard private school [an exclusive prep school on the South Side] were admitted at the house, where grief is mingled with horror and fear," Maurine wrote. Eight of Bobby Franks's Harvard friends carried the casket down the front walk and placed it in the hearse, an emotionally burdensome task for any fourteen-year-old boy. Bobby's parents and Josephine slipped out a side door, led by a private guard. Fearing for their daughter's safety, Jake and Flora Franks wanted to avoid the three hundred or so people who had gathered in the street to watch the procession depart for the cemetery.

The crowd was nowhere near as large or unruly as the one that had congregated outside the Stopa place a month before. Like the curious gathered around the Franks residence, Maurine also seemed less engaged by Bobby Franks's funeral than by Wanda Stopa's. Maybe it was the setting: The broad hallways and soaring ceilings of the Franks home were unlike anything she'd known growing up. The family's suffering, even with the killer or killers uncaught and the threat of more violence hanging over them, didn't seem as raw to Maurine as the Polish family's in the little walk-up on Augusta Street. The Stopas had been humiliated as well as grief-stricken. And they didn't have wealth to protect them.

The Franks family's suffering also wasn't the chief concern of the city's other newspapers. They were more interested in playing detective. The *Herald and Examiner* recognized that all of Chicago had become supremely fascinated by the search for those responsible for Bobby Franks's death. The paper's editors figured it would be a major circulation boon if they could involve in that search not just their police reporters but everyone in the city. In the Monday edition, the *Herald and Examiner* published a call to action, giving it greater play than the funeral report:

> How and why was Robert Franks, a fourteen-year-old heir to $4 million, killed? Police investigators may clear that up. But have you a theory now? Can you write a logical theory, telling step by step how the crime was committed and what motivated the participants? The *Herald and Examiner* will give a prize of $50 to the reader who writes the best theory. The winner also will be eligible for a share in the $10,000 reward if his theory should aid in the solution of the slaying. The judgment will take place when the slayers are apprehended, if they are, and if they are not, upon the logic and probability of credence obtained in the written theory. The theories should be written in condensed, concise form, cleanly written or typed, on one side of the paper, and should be addressed to the City Editor, *Herald and Examiner*.
>
> Somewhere in Chicago, behind a desk, or in a street car, or in a foundry, may be a keen analytical mind adapted but not trained to detection and the reconstruction of past events, as a hunter reconstructs the story of the chase from the muddy records of the spoor. It may be yours. Send in your theory.

Just a day before the funeral, Belva Gaertner had been confident that, with Beulah's case decided and soon to be off the front pages, she would now have the spotlight all to herself. A young boy being killed was terrible but hardly unprecedented in Chicago. And the murderer, undoubtedly a simple-minded pervert, uninteresting in every way, was sure to be caught at any moment. Belva had every reason to expect that her impending trial, scheduled to get under way at the beginning of June, would once again make her the leading story in the city. But it wasn't to be. The *Herald and Examiner* announced that within a few days of its appeal, it had received more than three thousand theories from readers about the Franks murder, with more coming every hour. No one could quite put his finger on it yet, but there was something different about this particular murder. No other news story could possibly compete.

Somehow the police made progress without the aid of the *Herald and Examiner*'s sleuthing readers. Within days of the murder, police turned their attention to Dick Loeb and Nathan Leopold, after a pair of eyeglasses found near the body was identified as Leopold's. The boys—both from wealthy South Side families, both intellectual prodigies who had graduated from prestigious universities by the age of eighteen—were brought in for questioning on Thursday, May 29, five days after Beulah's acquittal.

From the start, it seemed clear to reporters that the boys were not serious suspects. Police took them to a comfortable downtown hotel to be interviewed, not a police station. Prosecutors provided breaks and restaurant meals. The nineteen-year-old Leopold, in particular, was completely at ease as he faced questions from the police. "He caught them lightly and deftly, answering suavely," observed Maurine, one of the reporters covering the story. "He has not once taken the defensive. No question has shaken his calm or penetrated his urbanity."

The boys, by their relaxed manner and easy smiles, showed that they found the whole thing amusing. They claimed that they had been out birding in the area where the Franks boy was found. Some police officers accepted the explanation without reservation, believing the boys' relationship to the case was pure coincidence. After all, these were future leaders of the city, maybe the country. Still, the questioning continued, with the hope that perhaps Leopold or Loeb had seen something that would prove valuable to the investigation. Leopold's father, as horrified by the murder as the rest of Chicago, publicly promised that the family would cooperate with the police. "While it is a terrible ordeal both to my boy and myself to have him under suspicion, our attitude will be one of helping the investigation rather than retarding it," he told reporters. "And even though my son is subjected to hardships, he should be willing to make sacrifices, and I am also willing for the sake of justice and truth until the authorities are thoroughly satisfied that this supposed clue is groundless. I probably could get my boy out on a writ of habeas corpus, but there is no need for that sort of technical trickery. The suggestion that he had anything to do with this case is too absurd to merit comment."

The questioning of two brilliant sons of Chicago's elite meant that the departure of another woman from the Cook County Jail would slip by almost without notice. Kitty Malm, the most famous gun girl in Chicago just three months before and Belva's best friend behind bars, shipped out to Joliet on the same day that the police brought Leopold and Loeb in to be interviewed. It wasn't just that compelling new events—first Belva, Beulah, and Wanda, now the Franks murder—had overtaken the Wolf Woman's criminal exploits. Since her conviction, Kitty had become "a most docile prisoner," which was hardly interesting to newspaper readers. She was preparing for her time in the state pen by letting go of all resistance, by abandoning everything Otto Malm had taught her about how to handle herself around authority. "You'll not find me making any trouble if they put me under lock and key," she told the jail's matrons. "This rough stuff doesn't get you anything, anyway. If I have to go to prison for a long stretch, I'm going to behave myself and maybe they will let me out sooner."

In March a group of society ladies had made noises about taking Kitty on as a cause, at the very least to get her sentence shortened. The interest pleased Kitty, but witnessing the attention bestowed on Belva, she didn't put much stock in it. "Some other woman might get off, but not me," she said. She was right. Efforts to push her case up to the Supreme Court got nowhere. By May, there was no reason for her to remain at the Cook County Jail. "Kitty Malm was taken to the Joliet penitentiary today, there to spend the remainder of her life," the *American* reported in a brief buried deep in the back pages. The matrons had brought her three-year-old daughter in on Thursday morning for a "final visit" at the jail. Kitty didn't have much to say to her beloved Tootsie. There was nothing left to say. She hugged Tootsie close and tried, without success, to hold back the tears. The *American*'s reporter said the one-time "tiger woman" now "presented a pathetic little figure" as she was taken out of the jail. "Goodbye, Kitty, and good luck," one of the other prisoners said as she passed. The send-off cracked Kitty's already shaky composure: Tears bubbled in her eyes again, and she chomped on her lower lip in hopes of avoiding a breakdown. "Not much luck for me, I guess," she said in response. Tears rolled down her cheeks as the heavy door to the women's quarters swung open and she was marched through. The *Evening Post*'s headline—as in the *American*, it was buried far back in the paper—declared: "Kitty Malm Sobs as She Starts to Begin Life Term."

Reporter Owen Scott, seeing Kitty carted off in chains, noted the difference from Beulah Annan's triumphant departure from the jail five days before. "Her mistake," he wrote, "was in being 'hard boiled' and none too good looking."

⁂

By Friday, thanks to Nathan Leopold and Dick Loeb, interest in the Franks case had increased still more. The glamorous college boys had impressed everyone during a brief initial exposure to the press the day before, leading the police to make them available for a question-and-answer session with reporters. Leopold and Loeb had shown a remarkable ability to talk philosophy, history, and ethics at a high level, so Maurine's editors gave her a straightforward assignment: to record what they had to say at the press session, in the event that select quotes might be newsworthy, even independent of the Franks investigation.

Maurine, however, had something more in mind. She sensed that there was something unusual about the boys, aside from their wealth, charisma, and intellectual abilities. She was intent on doing "a character analysis, a study of their temperament." She later remembered that "the room was full of reporters and we were each allowed one question. I was the only woman. I asked Leopold, 'What three men do you consider the greatest who ever lived?' He named Nietzsche, Haeckel and Epicurus. I took an absolute gamble in asking it. I wasn't thinking about the crime. I was thinking about my story—how I could get two columns out of one question. So I got the books they had read, their educational background. Nietzsche believed in the superior man, Haeckel taught that there was no immortality of the soul and nothing beyond this life, and Epicurus advocated the right of the individual to do as he pleased."

Could anyone have come up with a more perfect synthesis to express the Chicago Idea? It seemed to Maurine that all Chicagoans thought the same way Nathan Leopold did, even if most of them couldn't articulate it nearly as well. Being guided by your own thoughts and abilities, living out there on the high wire and being rewarded for it: That was the Chicago way. Nothing else counted. If it were sensational enough, whether a scientific breakthrough, a rousing new style of music, or an underworld murder, it would be celebrated. "With that sort of philosophy as a foundation, one could begin to see how they might have done it," Maurine said. She was among the first reporters to seriously consider the possibility. She noted that the boys had mentioned "Oscar Wilde's remark, 'To regret an experience is to nullify it,'" and that they touted a belief that there was no God.

Leopold did most of the talking during the question-and-answer session. "In clear, precise language," Maurine wrote, "he dictated to the reporters a statement for the papers: 'The police are more than justified in holding me in custody for a limited period, as I am the victim of an unusual set of circumstances.'" He added, "'And won't you thank President Burton [University of Chicago president Ernest DeWitt Burton] and Dean Woodward of the Law School for their expression of sympathy and confidence in me?'"

Leopold, aware that he and Loeb were not going to face challenging questions about the case, brazenly showed off his high-dollar education at the press event. He tossed out the names of obscure philosophers and complex economic theories, the reporters struggling to keep up. (Maurine laughed at her fellow scribes' intellectual competition with the college boys, writing that "the most conceited tribe on earth—reporters!—nibbled their pencils and coughed suggestingly [*sic*] for spelling and definitions!") It seemed obvious to many there that the two brilliant friends just happened to have recently been in the same culvert where Bobby Franks's body was found. In a city of strivers, the wealthy were typically given the benefit of the doubt, and that was the initial response to the eyeglasses discovery. When told that Leopold and Loeb had been brought in as possible suspects, *American* reporter Howard Mayer, who knew the boys from the University of Chicago, exclaimed, "That's impossible." The early police questioning of the boys yielded nothing to alter that reaction. Prosecutors expected to release them by the weekend. "The most brilliant boy of his age

I've ever known," State's Attorney Robert Crowe said of Leopold, possibly to ingratiate himself with the young man and get his defenses down. But Maurine was not fooled.* She saw a scary narcissism in Nathan Leopold, noticing that he seemed to live "in a world of his own creating, and the people around him are more or less shadows." She immediately recognized the difference between breezy upper-class confidence (as exhibited by Leopold's father) and a dark, possibly sociopathic sense of superiority, noting Leopold's "slow, calm smile that admits the hearer cannot grasp his meaning." In Saturday's paper she wrote:

> He has built for himself a world beyond morality, beyond convention—yet he accommodates himself to the world in which he lives. And he does not preach his convictions to others, for he realizes that such meat is only for the strong.
>
> With his friends he smokes and drinks and "takes his pleasure where he finds it."

Based on a single, relatively brief interaction, Maurine proved remarkably perceptive. She took a risk in laying out such a damning interpretation of Leopold from an interview that ranged across centuries of philosophical thought but never got past the superficialities of the Franks investigation. Even though she knew the boys were likely to be released before the morning edition hit the streets, she didn't water down her conclusion. She closed the piece with a swipe at Leopold's touting of experience for its own sake: "If he's not connected with the crime—what an experience! And if he is connected—still it's experience!"

Maurine would find out, shortly after the article went to press, that she got it exactly right. Leopold and Loeb did do it—and, indeed, for no other reason than for the experience. For the thrill of it. Just a few hours after the group interview with reporters, at around one in the morning, Dick Loeb broke. Leopold, responding to his friend's confession, soon followed. (The same court stenographer who'd recorded Beulah's confession in her

---

*Nor were Alvin Goldstein and Jim Mulroy of the *Chicago Daily News*. Their dogged detective work would lead to valuable evidence, for which they would be awarded a Pulitzer Prize.

apartment on April 3 took down the boys' confessions.) State's Attorney Crowe, hailed in his campaign literature as "Fighting Bob," took charge of the case himself. He knew, or at least strongly suspected, that some of the assistant state's attorneys on his staff were on the take from gangsters. Dozens of police officers, maybe hundreds, had been corrupted by the Mob. So if the ambitious forty-five-year-old prosecutor, a Yale Law School grad and former chief justice of the criminal court, wanted to become mayor or governor (and he did), he'd have to make headlines with a different kind of sensational case, a case like this one.

"The Franks murder mystery has been solved. The murderers are in custody," Crowe declared outside his office at six in the morning. "Nathan Leopold and Richard Loeb have completely and voluntarily confessed. The kidnapping was planned many months ago, but the Franks boy was not the original victim in mind." A hasty collection of reporters, some expressing astonishment, rushed to file the news. The state's attorney was the hero of the moment. Within an hour, most of the city's papers had special editions on the street proclaiming the confessions.

The *Tribune* gave over almost its entire front page to Leopold and Loeb, justifying it by stating in an editors' note that "the solving of the Franks kidnapping and death brings to notice a crime that is unique in Chicago's annals, and perhaps unprecedented in American criminal history." The editors added: "The diabolical spirit evinced in the planned kidnapping and murder; the wealth and prominence of the families whose sons are involved; the high mental attainments of the youths; the suggestions of perversion; the strange quirks indicated in the confession that the child was slain for a ransom, for experience, for the satisfaction of a desire for 'deep plotting,' combined to set the case in a class by itself." The wall-to-wall reports marked only the beginning of the newspaper's obsession with the crime. In the flurry of activity following the confessions, editors directed a team of reporters to track down people who knew Leopold and Loeb. Maurine recalled later that the *Tribune* wasn't picky about its sources: "Anyone who had ever spoken to either of them was good material."

Having focused on Leopold on Friday, Maurine now turned her attention to Loeb on Saturday. She canvassed his family and friends, finding

shocked disbelief at every turn. Loeb, unlike Leopold, had a sweet disposition. He wanted to be liked by everybody.

"He couldn't have done it. We know he's innocent," said one Loeb ally.

"He is innocent and confessed merely to get sleep. It can be repudiated
when he comes to trial," said another.

Maurine granted that the disbelief was to be expected. "'Loeb' as the
name of a murderer falls strangely on Chicago ears," she wrote. "For the
people of that name are written in the book of Chicago's history as builders
and leaders in philanthropy, charity and educational movements."

"It's a damned lie!" said Richard Rubel hysterically. "I'm Dick Loeb's best
friend and he couldn't have done it! For a ransom—!" he looked about
at the magnificent home of his millionaire friend, at the garage stocked
with limousine, sedan, coupe touring car; at the tennis court where they
so often played.

"Why, those boys could have had all the money in the world! Why
should they do that?"

Maurine had some theories for Sunday's paper: "Were they bored by a life
which left them nothing to be desired, no obstacle to overcome, no goal to
attain? Were they jaded by the jazz-life of gin and girls, so that they needed
so terrible a thing as murder to give them new thrills?"

So it seemed. The next day, Monday, June 2, the day before Belva Gaertner's trial opened, Leopold would say of the murder of Bobby Franks: "It
was just an experiment. It is as easy for us to justify as an entomologist in
impaling a beetle on a pin."

Leopold remained cold, clinical, detached. His friend and partner, meanwhile, had fallen into desperate fantasy. "This thing will be the making of
me," Loeb told a police officer on Sunday. "I'll spend a few years in jail and
I'll be released. I'll come out to a new life. I'll go to work and I'll work hard
and I'll amount to something, have a career."

17

Hatproof, Sexproof, and Damp

Belva Gaertner wouldn't get the endless newspaper space for her trial that Beulah Annan did. The Bobby Franks murder case had suddenly heated to the boiling point and was beating out all other stories in competition for the public's attention. The famous Clarence Darrow had taken over the defense of Leopold and Loeb. Assistant State's Attorney Bert Cronson, one of the men who'd helped elicit the Midnight Confession from Beulah in April, had been assigned to the Franks case. He was considered the "ace" of the staff, better than McLaughlin or Woods or Harry Pritzker.

Still, the "double divorcee," as all of the papers constantly and salaciously called Belva, remained front-page news. Editors knew that the "stylish murderess," with her gorgeous outfits and regal bearing, would provide pictures that no other story could match. Chicagoans still wanted to see and read about her.

As expected, Belva dressed for court with care, determined to impress potential jurors as a woman of the upper classes, the kind of privileged, well-appointed lady who would naturally awe any ordinary man. Downtown's priciest shops helped out, sending dresses for her to consider, knowing that the outfits would be rapturously described in the newspapers.

Belva arrived at the Criminal Courts Building for jury selection on Tuesday morning, June 3. Paul T. Gilbert of the *Evening Post,* assisting Ione Quinby with coverage, treated it as if covering an appearance by screen star Mary Pickford.

The case of a negro was continued. A varied assortment of blacks filed out of Judge Lindsay's courtroom. The defendant shuffled back to the bullpen.

A moment's silence, then—

"Belva Gaertner."

A voice from the corridor leading to the county jail re-echoed the call. *"Belva."*

A trim figure entered, clad in navy blue. It was Belva Gaertner, the attractive young divorcee in whose sedan one night last March, after a hectic cabaret tour of the south side, the limp body of Walter R. Law, automobile salesman, was found, a steel-jacketed bullet in his head, an automatic pistol on the floor of the car. . . .

The room, packed from end to end, was ready for her. Spectators vying for sight lines huffed and stomped like spooked show horses. A small din erupted as Belva glided, cool and confident, through the door. "Her color was heightened by rouge," Gilbert wrote. "Her lashes had a touch of mascara. Cosmetics had been applied also to her lips, but the make-up wasn't overdone. . . . She might have been in a divorce court instead of at the criminal bar." Court fans seemed universally impressed.

"Say, she's got the Annan girl skinned a mile!" enthused an eyewitness.

"Not so pretty, but more class," came the response.

The exchange stuck with Maurine Watkins, who diligently recorded it. " 'Class'—that was Belva," she wrote for the morning paper. "For she lived up to her reputation as 'the most stylish' of murderess' row: a blue twill suit bound with black braid, and white lacy frill down the front; patent leather slippers with shimmering French heels, chiffon gun metal hose. And a hat—ah, that hat! Helmet shaped, with a silver buckle and cockade of ribbon, with one streamer tied jauntily—coquettishly—bewitchingly— under her chin."

Belva padded softly down the aisle, no doubt pleased to see the courtroom just as full for her as it had been for Beulah. She bowed to the judge. The *Daily News* wrote, "She looks younger and fresher since her incarceration—hardly like the same woman the police found cowering in her apartment, her clothing covered with the blood of the young married man who had been her companion during the fateful evening." The paper added that she wore a "smart white blouse" and "white kid gloves, as if for a matinee." The *Daily Journal*'s reporter decided that the "chin strap of her bonnet and her fresh white frilled blouse gave her an air of distinction, as did also her immaculate white kid gloves with yellow cuffs." Belva, her white-gloved hands held out before her, played to the crowd while at the same time appearing to be embarrassed by the attention. "Arrived at court, Belva adjusted her skirts modestly, pulled the choker more tightly around her neck and smiled demurely at everybody in general," Quinby wrote for the *Post.* Maurine described the defendant as a "perfect lady" in court.

Chicagoans across the city would be just as impressed as court spectators when papers started rolling off the presses later in the afternoon. As Belva stood alone before the judge, with the court fans no longer near enough to reach out to her and spoil the frame, news photographers exploded into action. The cameras clicked and flashbulbs popped, momentarily blinding everyone. One of the prosecutors, Samuel Hamilton, took offense at the fawning attention. He requested that the photographers be removed. Judge Lindsay, who'd seen worse when presiding over Beulah's trial, waved him off. "The cameras are not disturbing me nor the defendant nor the men called for jury service as far as I can see," he said. Belva smiled at the judge, and then gave Hamilton a quick, triumphant glare. Forgotten in all the hullabaloo was a small, thin figure in the front row. Mrs. Freda Law, dressed in black, sat alone, grim-faced and staring straight ahead.

"Are you ready?" Lindsay asked each set of lawyers.

Belva joined her attorneys at the defendant's table. Judge Lindsay addressed the potential jurors and then turned to the state. "Proceed," he said.

Hamilton got right to it. He strode up to the nearest juror candidate. "You understand the penalty is death or life imprisonment? Do you think that's too severe?" he demanded. The man paused, and then answered that he understood the penalty for murder. "If this were to be proved a cold-blooded murder, could you inflict the death penalty?" Hamilton asked.

The man swallowed. "I could."

With that answer, Freda Law quivered to life. "Mrs. Law, who up to this time had shown little emotion, leaned forward eagerly," wrote the *Post*. "Her eyes shone. She trembled slightly."

Hamilton moved down the line, taking turns with the case's lead prosecutor, Harry Pritzker. "Would you be willing to mete out the same punishment to a woman that you would to a man?" they asked each potential juryman.

Faced with this hard-hearted questioning of jurors, and with the comfort most of the men expressed with putting a woman to death, Belva finally showed some anxiety. "She clasped and unclasped the fastener of her fur choker nervously" and stared straight ahead, wrote the *Journal*. Her lead attorney, Thomas D. Nash, whispered something to her, soothing words.

The lawyer had a knack for calming down clients. For one thing, he looked the part of the quintessential defense attorney. Though just thirty-eight years old, his hair was a forbidding gray, and he had a voice and manner that instinctively provoked confidence. Nash had made a name for himself quickly in Chicago, winning election to the city council in 1911 when he was just twenty-five. In 1920 he was defeated in a run for judge of the municipal court, but the setback hardly dented his political influence. He remained the Nineteenth Ward's Democratic committeeman, a powerful position, and turned his attention to his thriving criminal law practice. "The list of Tom Nash's clients reads like a page from the who's who of vicious criminals," his opponent for the county board of review would charge in 1928. "Murderers, gun toters, robbers, gangsters and their political tools are included among the crew which pays retainers to Tom Nash." That was true. Johnny Torrio and Al Capone, among other prominent gangsters, were Nash clients. They came to him because he was good: smart, clever, personable. He could put any man, no matter what charge he faced, at ease.

Nash was just as conscientious about seating a jury as the prosecutors. He took seriously his client's preference for "worldly" jurors—"the kind of men," as Belva put it to reporters, "who realize that after a woman has had as many sweethearts as I have had, she can't love any one enough to shoot him." Because Belva had been so open about her preferences, the jury selection process sparked an unusual public debate in the newspapers. "She's wrong," one policeman told a reporter outside of court. "The kind she should get on a jury is the inexperienced, home man who is used to gentle women. A worldly man knows that the woman who has been on the primrose path is more likely to shoot than any other." But an automobile salesman said he "could certainly give a woman an impartial break on the story Mrs. Gaertner tells." Seconded a hotel clerk: "I believe that to a woman of a rosy past, a man is just a man. What they want is a good time and they don't care who pays for it. She wouldn't shoot for love." A coffee-shop owner, on the other hand, opined that "women who have a succession of sweethearts usually display violent attachment for the man who holds their interest for the moment. That's my observation, and I think Mrs. Gaertner's argument is all wrong."

Captain Patrick Kelliher of the Chicago Police expressed the fears of every prosecutor: "A jury of family men probably would not convict her," he said. "A jury of bachelors would never convict her. The average unmarried man about town has liberal views and is very tolerant of erring women."

That must have sounded good to Nash and his team, but the common-ness of the view also guaranteed that they wouldn't be able to finagle a jury solely of single men on the make, as Belva hoped. Pritzker and his seconds, Hamilton and H. M. Sharpe, were able prosecutors. Men who seemed vulnerable to irrelevant explanations for a woman's violent behav-ior were sent home. The defense, meanwhile, sought to jettison those from the other extreme. One man after another was dismissed after expressing prejudice against any woman who drank liquor or went to clubs. "Would you be prejudiced if it should develop that the lady had been drinking that evening?" Nash asked the jurors, an important question considering Belva's official statement that she was too drunk on the night of the murder to remember what happened.

There also was one more consideration for the attorneys: the so-called beauty-proof jury, like the one that had set free "Beautiful Beulah" Annan.

"Would you let a stylish hat make you find her 'not guilty'?" Assistant State's Attorney Hamilton asked a jury candidate. He asked other potential jurors similar questions about their susceptibility to high fashion and carefully rouged female faces. In the end, everyone the state accepted declared himself suitably armored against such feminine wiles.

Maurine Watkins, after the disaster of Beulah's trial, found the whole thing a farce. She wrote that many prospective jurors, wanting to be part of the trial at any cost, struggled to come up with what they thought the attorneys wanted to hear, and "the questioning went merrily on to find a hat-proof, sex-proof, and 'damp' jury, who would also accept circumstantial evidence as conclusive." Though she joked about it in the *Tribune*, Maurine worried that she'd get another "moron jury" that wasn't capable of doing the right thing. "The essence of Christianity is to think of other people," she later remarked. "That doesn't mean to give an easy break. The juryman with his maudlin sentiment may think he's practicing Christianity when he gives an acquittal and in some instances he may be, but there is just as much Christianity in having your sympathy with the man who was killed and in restraining the individual."

After a full day, most of the jury had been selected, and the trial was scheduled to get under way the next afternoon. Matrons escorted Belva back to the women's section of the jail, with reporters striding along behind them in the hope that the defendant would be in a talkative mood before deadline. They were disappointed. Belva smiled and said she felt fine but had nothing more than that to say.

≈≈≈

In the morning, Maurine's report once again made clear her sympathy for the city's prosecutors. "Demure but with an 'Air' at Murder Trial," the subhead teased. The story itself was even more direct. Like Beulah, Belva was trying to fool jurors with womanly razzmatazz.

Cabaret dancer and twice divorcee, Mrs. Gaertner was as demure as any convent girl—yesterday!—with brown eyes dreamily cast downward. Her lips were closed in a not-quite smile, the contour of her cheek was unbro-ken by lines, and rejuvenating rouge made her well on the dangerous side of 30.

It was another jazzy, satirical performance—and one that hit hard. Mau-rine described, in stark contrast to Belva's rouged, dangerous appearance, the sad, "sweet-faced" widow in the front row, decked in mourning attire, looking younger still than the aggressively made-up Belva and not at all dangerous. Maurine claimed that, of the two women, Mrs. Law "seemed more concerned."

If Maurine's eviscerating story in the *Tribune* bothered Belva or her lawyers, they didn't show it when they came into court.* Belva once again looked fabulous, with a new dress "that clung in soft folds to her body." She smiled dutifully as flashbulbs popped. ("I hear Belva got a lot of compli-ments on how she looked when she walked into court this morning," one inmate said to Ione Quinby when the reporter came through the jail later in the day.) With court fans once again blocking the aisle and falling over each other, Judge Lindsay kept the entrance theatrics to a minimum this time. He hurried along the questioning of more juror prospects, and the final four jurors were quickly identified and accepted. At two P.M., after a lunch break, Hamilton and Pritzker launched into their opening statement, declaring that they would prove Belva E. Gaertner had fired the bullet that killed Walter Law and had even tried to dispose of the body before decid-ing the dead man was too heavy to move.

Nash seemed unperturbed by this salvo. He waived an opening state-ment. He was counting on the fact, Maurine pointed out, that there were no witnesses: "Just a man found dead, slumped over the steering wheel of Mrs. Gaertner's car, a bullet in his head from her pistol left lying on the sedan floor." Maurine added with icy mockery that Belva was expected to testify on her own behalf, and that, with her defense based solely on her lack of memory of the murder, the testimony "will at least be unique."

---

*It's possible that they missed it, as the Leopold-Loeb case pushed Maurine's story back to page 4. The *Daily News* and the Hearst papers managed to find places on their front pages for Belva, even with banner headlines devoted to the Franks killing.

First, though, the state presented its evidence. Prosecutors brought out a pair of bloodstained silver dance slippers to show the jury. Belva "stared, chin in hand," as Assistant State's Attorney Hamilton insisted that the slippers put her up close with the victim at the time of his death. Taking the stand, Dr. William D. McNally, the coroner's chemist, described how he did his work, gesturing mindlessly with one of Belva's slippers, which he held in his hand while giving testimony. "Now, a small strip of fabric was removed and dissolved in a salt solution," he said. "Then the usual chemical tests were made—placed under a spectroscope, acetic acid, crystals obtained—indicating human blood."

The newspapers latched onto the stylish footwear. "They had been effective with the green velvet gown she had worn that fatal night. They had carried her through that last dance," wrote the *Daily News*, attempting to mimic the humorous bent in Maurine's stories. Maurine, of course, topped the competition, writing that it was Belva's "twinkling feet" in those silver slippers that "had danced her into Overbeck's [*sic*] heart, when she was Belle Brown, cabaret girl; that had carried her to—and from!—a bridle path romance with Gaertner, wealthy manufacturer; that had stolen her into a 'palship' with a young married man—and then to a murder trial." For all the florid newspaper prose they inspired, however, the slippers proved only that Belva had been at the crime scene, which the defense already acknowledged.

A more promising witness for the state was the coroner's physician, Joseph Springer, who testified that a gun "must be held within fifteen inches or so to make powder burns."

"From the absence of these, is it your opinion that he did not shoot himself?" Hamilton asked.

Springer nodded. "He did not."

The defense, almost completely mute until now, refused to accept so definitive a statement. Nash's associate, Michael Ahern, approached the witness and, saying he would pose as Law, asked Springer to hold the pistol at the correct angle and distance from the victim. Springer agreed, placed Ahern just so, and pulled the trigger. The gun clicked violently, drawing gasps from around the room. But Ahern didn't even flinch.

"There! You see," the lawyer said, twisting his arm to show how he could hold the gun himself where Springer had it. He imitated a man holding a gun to his own head and leaning away in fear, eyes clenched in anticipation of impact. "He could have killed himself."

"He could not!" Springer whined as Ahern strutted back to the defense table.

William F. Leathers, headwaiter at the Gingham Inn, was next. Belva had insisted from the beginning that she was too drunk on the night of the murder to remember what happened to Walter Law, and so the state wanted to suggest otherwise. "They ordered three bottles of ginger ale, family-size, eleven-ounce bottles. I waited on them myself," Leathers said. "No, their steps were not unsteady. They seemed perfectly sober when they were dancing." He added: "I wish that I had always remained as sober as they were."

As more witnesses took turns on the witness stand—a series of policemen followed Leathers—Maurine homed in on Belva's "virtuous calm" during the testimony. It irritated her. She ratcheted up her attack on the woman who had sat patiently and politely for numerous interviews with the young reporter over the weeks.

> Her sultry eyes never lost their dreaminess as policemen described the dead body slumped over the wheel of her Nash sedan—the matted hair around the wound, the blood that dripped in pools—and her revolver and "fifth" of gin lying on the floor. Her sensuous mouth kept its soft curves as they told of finding her in her apartment—4809 Forrestville avenue— with blood on coat, blood on her dress of green velvet and silver cloth, and blood on the silver slippers.

Not all of the observers present saw only steely calm. A reporter from the *Atlanta Constitution,* sent north specifically for the trial, declared that "Mrs. Gaertner lost her composure and trembled as the prosecution exhibited bloodstained clothing she wore the night Walter Law, an automobile salesman, was shot and killed in her sedan." The *Daily News* and the *Evening Post* also noted signs of nervousness in Belva as she listened to testimony.

Maurine refused to attribute such human emotions to the defendant. She worried that she hadn't been hard enough on Beulah Annan, that she'd underestimated her and thus helped free the beautiful killer. She would make sure there was no doubt about Belva Gaertner's guilt. This sense of mission, however, didn't cause her to lose her sense of humor. In fact, it sharpened her wit. She would pepper her trial stories with sly digs at Belva and the jury, at witnesses and lawyers and court fans. Dr. Springer, she wrote, "identified the gin bottle which was found lying on the floor of the car. Belva's jury, selected for their lack of prejudice in favor of the Volstead act, pepped up a bit at sight of this, and Belva herself leaned forward. But it was empty." Maurine laughed openly at the testimony of the Gingham Inn's Bert Brown, who claimed the establishment served "nothing stronger than ginger ale."

> According to his statement, the Gingham Inn is matched in dryness only
> by the Sahara; no liquor is sold there, no liquor is brought there, no liquor
> is displayed there on table, floor, or under cover.

In describing a policeman's testimony, Maurine even managed a playful swipe at Belva's vaunted clothes sense, skillfully insinuating along the way that the defendant was both a liar and a whore. Belva, she wrote, "couldn't shake her head nor nod approvingly at the testimony, for she doesn't 'remember,' but she could show impatience as the officer floundered in describing her clothes. But—to his relief—they were admitted in evidence; the mashed hat and rumpled coat, the 'one more struggle and I'm free' dress, and the flimsy slippers."

୬୧

The trial moved swiftly. Straightforward and uneventful, it was given to the jury on Thursday, having lasted less than two days in total. Belva, to the disappointment of the crowded room, did not testify.

As the state completed its closing argument, Maurine saw reasons to be optimistic. Freda Law's brief testimony, during which she identified a bloodied hat as belonging to her late husband, was so pathetic that surely even the hardest juryman's heart broke. Lieutenant Egan, who had interrogated Belva the night of the shooting, testified that she was only "intoxicated enough to be cunning." And there was no cynical, fanciful defense, like the one Stewart and O'Brien had put on for Beulah Annan. In fact, there was essentially no defense at all. Nash and his colleagues "refused to present evidence and waived their closing argument."

These reasons for hope soon suffered, however. Nash, in refusing a closing argument, declared the case purely circumstantial and asked for a dismissal. Judge Lindsay refused the request but, out of the hearing of the jury, agreed "that there was not sufficient evidence to cause the Supreme Court to uphold a verdict of guilty." Nash had done an excellent job of playing possum, coming alive at opportune moments to punch holes in the state's evidence. Lindsay said that he couldn't "tell the state's attorney what to do. But if the jury should bring in a verdict of guilty, I am confident the Supreme Court would reverse the decision, as the evidence is only circumstantial; strong enough to rouse suspicion of guilt, but not to convict."

Pritzker and his team ignored the judge's warning. They were willing to take their chances with the higher court. They asked for life imprisonment, not the death penalty. Lindsay gave final instructions to the jury, landing hard on the definition of reasonable doubt. He reminded jurors "not to assume that, because the defendant might have committed the crime, she necessarily did commit it." As the judge motioned to Belva, a reporter observed, they "turned to stare at the slim, youthfully rounded creature who'd never looked prettier." The defendant offered a small, brave smile as twelve pairs of eyes fell on her. At four P.M., the jurors left the room.

Belva was taken from the courtroom and placed in the adjacent prisoner bull pen, some ten feet from the room where the jurors were beginning their deliberations. Nash expected her wait to be short. Seeing as he had mounted no active defense, a swift decision would be a good sign. He'd simply asserted that the prosecution had no case—no meaningful evidence, no eyewitnesses. If the jury reached the same conclusion, they should do so quickly. There was either evidence or there wasn't.

So when the minutes ticked into hours, Belva's composure began to fray. She paced in the small holding cell, wondering what the jurors could be discussing behind that door. Were some of them "narrow-minded old birds" who'd lied about their opinion of liquor so that they wouldn't be dismissed from the jury? She knew self-righteous fanatics could be convincing when they got going; they could shame anybody. Belva chain-smoked cigarettes and, like Beulah before her, avoided chatting with the matron minding her, hoping to fight off a burgeoning hysteria. Her mind reeled with the possibilities, the rest of her life behind bars rolling out before her.

At last, shortly before midnight, the jurors sent word that they had a verdict. It had taken them nearly seven hours to reach a decision—"much longer," noted the *Daily News*, "than it takes most 'woman-proof' juries." When guards led Belva back into the courtroom, dark circles slashed under her eyes. She looked shaken, scared. She chanced a look at her sister, Malinda, who stood in the back.

The jury entered a few minutes later, tired and grim. Tension gathered about the defendant's table; Belva, rocking slightly, seemed prepared for the worst. A piece of paper was passed to the bailiff, on to the judge, and then back again. The jury foreman now unfolded it as if he had no idea what it said. When he announced the verdict—"Not guilty," in a clear, echoing voice—Belva let out a gasp and clutched at her stomach. She "laughed and cried in one breath" and swung around to see her lawyers' reactions. "I'm so happy," she managed, her voice breaking. She sat, as if exhausted, and then climbed to her feet. "I want to leave this place and get some air." Suddenly overcome by emotion, she hugged a deputy sheriff, surprising the man, who reflexively returned the embrace. She bounded over to the jury. She thanked them, tears in her eyes, reaching out to grasp their hands. As Belva posed for pictures with the jury, Walter Law's widow once again went almost unnoticed. Freda Law cried softly, hugging herself and her sister in the back of the room. When a reporter approached, she lashed out. "There's no justice in Illinois!" she spat. "No justice! Walter paid—why shouldn't she?" She quickly left the courtroom. Harry Pritzker saw Mrs. Law storm out. Defeated, appalled at the verdict, he didn't want to talk to the press. "Women—just women," he said, shaking his head as he gathered his papers and marched from the room.

After the courtroom had emptied, Belva crossed the bridge of sighs to the Cook County Jail, Malinda a step behind her. She packed her "wardrobe" and said good-bye to the inmates. She waved off the reporters who followed her on this final trek to the jail. "I'm going to remarry Mr. Gaertner and forget all this on a second honeymoon to Europe," she said, as she glided out of the building and into the early morning air.

William Gaertner didn't yet know that he was about to marry again. Up past his bedtime, he had gone home before the verdict came in.

≈≈≈

Even with the Leopold-Loeb drama gripping the city, Belva Gaertner earned prime placement on the city's front pages on Friday. The *Daily Journal* trumpeted: "Belva 'Checks Out' of Jail." The *Daily News* reported stolidly, "Jury Takes Eight Ballots; 'I'm So Happy,' She Declares After Verdict." The *Evening Post* offered the blandest headline—"Mrs. Gaertner Given Freedom on Murder Charge"—and the blandest report. Ione Quinby, her work consistently overshadowed by Maurine's sharp coverage of the Beulah and Belva trials, had done the unthinkable: She gave over the prized verdict story to a junior colleague.

In the *Tribune,* unsurprisingly, Maurine did not hide her disgust at seeing a second murderess walk free. For the first time, a sour, humorless note dominated her prose.

> Belva Gaertner, another of those women who messed things up by adding a gun to her fondness for gin and men, was acquitted last night at 12:10 o'clock of the murder of Walter Law. "So drunk she didn't remember" whether she shot the man found dead in her sedan at Forrestville avenue and 50th street March 12—
>
> But after six and one-half hours and eight ballots the jury said she didn't.

Maurine was angry, just like after Beulah's acquittal. She couldn't believe it had happened again. But she tried not to wallow in her fury. The next day, Saturday, June 7, she wrote a follow-up that showed she had managed to take a breath and find her sense of humor again. With Belva's acquittal on Thursday night, and with Leopold and Loeb indicted for murder just a few hours later on Friday, she recognized that the women's quarters of the Cook County Jail would no longer be the focus of the city's attention. An era had passed. "Only four women, the fewest in years, are now waiting trial for murder—for they're getting out even faster than they're getting in!" Maurine wrote. "And the two who walked to freedom in the last two weeks, 'pretty' Beulah Annan and 'stylish' Belva Gaertner, robbed the women's quarters of their claims to distinction and plunged murderess' row into oblivion."

Maurine jokingly lamented that the pretty and interesting girl gunners, which the city once supplied in seemingly inexhaustible numbers, were all gone from the jail. Two of the remaining murder suspects were black women, and the other two—Helen Cirese's clients, Sabella Nitti and Lela Foster—were middle-aged and dowdy. Makeup and new clothes surely wouldn't be enough for any of these four to gain acquittal, Maurine wrote, for they "will lack the advice of Belva, known even in some other circles as an expert in dress."

18

A Grand and Gorgeous Show

Five days after Belva walked out of the Cook County Jail for the last time, Maurine returned to Nathan Leopold and Dick Loeb. The "boy killers" continued to rule every newspaper in the city, and correspondents began to arrive from around the country to report on the case.

Even now, after nearly two weeks in jail, Leopold and Loeb lacked the barest semblance of remorse. These intelligent young men, brought up with every advantage, had done what they'd done purely for the "experience," they said, as a sort of personal scientific experiment. Said Loeb, "I know I should feel sorry I killed that young boy and all that, but I just don't feel it. I didn't have much feeling about this from the first. That's why I could do it. There was nothing inside of me to stop me."

Reading such an admission sickened people across the country, Maurine included. Sent out to cover the boys' arraignment, Maurine attacked from the first sentence. She noted that it was Loeb's nineteenth birthday, but "Dickie" didn't much interest her. The good-looking boy seemed pathetic, desperate to be liked—the weak half of the malevolent duo. It was the haughty Leopold, with his slicked-back hair, swarthy complexion, and smug, half-lidded gaze, who truly repulsed her.

Maurine had little interest in imparting any actual news with her report; she was out simply to ridicule, to hit the two wealthy criminals where she knew it would hurt them most: their egos. (The approach apparently worked. Even twenty-five years later, Leopold would profess a deep hatred for the *Chicago Tribune*.) The reporter, taking a shot at Leopold's atheism, snorted that "it was a big day in itself to Mr. Nathan Leopold Jr., that gentleman who first won fame because 'he loved the birdies so.' How it must have delighted his egocentric soul—your pardon, Leopold!—his egocentric *mind,* to know that the crowd had begun gathering before 7 o'clock that morning. By 9—an hour before the performance—there were S.R.O. signs and the hallway to Judge Caverly's court was jammed with sturdy determinists who broke down the door for a chance glimpse."

The crowd, in fact, astounded Maurine almost as much as Leopold did. She watched as court fans, even more than had turned out for Beulah and Belva, jockeyed for position in the hallway of the Criminal Courts Building three hours before the arraignment, and then, when the doors opened, rushed for seats as if fleeing a tornado. She scrutinized men and women "packed in separate quarters like a Quaker meeting": "gum-chewing flappers" and "housewives sentimentally inclined" on the right, men "with loud ties and shifting eyes" on the left. Even courthouse professionals, who dealt with degenerates every day, wanted to see these killers: "Lawyers and stenographers from other courts lined the walls and filled the benches. Reporters sat—or stood—on tables and chairs, and cameramen formed an impregnable line back of the 'bench.'" Leopold's father, Nathan Leopold Sr., found himself surrounded by reporters. He had nothing to say to them. "Why come to me?" he croaked, tears in his eyes, still unable to fathom what his son had done and what had happened to his family. "What did I do? Why come to me?"

For weeks Maurine had been tinkering with an idea for a stage play based on the Beulah Annan case. She wanted to create a deeply cynical satire of the celebrity mania that she saw as the dominant feature of twentieth-century urban life. The sight before her only confirmed that she had chosen the right subject. Maurine didn't bother approaching the senior Leopold like the other reporters. By now supremely confident in her satiric style, she remained an observer and posed the whole scene as the equivalent of a play. Labeling Leopold "the Master" and Loeb "his dutiful friend," she wrote, "The judge entered; Superior Court, criminal branch No. 1, was opened. Camera men poised their flashlights. All turned breathless to the door that leads from the 'bridge of sighs.'"

The stage was set. "The Master" entered. Accompanied by his dutiful friend and their two attendants—faithful attendants chained to their wrists by "come-ons."

Still poised and self-possessed. And prison life, where they've done without wine, women and song, has helped them physically. Both were carefully groomed, and Dick wore a brand new suit for the "party." His brown eyes searched the crowd half fearfully for his brother, Allan, and the weak, sensuous mouth half parted.

But the "hypnotic" eyes of Nathan, with the whites gleaming 'neath the pupil, sought no one. He swept the crowd with a glance; just a mob, important only because they wanted to see him.

The boys' guards—their "faithful attendants"—had to put their shoulders down like halfbacks to ward off the pushing, grasping spectators. The guards pulled the boys down the aisle to the bench. Judge John R. Caverly glowered down on them. He reminded them that they had been indicted for murder and then asked if they pleaded guilty or not guilty.

"Not guilty, sir," said Leopold, followed by Loeb, straining to match his friend's tone of cool indifference: "Not guilty, sir." ("They never forgot the 'sir,'" Maurine pointed out. "Millionaires are bringing etiquette to our courts!") With the pleading out of the way, State's Attorney Crowe requested a trial date of July 15. The redoubtable Clarence Darrow, however, demurred. "We need time to prepare the case, and time," the defense attorney said, indicating with a flick of his eyes the mob behind him, "for public sentiment to die down." Darrow got a promise of time, and then Leopold and Loeb were led out of the courtroom and back to the jail. "The crowd," wrote Maurine, "filtered out slowly. Satisfied: they had seen the millionaire murder confessors."

◦◦◦

Maurine knew, now that the legendary Darrow stood for the defense, that the circus atmosphere would only get worse in the weeks ahead—and she was right. "The case was really ridiculous. . . . Can you imagine it?"

she later said. "It was just a grand and gorgeous show. Things being what they are, I don't see why the state doesn't charge admission to trials and lighten the taxes."

This statement, made in 1927, was bravado, an effort to be amusing and to sell herself to a New York journalist fashioning a feature story about her. By the time of this interview, nearly three years after the trial, the stomach-turning, horrified reaction to the "crime of the century," if not interest in it, had begun to fade from memory. But as the case was unfolding, when Maurine was looking up close at Leopold's smirking eyes and Loeb's friendly grin, she undoubtedly was as shocked as most Americans. Leopold's cool insistence that the murder was as justifiable as an entomologist killing a beetle, and his scoffing denial of the existence of God, could only have rocked her. Maurine's hard-boiled reporting style made for addictive reading, and it also made her a rising star at the *Tribune*, but it was an act. It was a heightened, fantasy version of herself, one that began to break down when faced not with the silly, mindless evil expressed by Beulah Annan and Belva Gaertner but with the calculated abominations of soulless young men with first-rate intellects.

"I was on the case until the trial started and then I had to do movie criticisms," Maurine recalled in that 1927 interview. "I thrived on murders, but the pictures had given Mae Tinee a nervous breakdown and I had to sub for her. Pinch-hitting was a very tame life after killings. Homicide was such a natural, normal fare out in Chicago."

It's possible Maurine was reassigned to movie criticism against her wishes just as the most sensational crime story in the city's history picked up momentum, but that seems unlikely. Newspapers were throwing every available reporter onto the story. (Plus, Mae Tinee was a pen name—a play on the word "matinee"—for an array of *Tribune* film reviewers.) It's much more likely that Maurine requested reassignment. She had excelled on the police beat, becoming a "name" reporter within weeks of starting at the paper. But it had exacted a toll. Leopold and Loeb, college boys from wealthy, influential families, accomplished students and professed atheists, represented everything that was wrong with the new modern age—everything Maurine's parents surely had warned her about when she went to the big city. She couldn't easily make light of such boys. Their murderous act was too horrible, too deliberate and vicious—too powerful.

∾∾

By the middle of 1924, after having interviewed some two dozen suspected murderers in less than six months on the job, Maurine Watkins had tired of the police reporter's life. Just as important, the beat had begun to tire of her. The Bobby Franks story did not lend itself to the cynical, lighthearted, murder-as-entertainment ethos that Maurine had brought to crime reporting. The thrill killing of a teenage boy just went too far. If, as Maurine said, she was conscripted into the movie-reviewing job, this may have been the real reason for it. The tongue-in-cheek writing style that Maurine had perfected—and many other police reporters tried to imitate—was about to become obsolete.

Early in July, the *Tribune* announced plans to broadcast the Leopold-Loeb trial on the company's fledgling radio station, WGN. In the nearly four years since the nation's first commercial station, in Pittsburgh, had gone on the air, radio's popularity had soared, and the Tribune Company decided it wanted to dominate the Chicago radio market as it did its newspaper market. It figured broadcasting the trial was a good way to do that. But management was surprised to receive hundreds of letters from Chicagoans asking them not to broadcast the trial, fearful that innocent ears would be subjected to a most horrid reality. The paper's competitors, worried about the *Tribune*'s reach through the new medium, stoked the negative response. The *American* called the *Tribune*'s broadcast plan "the finest and most powerful appeal ever made in this city to the moron vote." The *Tribune* tried to sway public opinion, arguing that the "broadcasting of the trial will be kept clean. Sensation there will be. Sensation is a part of life. It is an inseparable part of a trial for life. But there will be no filth." The public was not moved by this appeal, though. The trial did not go out over the airwaves. The *Tribune* quickly tried to regain the high ground on the issue, declaring that the sensational coverage of the story in the city's papers had "become an abomination." The rules, quite suddenly, had changed.

That same month, Maurine turned almost exclusively to film criticism and light features. She wrote that Pola Negri had "the spark" of stardom in *Lily of the Dust,* and she joked that "the weather's the best part" of *The Marriage Cheat,* a slow-moving drama set in the tropics. She reported on child star Jackie Coogan's appearance in Chicago, where the nine-year-old actor got to be mayor of the city for ten minutes. "He looks just like himself!" she quoted an enthusiastic young fan as saying when catching sight of the actor in the flesh.

Maurine wasn't the only prominent female police reporter on the sidelines for Chicago's "crime of the century." The *Evening Post*'s city editor did not put Ione Quinby on Leopold-Loeb duty, likely deciding the subject matter was too rough and perverse for a woman. With all of the high-profile murderesses gone from the Cook County Jail, Quinby found herself back on the women's pages. This did not sit well with the "little bob-haired reporter." Covering a society yacht party on Lake Michigan one night, she grew so bored that she removed her clothes, climbed up onto the railing, and dived into the water. Guests rushed to the side and watched her kicking for the shore. No one knew how the reporter—sopping wet, all but naked, and possibly drunk—managed to get home once she reached the beach. Years later, when an editor asked if the oft-told story about her stripping and diving off the boat was true, Quinby offered an impish smile. "Oh, yes, I did that," she said. "The water was very cold."

Maurine, for her part, wasn't nearly so put out. By this point, she was simply marking time until classes began at the newly established Department of Drama at Yale University, where her former teacher, George Pierce Baker, was setting up shop after thirty-six years at Harvard. She'd begun writing her play based on the Beulah Annan case, and Baker had invited her to New Haven to work on it. She now focused on the play, not her day job. Before the end of the year, Maurine would resign from the *Tribune* and head out of town, first for a stopover in Indiana to see her parents and then on to New York. She had accepted a job as a junior editor at a magazine in the city and planned to take the train to Connecticut for class. Her experiment in Chicago was over. Now the real test—discovering if she'd truly learned anything—would begin.

19

✤

Entirely Too Vile

George Pierce Baker had changed little since Maurine had sat in his Harvard playwriting workshop three years before. With his formal manners, his high-buttoned coats, and an ever-present pince-nez squeezed onto the bridge of his nose, the theatre professor could be a forbidding figure to students. He had a heavy, echoing voice, and he threateningly chopped his arms as he lectured, but he sometimes seemed to favor his female students, "speaking to them half in confidence, half in apology for being so obvious."

Baker may have intimidated Maurine back in Cambridge, but now she was more mature and worldly, and it showed in her work. She came to Yale with an ambitious comedy already mapped out, the characters vividly drawn. With his most talented students, Baker believed his chief task was to provide encouragement. "The finer the spirit of the young artist the more unsure and secretly timid he is in trusting his instincts for expression," he wrote. Baker saw the potential of Maurine's project right away, and he sought to shore up her confidence to allow her to do her best work. The relationship between teacher and student quickly grew warm at Yale.

Maurine titled her play, which was set in Chicago, *The Brave Little Woman*. Its main character was Beulah Annan, renamed Roxie Hart.* The married Roxie, like Beulah, shoots down her boyfriend when he tries to

---

*Roxie Hart was the name of a woman who'd been involved in an extramarital affair gone awry near Maurine's hometown when Maurine was in high school. Roxie's boyfriend murdered a man in an attempt to keep the affair a secret, leading to a trial that was widely reported in Indiana.

leave her. When reporters get a look at Roxie's gorgeous face and figure—
and take note of her willingness to do anything to stay in the papers—they
make her into a huge celebrity. But Maurine wasn't simply writing a memoir for the stage. *The Brave Little Woman* focused on the criminal-justice
system, "sensation journalism," and the stupidity of old-fashioned notions
of chivalry in an era of pretty young women wielding guns and sex to get
what they wanted. It endeavored to expose the utter corruption of both
the legal system and the newspaper industry—how lawyers and reporters were interested not in justice or truth but in making themselves look
good. The average American's desperation for public attention, Maurine
believed, only egged on such unscrupulous professionals. "Nobody but
a newspaper worker knows to what extent not only indecent but decent
people will sometimes go to 'get publicity,'" noted the *Chicago Herald and
Examiner*'s Ashton Stevens.

This obsession for publicity was something new in society—some pun-
dits believed it to be the scourge of the twentieth century. Maurine recognized that it made the newspapers, just as much as the people they
covered, what they were—and she zeroed in on it. "Here you're gettin'
somethin' money can't buy: front-page advertisin'," a gruff reporter named
Jake, recognizing the circulation potential of such a beautiful girl gunner,
tells Roxie after her arrest. "Why, a three-line want ad would cost you two
eighty-five, and you'll get line after line, column after column, for nothin'."
Jake continues:

> Who knows you now? Nobody. But this time tomorrow your face will
> be known from coast to coast. Who cares today whether you live or die?
> But tomorrow they'll be crazy to know your breakfast food and how did
> yuh rest last night. They'll fight to see you, come by the hundred just for
> a glimpse of your house—Remember Wanda Stopa? Well, we had twenty
> thousand at her funeral.

One of Baker's lectures about comedy had a particular resonance for
Maurine as she worked. The Victorian writer George Meredith wrote that
classical comedy "proposes the correcting of pretentiousness, of inflation,

of dullness, and of the vestiges of rawness and grossness yet to be found among us. [Comedy] is the ultimate civilizer, the polisher." Expanding on Meredith's writing, Baker added farce to the discussion, pointing out that classical comedy "presents us with the imperfections of human nature. Farce entertains us with what is monstrous." Classical comedy, Baker insisted, made human imperfections funny for "those who can judge." Farce, on the other hand, was "intended for those who can't judge."

Here was where Maurine made a leap, where she moved beyond her mentor. She chose not to make a distinction. From her experiences as a reporter in Chicago, she'd determined that human imperfections, individual and collective, had become monstrous. Real life had become farce. Her play would not only make no distinction between traditional comedy and farce, it also would make no distinction between comedy and tragedy. They were all one and the same in a superficial modern world of mass communication and overpopulated, spirit-crushing cities, a world that produced anonymous men and women seized by insecurity and a frantic desire for money, status, and attention.

In jail while awaiting trial, Roxie spends her time pasting news clippings into a scrapbook, happy to be noticed and unconcerned that it's because she killed a man. When the newspapers begin to show interest in another murderess, she feigns pregnancy to grab back the headlines. Roxie is so beautiful, and so ruthless in promoting herself, that it simply doesn't matter that she has committed murder. "Oh, I feel so sorry for her when I think of all she must have gone through to be driven to a step like that," the reporter Mary Sunshine says to Roxie's lawyer, Billy Flynn. "But she has everyone's sympathy—that will help her in this awful hour." The sob sister pulls a handful of telegrams and letters about Roxie out of her bag to show the counselor. "We're paying ten dollars a day for the best letter, you know, and some of these are just too lovely."

All of Baker's students were required to read their drafts in class and were subjected to criticism from the room. The students often tried to prove their powers of insight, and impress their professor, by throwing haymakers at each other's work. But Maurine, reddening in embarrassment, her voice tiny, left everyone gasping in delight and amazement when she read. Her Roxie was the moron triumphant, counting on her fellow morons—on the newspaper staffs, on the jury, everywhere in this twisted new America—to save her. The play was shocking—and it was hilarious. Baker, in particular, was thrilled with the result. He believed Maurine had produced that most rare thing in art: something original. Baker taught classical Greek comedy as the baseline, but he pointed out that "when we have what might be called vernacular comedy as distinguished from classical comedy, when all the conditions of our comedy are freer and more spontaneous than that of the classical comedy, it is absurd that we should apply the definitions and test of Aristotle to our comedy and get any really valuable results."

Maurine Watkins, he believed, had found a true American style.

☙❧

Maurine finished the play by the end of the term. Now titled *Chicago,* it didn't get to be the first production of Yale's new drama department, as she probably had hoped, but this didn't mean she was being slighted. Nearly every year, Baker selected a play from the workshop and helped place it with professional producers. For 1926, he chose *Chicago.* Baker introduced Maurine to New York agents, and from there momentum gathered swiftly. Sam H. Harris, George M. Cohan's former partner, snapped up the play. In October, the *New Yorker* magazine, in a fawning, half-joking "Talk of the Town" item, declared that Harris had accepted Maurine's play about a "gaudy murder trial," even though there was a problem with it: the title. "Mr. Harris' admiration for the play is warm but, after all, he has business interests in Chicago and would like to be able to drop out there from time to time without adding to the familiar depression of such a pilgrimage the disquieting prospect of being obliged to join our feathered friends." The best solution, the magazine surmised, was a change of title, from *Chicago* back to *The Brave Little Woman.* But Harris's reception in the Second City clearly didn't concern the producer as much as the *New Yorker* thought it might. Harris had more than a dozen projects in the works during the summer and fall of 1926, including a Marx Brothers tour of their Broadway hit *The Cocoanuts.* Despite such a full plate, he aggressively moved *Chicago* forward, its new title intact. Early in the fall, George Abbott signed on as director, with a planned New York opening by the end of the year. Rising stage ingenue Francine Larrimore was cast as Roxie.*

It was a big leap from Baker's classroom straight to Broadway, arguably the highest level of commercial theater in the English-speaking world and unquestionably far more prestigious than the movies, which were still silent. But Maurine believed *Chicago* deserved it. She was proud of what she'd written. She had put down on the page, in a great cathartic explosion, all of her frustrations as a police reporter—"the result," she said, "of watching justice and publicity in their relation to crime." She knew the play was likely to be controversial. There was nothing uplifting about *Chicago*, though she believed it was deeply moral. "It seems to me that the purpose and treatment of a subject should determine the morality rather than just the choice of your theme," she later said, in defense of her work.

For his part, Baker worried that Maurine would come under pressure from people who didn't fully understand what she was trying to accomplish with the play. He warned her to hold tight to her principles as the director worked with his cast to find the right tone and timing for *Chicago*, fearing Abbott or Harris might undercut its purpose to "force as many laughs as possible." Baker believed Maurine had written more than merely a good comedy. "You wrote something that might have an effect on the conditions you ridicule," he told his student. "It may well be turned into something which will have no such effect." Baker's fears were strong enough that, even after advising her, he couldn't leave it to Maurine to defend the work's integrity. Knowing that his reputation depended on his students' success, he strongly supported the play publicly. "It is a comedy, intensely satirical, treating the sentimentalization of the criminal in this country by the public, newspapers, lawyers, and even courts," he wrote to the Theatre Guild just before *Chicago* opened. He added: "Whatever happens to the play, I know it was written with honest intent and with the knowledge of facts existing for Chicago, though not perhaps for other cities to the same extent."

---

*Jeanne Eagels, a bigger star than Larrimore, was originally cast as Roxie, but the troubled actress abruptly left the show after rehearsals began.

Baker had good reason to be concerned about *Chicago*'s prospects. One prominent playgoer at its pre-Broadway run in New Haven, John Archer of the Yale Divinity School, called *Chicago* "entirely too vile for public performance." He added: "Why flaunt that sort of life within the realm of drama? Why not leave the lid on the sewer and keep the stench from the nostrils of our Eastern public?"

Though just an unknown former reporter and fledgling playwright, Maurine wasn't about to let the attack go unchallenged. That was her life up there on stage. "I quite agree with Professor Archer that the situation in the city of Chicago is deplorable," she responded in the *New Haven Register*. "What surprises me is that he of all people, a divinity professor, should condemn the action of calling attention to evil. Does he suppose the way to combat evil is to ignore it? I wonder whether, in his sermons, Professor Archer pretends that the world is a rose garden, and scrupulously avoids the unpleasant side of things. More than likely he speaks of evil conditions himself."

That was what Maurine had been doing as a reporter in Chicago—combating evil. She wanted people to know that. If she now helped bring about a wider understanding of that evil, even if it had to be turned into rank comedy to do so, that was for the good. The sharp response shut down the minor controversy, but Maurine recognized that more of the same surely waited in the big city. Like Archer in New Haven, theater censors were on the march in New York, for the Jazz Age had belatedly arrived on the city's stages in 1926, throwing all sorts of licentious shocks at audiences. "Liquor runs deep down the course of this season's theatre in New York," wrote Gilbert W. Gabriel in *Vanity Fair*. "Scarcely a play is staged without the bravado of some one or two scenes of secret and melancholy drinking." On top of that, thanks to Mae West's career revival as playwright and performer, there was sex. Manhattan's district attorney, goaded by the influential New York Society for the Suppression of Vice, empowered a "play jury" to attend plays and vote on their moral stature.

The jury quickly attacked West's off-Broadway play, *SEX*, along with two prominent Broadway shows, *The Captive* and *The Virgin Man*, for their "tendency to corrupt the morals of youth." Police raided all three productions on the same night and dragged the casts off to jail. A police sergeant, Patrick Keneally, had been sent out to the plays beforehand to make notes on their transgressions. When *SEX* went to trial, in February 1927, Keneally focused on West's "kootchie" dance in the show, testifying in a room full of sucked-in breath that "Miss West moved her navel up and down and from right to left." The jury convicted West and her producers and sentenced them to ten days in jail, along with a $500 fine each. Both the author and producer of *The Virgin Man*, about an undergraduate undone by a bevy of "seductresses," received similar fines and jail sentences.

Into this tense, nervous atmosphere arrived *Chicago*, which opened at the Music Box Theatre on December 30, 1926. The play had drinking, *and* it had sex. If you weren't of a mood to recognize it as satire—and members of the New York Society for the Suppression of Vice tended to take all art literally—you saw only the most horrific debauchery: remorseless murderers celebrating their bloody acts and being celebrated for them. At one point in the play, the jailed Roxie, surrounded by male reporters but without the slightest shame, decides to remove her garters so she can auction them off to her fans. "Here, take these, too!" Roxie tells Jake as she "gives herself a reflective wriggle" and then pops the elastic band free.

JAKE [*waves them aloft*]: Bravo! 'You've read about 'em, boys, here they are: what am I offered for the Famous Turquoise Garter?' [*Breaks off in alarm as she seems bent on further disapparelment.*] Stop! This is *not* strip poker!

ROXIE [*straightens with dignity*]: I was only *rollin'* my stockin's. [*They drop to her ankles and* JAKE *retreats.*]

Not even Mae West's play was so depraved and cynical as this daring new production. The New York correspondent for the *Chicago Tribune*, writing on opening night, noted that *Chicago* arrived from its out-of-town tryout with a reputation "as a shocker unfit for human consumption and all Broadway attempted to get into the Music Box where Sam H. Harris staged it." After seeing it, however, the local critics sought to mitigate any shocks caused to the citizenry. Recognizing an original and ambitious production rather than a moral hazard, they immediately embraced the play, perhaps hoping to preempt the censors.* "My hat is off to the genius of the young Miss Maurine Watkins, who has contributed to the American theater the most profound and powerful satire it has ever known," wrote novelist and critic Rupert Hughes. "Best of all, [*Chicago*] is a satire by a woman on the folly of men in their false homage to woman, their silly efforts to protect her while she dupes them." The play was more than a thumping entertainment, he continued. It sought to "put an end to the ghastly business of railroading pretty women safely through murder trials by making fools of the solemn jurymen."

Hughes's review was representative of the norm. In the *New York Times*, Brooks Atkinson warned off potential moralist outrage, insisting that "*Chicago* is not a melodrama, as the prologue indicates, but a satirical comedy on the administration of justice through the fetid channels of newspaper publicity—of photographers, 'sob sisters,' feature stunts, standardized prevarication and generalized vulgarity."

Jump-started by the critical reaction, *Chicago* began to consistently play to packed houses. Maurine Watkins had caught the Zeitgeist, and not just in New York. Plans for a tour were undertaken, first to the title city itself and then to Los Angeles. The bloodletting in Chicago, the heart of Prohibition-driven gangsterism, had become a national topic, and thanks to Maurine, making fun of Murder City was now de rigueur. Two months after the play opened, humorist Will Rogers picked up on the subject, joking in a newspaper piece that Detroit's leaders had come to him and complained, "What's the use of having all these robberies and killings [in our city]? No one ever reads about them. Chicago seems to be the only place most people think that can put on a murder." Rogers's answer to Detroit's problem: Go for quality, not quantity. "It's best not to have a woman do the murdering," he wrote. "A case like that holds for a while, but when it comes to a trial it loses interest, for the people want to see a case where there is some chance of conviction."

---

*The raves may have helped. There's no record of the play jury offering comment on *Chicago*.

❧❧❧

With *Chicago*'s unexpected box-office success, Maurine began fielding interview requests. The *New York Times,* in profiling the new playwright three days after the opening, gave credit to George Pierce Baker and joked that Maurine's final grade under the well-known professor "will be determined by the manner in which the play is produced. And [Baker] has promised that what the Chicago Chamber of Commerce has to say won't count."

The profile praised Maurine's talent and manners, but a more telling passage came in the brief description of her journalism career. The paper stated that it was "the experience of reporting the Leopold-Loeb case that supplied her with much of the material for *Chicago.*" A *New York World* feature on Maurine later in the month also dwelled on Leopold and Loeb, quoting her at length on how she decided what to ask the thrill killers when she had the opportunity and what she thought of the "crime of the century" spectacle.

That Maurine would expound freely on Nathan Leopold and Dick Loeb is not surprising: It made sense for an unproven playwright writing about the newspaper world to buttress her qualifications by highlighting her role in such a famous story. But in both the *Times* and the *World* interviews, she failed to mention that her play was actually based on a different trial. In fact, almost none of the numerous feature stories and reviews about *Chicago* in the New York press mentioned Beulah Annan. By this time, more than two years after the fact, Beulah and her trial had been forgotten outside the Second City. In contrast, articles about the play frequently referenced the infamous Leopold and Loeb.

In keeping the true inspiration for *Chicago* quiet, Maurine may have been worried that she'd hewed too closely to real events to be worthy of the acclaim she was receiving for writing a brilliantly original play. After all, some snippets of dialogue in *Chicago* came straight out of William Scott Stewart's and W. W. O'Brien's mouths during Beulah's trial. Key plot points—such as Roxie's pregnancy announcement—were also lifted directly from real events. Some of Maurine's stage directions and scene descriptions were taken nearly word for word from her *Tribune* articles. The details of Roxie's shooting of her boyfriend tracked exactly with the real thing, including the blaring jazz music on the phonograph and the children playing outside the window. Physical descriptions of Roxie also borrowed from Maurine's *Tribune* descriptions of Beulah.

Moreover, Beulah wasn't the only real-life murderess to make it onto the stage in *Chicago*. Belva Gaertner, in the form of the relatively minor character of Velma, was represented down to the smallest details, including Belva's claim to have been so drunk that she didn't remember anything about her boyfriend's murder. Velma is described as being in her "late thirties, with smooth sallowed features, large dreamy eyes, and full lips that have a dipsomaniacal droop." Velma, like Belva, is a wealthy society lady who pays an Italian immigrant prisoner to make her bed every morning. Sabella Nitti, Kitty Malm, and Elizabeth Unkafer also got lifted from the newspaper and dropped down into the play intact.

Maurine even offered herself up, tangentially, as "the woman from the *Ledger*" who doesn't buy into the sham public persona Roxie puts on for the sob sisters. "I won't see her," Roxie says petulantly, when Billy Flynn tells her the reporter is coming to the jail for an interview. Flynn replies, "You've talked so much, you can't stop now. If you tell enough lies they're bound to forget a few!"

All of these similarities, now that the play was actually up and running, appear to have made Maurine a bit nervous. The play was advertised as a satire based on broadly identifiable conditions in the country; she wasn't supposed to be retrying an old case on the stage. The furthest she went in acknowledging the extent of her inspiration was to write, in a letter to the editor in the *New York World*, that she "was portraying conditions as I actually found [them] during my newspaper work. For while the play may sound like burlesque or travesty in New York, it would pass for realism in its home town." Again, she did not mention Beulah Annan.

Of course, that was Maurine Watkins in sophisticated New York. When *Chicago* arrived in Chicago in the fall of 1927, after running for 172 performances on Broadway and being sold to Hollywood, there would be no ducking the truth. There was no reason to do so.

20

The Most Monotonous City on Earth

On Sunday morning, October 9, 1927, the Twentieth Century Limited chugged slowly through Gary, Indiana. Heavy clouds pulled the sky down to the rooftops like a cap. The train swung north into Chicago's sprawling industrial suburbs, open fields giving way to "crooked, ill-paved streets lined with bleak houses and thick with the murk of factory vapors." For mile after mile, passengers watched one ramshackle structure worse than the last roll past, swimming in crashing waves of bilious smoke. Men and women pressed their noses to the windows. A sheltered, properly raised young woman, a woman like Maurine Watkins had once been, could be forgiven for looking out the window of her compartment and thinking some dreadful natural disaster had occurred. The traveler coming into Chicago for the first time saw a ghastly, dirty farce of a city. It was "the most monotonous city on earth," proclaimed New York businessman Edward Hungerford on his initial trip. "Chicago, with the most wretched approaches on her main lines of travel of any great city of the world."

To Maurine, of course, it looked like home. Once the train settled into LaSalle Street station, she stepped onto a red carpet that had been laid out for the passengers and walked through the station. Out at the taxi stand, a driver assumed control of her baggage and drove her to the Drake Hotel, where she registered and went up to her room. Maurine had looked forward to her return to the city for weeks. *Chicago*'s press agent planned to send newspaper photographers over to the station to meet her, but Maurine didn't want to show up her old colleagues who hadn't left town and become famous. She conveniently forgot to tell the publicity man when she was coming. Just to be safe, she stayed shut up in her room all day, as if she didn't know a soul in the city or where to go.

When Maurine finally stepped from the Drake that evening, small, beautifully dressed, and alone, she climbed into a taxi and directed it to the Harris Theater, where she paid the driver and walked quickly up to the box office. It thrilled her to be going to the theater, her favorite pastime, and especially to be going to this play in particular, her own hit comedy. But she hadn't planned ahead. The best available seat at this late hour, the ticket seller told her, was in the sixteenth row. Maurine smiled and told him that the sixteenth row was perfect; she was "glad it was not in the fifth or sixth row." Mystified by the response—it certainly took all kinds to fill a theater—the man completed the transaction without further comment and gazed over her shoulder to the next patron. Maurine stepped toward the doors, happy to be unrecognized, something that hadn't been possible for Belva Gaertner or W. W. O'Brien when they attended the play two weeks before.

It took all of ten seconds from the opening curtain for Francine Larrimore to have the packed house choking with laughter. Maurine laughed too. Oh, Francie was so wonderful! Maurine could enjoy the beautiful, gangly girl's performance night after night. Watching Larrimore bound about the stage, Maurine was convinced anew that the actress had captured the character perfectly: "a hint of a Raphael angel—with a touch of Medusa." You'd never know she was such a darling girl offstage.

"Why did you kill him?" a copper asked Larrimore.

The actress, an alley cat all of a sudden, screeched: "It's a lie! I didn't! Damn you, let go!" She chomped down on the policeman's wrist with sharp incisors, and he yelped and flung her off.

"So it was you," said the sergeant, a bit slow on the uptake.

"Yes, it was me! I shot him and I'm damned glad I did! I'd do it again—"

She didn't get to finish her confession—she never did. A reporter cut her off: "Once is enough, dearie!"

The audience erupted at the line, the whole theater reverberating with tittering echoes, as Francine Larrimore slowly started to fall apart.

"Oh, God . . . God . . . Don't let 'em hang me—don't . . . Why, I'd . . . *die!*"

The elegantly dressed men and women around Maurine crashed into hysterics yet again. They pounded on their armrests, cackled in delight. Maurine was delighted with the line as well. The success of the play gratified her. And yet when the second of the play's three acts closed, she apparently had had enough. She got to her feet and headed for the door. Eddie Kitt, the manager, smiled at her approach, grinning as any man instinctively did at the advance of a pretty young woman. Maurine asked him to escort her backstage. Kitt paused—this was an unusual request in the middle of a play—but then the young lady's smile, the dancing eyes, the loose, pulled-back hair, all clicked together in his brainpan, and he did as he was asked.

When the curtain rose for the third act, Maurine Watkins still was not in her seat—she was walking quietly, purposefully, across the stage, in full view of the audience. She sat next to the actress playing Mary Sunshine, her perfect doll's cheeks bulbous and reflecting light, blue eyes surveying the scene. Mr. Tilden, the stage manager, leaned forward from the wings to see what was happening.

Francine Larrimore glared at Maurine, but it was a look of surprise, momentary surprise. She wasn't really upset.

"What kind of look?" the lawyer asked. "Describe it to the jury."

Larrimore's eyes swung from Maurine to her questioner. "I can't describe it," she said. "But a terrible look—angry—wild—"

"Were you afraid? Did you think he meant to kill you?"

"Oh, yes, sir! I knew if he once reached the gun . . ."

"It was his life then or yours," the man said, his voice rising just enough to make everyone realize he was saying something important now.

"Yes, sir," said Roxie Hart, finally lifting her wavering eyes to meet his. She took a deep breath, her cheeks cherry-red all at once, then: "He was coming right toward me, with that awful look—that wild look . . . and I closed my eyes . . . and . . . *shot!*"

∞∞∞

Maurine loved being a part of the production. She'd been a reliable background player for months on Broadway, putting aside new writing assignments each evening to head over to the theater. She even understudied a couple of the minor roles. She couldn't help but want to be involved in all the fun. She'd had plenty of laughs during the real events on which the play was based, just like some of the other faces in the audience here in Chicago. She hadn't realized how much she missed the city and her former life until the play started. New York was surprisingly tame: Its murder rate was more than 50 percent lower than the Second City's. At one point, Maurine took a trip to supposedly wild Baltimore but found none of that old Chicago feeling, to her disappointment: "Nary a cherub with happy days in her arms or revolver in hand, and I strolled particularly through ladies' retiring quarters," she wrote to her friend Alexander Woollcott, the Broadway drama critic. But now she could have as much of her late police reporter's life as she wanted—at least her fantasy version of it. When she arrived in Chicago, the silent-movie adaptation of her play was shooting across town under the guidance of the legendary Cecil B. DeMille, its producer. It was being made under great secrecy, and everyone was talking about what they didn't know—everyone except Maurine, who never gossiped. Francine Larrimore was committed to the stage show, so the former Mack Sennett bathing beauty Phyllis Haver, best known as the vampire in Emil Jannings's *The Way of All Flesh*, took the lead for Mr. DeMille. Maurine didn't know what to think about that. The whole endeavor was challenging, turning such a talky play into a silent film. Haver would admit that herself, saying: "It is bad enough to get in tune with any character but when one jumps up and down the octave whamming out this discord and that, the task is nerve wracking."

Having the movie shooting in town was exciting, but the actors and crew mostly kept to themselves during production, and Maurine didn't impose herself on them. The play, on the other hand, was here for everyone, right now. And everyone seemed to love it, especially the critics. "Miss Watkins is uncannily keen, and *Chicago* is one of the brilliant satirical plays of the times," wrote C. J. Bulliet in the *Evening Post*. The *Tribune* said the play "is as rich a reason for laughter as has in many years been proffered to those of us who think we are civilized, educated, adult, responsive, transilient [*sic*], literate, something more than half-witted, what used to be called 'aware,' and what is now miscalled 'sophisticated.'" Whether or not Maurine needed to fear being found out in New York, Chicagoans felt flattered that real events in their city had made it to the Broadway stage. The *American* observed that "Good-natured Chicago laughed loudly and gossiped incessantly between the three acts at the clever burlesque on the stage, [at] county and city and bar and newspapers and police—at the hectic jazz times which could make possible an evening of entertainment, with women swearing like troopers, in this 'what price bullets' production."*

Praise for Francine Larrimore, as Roxie, was also unanimous. The *Daily News* enthused that the actress's performance was "faultless," adding that her "moods and tantrums, her wiles and witchery are superb." The *Herald and Examiner* insisted that Larrimore was "the solar plexus of this shrill satire. She gives herself to it body, nerve and adenoid. She is comical with a passion that sometimes wrings tears—yours as well as her own." When the play opened, Chicago was preparing to host the heavily anticipated heavyweight championship rematch between Jack Dempsey and the man who took his title the year before, Gene Tunney. The *Herald and Examiner*'s critic remarked, "Should Dempsey next Thursday night attack Tunney, or Tunney attack Dempsey, as Miss Larrimore tackles Roxie, it will be over in the first act."

Beulah Annan was not available to see Larrimore's knockout interpretation of her, but her lawyer, W. W. O'Brien, and Belva Gaertner showed up for the premiere. "Gee, this play's sure got our number, ain't it," Belva offered with a smile. "Sure, that's me," she added when a *Herald and Examiner* reporter asked her about the character of Velma. She also said, generously, "Roxie Hart's supposed to be Beulah Annan. She was the most

---

Chicago was indeed filled with awful swearing, which embarrassed Maurine. As she was the author, she was now hard-pressed to claim no acquaintance with such language. She tried, though: A rumor floated around that she had left blank spaces in the script where the swear words were supposed to go, to be filled in by the director and actors.

beautiful woman ever accused of murder." O'Brien, recognizing his own words in the script, called *Chicago* "the finest piece of stage satire ever written by an American."

Maurine's old compatriot, Genevieve Forbes, also took in the show. She was just as fascinated as Maurine with the reimagining of their newspaper lives. The production recalled gayer journalistic times in Chicago, "of those local ladies who tarried on the fourth floor of the building at Dearborn Street and Austin Avenue long enough to get themselves into a play." Like Maurine, she had become nostalgic for the old days. Crime in the city was all gangsters now—bootleggers with tommy guns and cold hearts. They didn't shoot for love, like the women she and Maurine had written about. A few days after Maurine took in the play, Forbes decided to remind any Chicagoan who might have forgotten about the city's murderesses of yore. In the *Tribune*, she wrote an open letter to theater management requesting "a block of seats, that I may take as my guests the women whom Maurine interviewed that May day now more than two years ago."

"Beulah Annan ought to have the aisle-seat," she continued. "For it was she—too beautiful to work in a laundry, but a sufficiently good shot to get her man with one bullet in the back—who is the Roxie of the piece. . . . Beulah went free: else, there might have been no play." Forbes knew the real Roxie still had star power. It had been incorrectly "whispered about" (principally by the *American*) that Beulah would attend the show on opening night, leading theatergoers to scan the crowd at every opportunity. But Forbes hoped she would make an appearance now, seeing as the reporter was issuing a formal invitation.

The next best seat, Forbes insisted, "ought to go to Belva Gaertner, Cook County's most stylish murderess." She wrote that Belva, remarried to the millionaire William Gaertner, was strikingly portrayed in *Chicago*. "One thing, however, is all wrong with her stage descendant. The Velma of the play goes before the jury in a vivid green gown; and everybody knows that Belva's favorite color was café-au-lait. A trivial point, but irksome, perhaps, to Belva."

Then there was the character of Moonshine Maggie. She was "a tangent form of Sabella Nitti, the farm-lady who achieved fame as instant as

Byron's when she was heralded as the first woman in the county to receive the death sentence. It was for the murder of her husband. But she tarried in jail long enough to learn the value of a hot bath, a manicure and a smart hair-do. . . . *She'd* love the theater!"

Last but far from least was the murderess Forbes covered more closely than any other. The character "Go-to-Hell Kitty," she wrote, "is Kitty Malm, who packed a gat where most girls harbor their love-letters. She's a life-timer at Joliet; but, if the Harris theater management throws in an extra ticket for a guard, I'll try to get permission for Kitty to come along."

The open letter was all in fun, of course, so there was another name that hung over the production that Forbes did not mention: Wanda Stopa. There was simply nothing amusing about her story, even with Francine Larrimore up on stage. And besides, Wanda had even less opportunity to attend the show than Kitty Malm.

⚜

Despite the raves Francine Larrimore received as Roxie Hart, Maurine had proved to be the biggest star to come out of the production. Reporters and critics had a difficult time believing she could be the writer of such a hard-edged, hard-hearted satire. (She heightened this sense of implausibility by saying she was twenty-six years old, though she was now thirty.) "She is blonde, comely, chic, and considerably under thirty—a pleasant way to be," the *New Yorker* declared in October 1926 when announcing the play. After *Chicago* opened, the magazine weighed in again, noting that the "popular opinion is that she is one of the prettiest unmarried girls who ever wrote a successful Broadway play."

The *New Yorker*'s theater writer was hardly alone in his crush. Every-body loved Maurine Watkins, and it was easy to understand why. That other popular stage authoress of the moment, Mae West, was a threat—her stated goal was proving the equality of the sexes. Not so *Chicago*'s scribe. She had sweet, old-fashioned manners, and her satire showed not how accomplished unfettered women could be, but how wicked. *Vanity Fair* thrilled to this "seraphic young person from the South," and the *New York World* marveled at her "distinctly feminine manner." The *New York*

Times's theater correspondent, on meeting Maurine, wrote that she was "more easily suspected as the author of poetry such as that penned by Edna St. Vincent Millay, than of a play like *Chicago*."

Now that Maurine had achieved celebrity status, it was inevitable that she would be recruited to be a celebrity commentator on the news of the day, the latest trend in the newspaper business. In January 1927, the *New York World* hired her to liven up the silly and already sensationalized Browning divorce case. Frances Browning was the sixteen-year-old wife of Edward W. Browning, a fifty-two-year-old real-estate millionaire. He called her Peaches. She called him Daddy. Not long after a series of lovey-dovey public appearances by the newlyweds, Peaches ran out on Daddy and sought a divorce. She insisted that her husband had forced her to walk around their residence naked and that he'd thrown phone books at her and burned her with acid.

The shocking charges notwithstanding, Daddy Browning had little to worry about from the court of public opinion. A swarming crowd gave him an ovation when he arrived at the courthouse in suburban White Plains, where the case was to be decided. Why not? He dressed beautifully, he had exquisite manners, and his name appeared in the New York papers a lot. Just a few years before, that wouldn't have been enough to engender the public's admiration, but this was now the age of moving pictures and public relations. People greeted Browning on the street like a war hero. Besides, his estranged wife didn't meet the public standard.

"She's too fat," a girl outside court announced loudly as Peaches made for a taxi on the case's first day.

"I don't call her pretty," agreed a fellow court-watcher.

"*Gold* digger," hissed still another spectator.

Witnessing all of this, Maurine saw an excellent opportunity to bring an even higher profile to *Chicago*, which was still in the first month of its New York run. Her coverage of the divorce would be less about the Brownings than about Maurine herself and her play's themes.

The *World* had no problem with this angle. An editor's note pointed out that "Miss Watkins," having revealed the *real* Chicago on the Broadway stage, was now "investigating scientifically the road to fame in our own fair city." As expected, that investigation's results amused the playwright-reporter. "Chicago was never like this," she wrote, leaning hard on her new public persona as a cynical Midwestern wisecracker in the Big Apple. "The Brownings would have been dismissed with a couple of 'moron' headlines; the whole Gold Coast could wash its linen on the Lake Shore without moving journalistically from that cemetery known as the Social Column. In Chicago you must shoot, not sue, your way to glory. Her front pages drip with blood, whereas New York's are smeared with dirt."

This made for an entertaining premise, and allowed Maurine to tout her play to a wide audience, but it obviously wasn't true. New York's papers could bathe happily in blood, and often did. Maurine helped prove this just three months after the Browning pas de deux, when another New York paper, this time the *Telegram,* hired her for another trial. Ruth Snyder, a onetime stenographer, and her corset-salesman boyfriend, Henry Judd Gray, were charged with murdering Snyder's husband so they could collect on an insurance policy and run off together. Reporters from every newspaper in the tristate area—and many more throughout the country—flooded the courthouse in Long Island City for this latest "crime of the century." Among those who signed up to cover the trial were novelist Fannie Hurst, celebrity evangelist Aimee Semple McPherson, actress and socialite Peggy Joyce Hopkins, even an ex-wife of Rudolph Valentino. Maurine would share space in the *Telegram* with popular philosopher Will Durant.

The *Telegram* hoped that Maurine's good looks and satiric charms would lure readers to imagine a "palship" with the plucky young playwright-reporter, causing them to pick the *Telegram* over its many newsstand competitors. With an alluring inset photograph accompanying each report—Maurine looking gorgeous in a practical, no-frills way, her hair pulled back and her face freshly scrubbed—she was the all-American girl commenting on the all-American sport. There was, however, a problem. Unlike the cases of Belva and Beulah, every aspect of this story was revolting. The nature of the crime—Snyder's husband was viciously garroted, after numerous previous attempts on the man's life—stood athwart all of the defense's efforts to make Ruth Snyder and Judd Gray sympathetic.

Time magazine pointed out that the "details, unusually gruesome, included poisoned whiskey, picture wire, binding, gagging, taking turns at skull-smashing with a window-weight, and $104,000 in life insurance."

From the start, Maurine hit the wrong note. "Strike up the band, for the show starts today!" she declared on April 18, under a byline that read "Maurine Watkins, Author of 'Chicago.'" As the trial careened toward a verdict, she mocked the two defendants for blaming their actions on the magnetic influence of the other:

Scene reconstructed from Snyder-Gray testimony:

"Oh, Mumsie, you're terrible to want to kill your husband! But I'll buy the chloroform for you—and what about a little sash-weight?"

"O Lover Boy, you mustn't come back to kill my husband! But here's the sash-weight, and I'll leave a couple of doors open and you'll find a bottle of whiskey up in Mamma's room."

"Oh Mumsie, I can't do it! Have you got the cotton waste and picture wire?"

O Judd, you really mustn't do it! Have another drink and the revolver's there on the piano."

Maurine undoubtedly recognized that Snyder, with her wax-figure countenance, stout figure, and carefully planned viciousness, was no Beulah Annan. She enjoyed tweaking Snyder, but mostly she gave the trial and its defendants short shrift, focusing instead on what was now her pet theme: the excesses of the mass media. More than a hundred seats in the courthouse had been "ticketed for the press," she pointed out. And that was just for starters. A "special room" had been given over to stenographers, another for a wire room, and an elevator was reserved for the use of messenger boys, for "what tragedy if the color of Ruth Snyder's hose or Henry Gray's breakfast menu should miss the early edition of the *Houston Press* or the *Rocky Mountain News*!" Maurine looked around at her fellow reporters, all doing the same job she was, and acted offended. "For a few days, at least, perhaps for a few weeks, the stenographer who married her boss will get attention such as Queen Marie [of Romania] enjoyed, and the corset salesman of East Orange will take his place with the Prince of Wales."*

In the end, the assignment brought Maurine nothing but a paycheck she no longer needed. The public greedily consumed coverage of the trial but never warmed to the story or its correspondents. Both Snyder and Gray, with a sigh of relief from millions of newspaper readers, were convicted. In January 1928, they were put to death in the electric chair.

శిశిశ

With Maurine's profile higher in the winter and spring of 1927 than many Broadway leading ladies, newspaper editors weren't the only ones seeking out her services. Every theater producer in New York wanted her on his next project.

The first assignment Maurine accepted was an adaptation of Samuel Hopkins Adams's novel *Revelry*, a fictional look at corruption in the Harding administration. Maurine diligently set to work, but with a busy schedule that included celebrity journalism and occasionally appearing as an extra in *Chicago*, her new star status quickly began to weigh on her. Reconnecting with the judgmental George Pierce Baker, who thought she had overcommitted herself, didn't help her anxiety. "Feel depressed," she wrote to Alexander Woollcott in longhand. "Just returned from Yale—first attendance since . . . *it* happened. Dear Teacher thinks I'm close by the precipice of utter ruin and that *Revelry* will push me completely over."

Baker, it turned out, wasn't far wrong. Thanks to *Chicago*, Maurine suddenly had become the go-to writer for hard-hitting, wisecracking satire that tested the bounds of legal decency. She'd barely gotten started on *Revelry*, a project certain to provoke outrage in some circles, when she accepted another hot-button assignment—adapting Herbert Asbury's scandalous *American Mercury* magazine article "Hatrack," the story of a "rebuffed churchgoer and sought-after prostitute" in the small Missouri town where Asbury grew up. "Our town harlot in Farmington," wrote Asbury, "was a scrawny creature called variously Fanny Fewclothes and Hatrack, but

*On the first day of the trial, Maurine highlighted her own celebrity status by taking *Chicago* star Francine Larrimore with her to the Long Island City courthouse to watch the proceedings.

usually the latter in deference to her figure." During the workweek, Fanny was a "competent drudge" on the domestic staff of one of the town's proudest families, but on Sundays she unself-consciously sold her body, taking her clients to lie down on the cool slabs in the town's Masonic and Catholic cemeteries. Upon publication in the *American Mercury*, the piece was deemed indecent and barred from being sent through the U.S. mail.

These were two assignments, like the Snyder-Gray trial, for which Maurine was constitutionally unsuited. *Chicago* was all flash and bang, and its subject matter—sensation journalism and celebrity-lust—was ideal for such eyes-wide-open comic treatment. "Any play which can batter away with unrelenting ridicule for three whole acts—and without a single sop to the sentimentalists—deserves a bonus of unabashed hurrahs," *Vanity Fair* wrote of *Chicago*. That it did, but *Chicago* was also sui generis. A recently deceased president and a sad small-town prostitute did not so easily lend themselves to Maurine's broad-stroke, incriminatory humor. Adaptations are always tricky, and for these in particular, Maurine needed a rapier, not the cannon that was her comic weapon of choice.

Revelry, her much-anticipated follow-up to *Chicago*, in fact proved fated for disaster before it even reached New York. In Philadelphia, the play was withdrawn shortly after it opened in September when a judge denounced it as "false, base and indecent, and slanderous of the dead." In dealing with a fictional version of the late president, Maurine had been asked to walk a fine line in writing the adaptation, and she had failed. The company that owned the Philadelphia playhouse in which the play was booked announced, "While the play had been rendered unobjectionable in other respects by the censors, the Stanley company considered the theme so essentially unpatriotic that any further revision would be useless."

That was not the official death of the production, but it might as well have been. When the New York critics got a look at it, the play hung in a dispiriting critical purgatory, garnering neither applause nor outright attack. "The play that Miss Watkins fashioned is, if somewhat disappointing, not worthless," wrote Edmund Wilson in the *New Republic*. "Its tone carries a certain sarcastic gravity; Miss Watkins has restrained, in the case of these national themes, her gay brutality, and has enjoyed herself less with naughty exposures." George Jean Nathan, in the *American Mercury*, added that "there is so much profanity and cussing that along toward ten o'clock one begins to suspect the author of concealing her inability to key up dramatic intensity in loud invocations of the Saviour and allusions to kennel genealogy." The play closed after only a month on Broadway.

With *Revelry*'s embarrassing reception, Maurine began to realize that Baker had been right: She had overextended herself and, perhaps as a result, not given her best to any of her projects. Just days after the *Revelry* brouhaha in Philadelphia, she wrote to Woollcott, then drama critic at the *New York World:* "Does your department pay damages to guileless souls who believe every word written therein? Basely deceived by a statement that out of five plays bought only one is ever produced, I went around this summer busily and merrily signing contracts for old plays, dramatizations, adaptations, or what have you. Came the fall and dawn; and managers' intentions, if not honorable, proved serious, with the result that I am even more busily if less merrily trying to buy out of various transgressions." She added that she had learned a hard lesson: "Don't sell a play till it's written."

✎✎✎

Two days before Christmas, 1927, the movie version of *Chicago* opened. Maurine now learned another lesson, if she didn't already know it: New York and Chicago truly weren't like the rest of the country. America's middlebrow critics—and the broad public they served outside the urban culture centers—feared the kind of cynical, in-your-face social commentary she served up in her play. Nelson B. Bell, a *Washington Post* film critic, even argued that *Chicago* benefited from being watered down by Hollywood. "Maurine Watkins certainly can harbor no feelings of resentment over the manner in which the producers of films have treated her melodramatic travesty, 'Chicago,' in translating it from the articulate stage to silent drama," he wrote. The chief change that made the film adaptation palatable to Bell was a reimagining of Roxie Hart's husband. In the movie version, Amos Hart has a backbone, and when he realizes Roxie's immoral nature, he "casts her firmly and not gently out of his life." Bell called this a "wholly commendable act" and, not realizing the whole thing was supposed to be funny, added that it "gives the drama an excuse for being."

The movie, produced by Cecil B. DeMille and directed by Frank Urson, opened to a mixed critical reception and good box office sales, but the renewed attention on her work didn't help Maurine's playwriting struggles. Two weeks before the film's release, still reeling from *Revelry*'s failure, she gave up on Herbert Asbury's story. The *Chicago Tribune* reported that "Miss Maurine Watkins has torn up her notes and memoranda, and has asked that she be let out of the contract to dramatize 'Hatrack.'" Baker wrote to Maurine from Yale, trying to buck her up. He told her it was time to write another original work. "I can understand that you may not have had a wholly happy experience in spite of your success in the theatre world, but you cannot afford not to have something worthy of you on the New York stage within a year. Otherwise, you will have to begin again."

Maurine did have an original play in the works, but it didn't appear to be a top priority. She was just trying to hold on, to survive the scrutiny and expectations. The past year had drained her. She understood publicity and sensation, those conjoined twins of the burgeoning tabloid era. Three years before, she'd expertly whipped them up for Beulah Annan and Belva Gaertner. The two alleged murderesses, on trial for their lives, had reveled in the public's attention. But Maurine, with one of the most successful new plays of recent years, could not match their enthusiasm when it was her turn in the spotlight.

The thirty-year-old playwright seemed to understand that the cost of continued success in New York would be high. The country's largest city, like Chicago, roared on at an ever more frenzied pace. No one seemed to have learned anything from the story of Roxie Hart. Mae West was a bigger star than ever now, thanks to her arrest and conviction for *SEX*'s "indecency." ("I expect it will be the making of me," she'd said as she was led to jail.) Newspaper readers, and so newspaper editors, wanted more and bigger shocks. The *New York Daily News* sneaked a camera into Ruth Snyder's execution; the resulting page-one photo of the woman sizzling in the electric chair—with a huge banner headline, "DEAD!"—sold out newspapers in a few hours. Literature followed the crowd: The Snyder story inspired Sophie Treadwell's *Machinal* on stage and James M. Cain's *Double Indemnity* in print. The pressure on writers to produce work that was deemed new and tough and exciting could be intense.

In response, Maurine began to retreat into herself, her old shyness rearing up again. Despite being a popular member of a celebrated group of New York artists and journalists—indeed, right now she was the most acclaimed of the bunch—she sometimes couldn't bear to leave her residence. "I am not coming for a drink today—not even for orange pekoe," she wrote in a typical letter to Woollcott. Maurine treasured her friendship with the garrulous critic, but their correspondence was dominated by her apologetic refusals to attend social events, no matter what carrot he dangled before her. "If it's one of those 'yes-or-no-and-stick-by-your-guns' affairs, it must be 'no,'" she wrote in another letter, "for God alone knows where I'll be next Monday and He won't tell—I've asked Him." She insisted to Woollcott that she was "by nature a recluse."

Maurine now increasingly turned to short story writing, possibly for the greater control it offered, the freedom from the demands of producers looking for the next commercial smash. But her themes and subjects changed little. Her stories frequently involved scheming women on the edge of respectability, women willing to do almost anything to get what they wanted. One, "Butterfly Goes Home," once again fictionalized Beulah Annan's life, following a beautiful cipher through the press's infatuation—"newspapermen swore to the tawny gold of her hair and the delicate pink of her flesh . . ."—and on to a tragic ending. It seemed important to the former crime reporter to provide the correct conclusion for Beulah. Maurine had gone to Chicago to confront sinfulness, after all. God created evil so that man—and woman—could create good, and Maurine struggled with the fear that nothing good had come of her time in the city. Despite her public response to Professor Archer, she realized she hadn't gotten closer to God through her work. Instead she had come to believe that "the feminine temperament can, perhaps, be more primitive than the male," that "the female of the species is really more deadly."

At the end of the 1926–27 stage season, *Chicago* was chosen as one of the best plays of the year by *New York Daily News* drama critic Burns Mantle and included in his prestigious theater annual. Most writers would have sought out more work, and more attention, after such an accolade, but Maurine withdrew further into herself. In a letter to Woollcott, she wrote: "Six months from now, if life keeps on happening, my chief worry will be what the angels are wearing this season. (Optimist!)"

Epilogue

The acquittals of Beulah Annan and Belva Gaertner ignited debate over whether it was time for women to serve on juries in Illinois. One headline, published a week after Belva's acquittal, declared:

A WOMAN JURY TO TRY
WOMEN SLAYERS URGED

CLAIM NOW THAT PRETTY GIRLS GET FREE,
UGLY ONES SENT TO PEN

Women's groups lobbied for women to be included on juries—Sabella Nitti's lawyer, Helen Cirese, was among the most vocal supporters—but the Illinois legislature could not be convinced. Seven years later, in 1931, Illinois voters passed a women jurors law on their own—only to see the state Supreme Court knock it down. Finally, in 1939, fifteen years after Beulah and Belva's murder trials, the legislature passed a law allowing women to serve.

There was at least one immediate and unexpected benefit of the new law. In the four months after women began being admitted to Illinois juries in September of 1939, the percentage of men asking to be excused from serving dropped dramatically. "Chicago men have suddenly become delighted to serve as jurors," wrote the *Tribune*. "And the only reason the jury commissioners and court officials can even suggest is this: The women jurors."

Beulah Annan never made it to Hollywood. Her popularity with the press collapsed almost as soon as she left the Cook County Jail, causing her to retreat from the spotlight. Many reporters had bought into W. W. O'Brien's reimagining of her as a naive innocent, and they didn't appreciate looking like suckers when Beulah walked out on Al right after her acquittal. "It was with a gesture of contempt for his unworldliness that she announced that she was through with him," the *Washington Post* sneeringly wrote in July 1924. "He is, she observed, too old-fashioned, too conservative, for one so sophisticated, so beautiful as herself."

It didn't help that she never gave birth to the child she had so publicly announced she was carrying while awaiting trial. There's no evidence that she was ever pregnant. In January 1927, six months after her divorce from Al was finalized, Beulah moved to Indiana and married twenty-six-year-old boxer Edward Harlib, reportedly "despite the bitter opposition of Harlib's family." The marriage lasted less than four months. At a divorce hearing, Beulah told of "blackened eyes and broken ribs at the hands of her former pugilist husband," but she didn't claim spousal abuse as the impetus for the court action. It was her discovery that Harlib had never divorced his first wife. Beulah returned to Chicago and took a small apartment with her mother.

Chicago opened in the city that fall, but Beulah didn't attend the play. By then, she found herself bedridden on and off for weeks, her strength sapped. Early the following year, doctors diagnosed tuberculosis, and she entered the Chicago Fresh Air Sanitarium. She registered under the name Dorothy Stephens. By now she was barely recognizable. "She wasn't very beautiful," said a friend. "She was thin and faded. All she seemed to care for besides her mother were her canaries and cats." Just weeks after her arrival at the sanitarium, less than four years after she'd dominated Chicago's front pages, "Beautiful Beulah" Annan died. The press didn't report it until nearly a week later. On March 14, 1928, the *Tribune* wrote, "Chicago, so long and so vividly aware of her existence, first as the central figure of a lurid murder trial and later in the thinly disguised role of the heroine of the sensational stage and screen success, 'Chicago,' was totally unaware of her passing."

Al Annan, alone and saddled with Beulah's legal bills, cut a pathetic figure in the weeks after his wife walked out on him. "I cannot make myself realize that Beulah has given me up," he said. "When we married we took solemn vows that it was for better or for worse, and that it was to exist until death parted us. . . . I shall love Beulah with a love that cannot be destroyed. Beulah is no different than any other woman. She is naturally weak and needs protection. She will come back to me."

Al would be disappointed on that score, but Maurine Watkins, for one, refused to offer any sympathy. She mused publicly that Al's willingness to endure so much abuse from his wife "may mean that men are more faithful than women—or merely that they enjoy more the glamour of heroic martyrdom."

Ten years after Beulah left him, Al, now forty-nine years old, was convicted of manslaughter for beating to death a woman named Otilla Griffin during a drunken argument in the apartment they shared in Chicago. He struck her at about three in the afternoon but didn't call police until three hours later. Al never served any time, however. The judge granted a request for a new trial, and two weeks later the case was dismissed for lack of evidence. William Scott Stewart helped with the defense.

Belva Gaertner remarried William Gaertner in May 1925. This one didn't turn out any better than the previous attempt. After moving into a luxurious new North Side apartment with her husband, she took to getting drunk every night. She also set out on a new round of adulterous affairs. William, now sixty years old, tried to be firm this time, but when he confronted her about her drinking, she flew into a rage and hit him in the head with a mirror.

The breaking point of the marriage came on July 5, 1926, when William returned from work and found a strange man in his bedroom. Belva, upon realizing her husband was home, "shrieked and leaped at him." She screamed that she would kill him, and William took the drunken outburst seriously enough that he retreated to an empty room and locked the door. This cowardice apparently infuriated Belva even more, for her "assault upon the door was so ferocious that he barricaded himself with chairs and bed." When William finally escaped the apartment, he didn't come back. He filed for divorce later in the month.

In response to her husband's suit, Belva claimed that it was William, not she, who had an "extreme and abnormal sex passion," and that her husband's perversion had left her nerves "sorely and permanently impaired." But, as with Beulah, the Fourth Estate could no longer be swayed to her side. She received overwhelming bad press, with one newspaper calling her husband the "most patient soul" since Job. Another paper referred to her as a "cave-girl."

After the divorce, Belva eventually relocated to Southern California to be near her sister. She traveled to New York, Europe, and Cuba for extended vacations but stayed out of the newspapers. She never married again. After years of seeking solace in the arms of others, she may have finally found some contentment on her own. When William Gaertner died in 1948, nearly twenty years before Belva, he left the bulk of his estate to her.

Katherine Malm was a model prisoner at Joliet State Penitentiary. She became proficient in typewriting and shorthand in hopes of a career as a stenographer one day. Known for being cheerful and helpful, she gained trusty status and worked as a clerk in the prison's main office.

During the first year of Kitty's imprisonment, the *Chicago Evening Post* sent Ione Quinby to the prison every month to check in on her. Quinby often brought Kitty's three-year-old daughter with her. "Each time," the reporter recalled years later, "I would pick up Tootsie, telling her that we were going to see her mother in a hospital. I remember that the first time we drove up in a cab, Tootsie cried, 'What a beautiful hospital!' It was a big, gray-stone, fortress-like place."

Kitty tried to win early release in 1930 and 1931, failing both times. In response, Quinby began to agitate for her parole, saying that Kitty was "no more a murderess than I am." Elsie Walther, a prisoner advocate working for the Church Mission of Christ, became an ardent supporter and secured the backing of Chicago's Episcopal bishop. Even the man who prosecuted Kitty, Harry Pritzker, joined the effort to secure parole for her.

But luck still wasn't with her. On December 19, 1932, the parole board again rejected her application for release. Just days later, she fell ill. What appeared to be a cold or the flu turned out to be pneumonia. Kitty's mother and daughter were hastily summoned to her bedside in Joliet's infirmary. Katherine Walters Baluk (Malm) died on December 27. She was twenty-eight years old.

Otto Malm, like Kitty, was sentenced to life imprisonment in 1924. But while Kitty's reputation improved behind bars, Otto's only worsened. In 1931, he was involved in riots at Stateville Penitentiary and declared insane by the state of Illinois. He was given an additional life sentence after killing a convict.

In 1931, **Ione Quinby** saw her first and only book published, by Covici Friede. *Murder for Love,* about female murderers, included a chapter on Wanda Stopa, but because of Quinby's belief in Kitty Malm's innocence, not one on Kitty. The following year, the *Chicago Evening Post* folded, putting Quinby out of work in the midst of the Depression. Also in 1932, she married a fellow journalist, Bruce Griggs, but just thirteen months after the marriage, Griggs died in an automobile accident.

In 1933, the *Milwaukee Journal* hired Quinby. She soon began an advice column as "Mrs. Griggs" that would make her a statewide celebrity in Wisconsin. In a 1953 profile, *Coronet* magazine stated that she had "helped countless girls in trouble, and has had many babies named for her out of gratitude." Year after year, Quinby's column remained the paper's most popular. "Whenever we had a tour come through the newsroom, the one person everyone always wanted to see was Ione Quinby Griggs," remembers fellow reporter Jackie Loohauis-Bennett. "They'd stop near her desk and watch her there typing away."

Quinby wrote her column for more than fifty years, until her retirement in 1985 at the age of ninety-four.

By the summer of 1924, **Genevieve Forbes** could feel her status as the top "girl reporter" at the *Tribune* slipping away. Even after Maurine Watkins left the paper, Forbes's confidence never quite returned. Convinced she was failing on the women's crime beat, she declared in 1927, "Once upon a time, perhaps, there was a lovely lady behind the bars who told the story of her life more easily, honestly, and spaciously to the woman reporter than to the man. But I've never met her." She argued that women in jail would much rather please a male reporter, despite "the stalwart assurances of some lady reporters that they can get the 'woman angle' where masculine tactics fail."

Forbes met her future husband, fellow reporter John Herrick, while working on the Leopold-Loeb case, and in 1930 they moved to Washington, D.C., to cover politics. After World War II, she and Herrick turned to the theater, with little success, leaving her "more deeply and depressingly convinced than ever that I write badly."

W. W. O'Brien's greatest triumph came a year after Beulah Annan's acquittal, with the sensational "Millionaire Orphan" murder trial. He and William Scott Stewart won an acquittal for William D. Shepherd, who was accused of poisoning his wealthy young charge, Billy McClintock. O'Brien, along with his partner, was now one of the most prominent and sought-after defense attorneys in Chicago.

The following year, in 1926, O'Brien represented the bootlegger Joe Saltis, who faced a murder charge. Saltis was allied with Hymie Weiss, who had become Al Capone's greatest competitor and enemy. After jury selection for the case, O'Brien was walking with Weiss in front of the Holy Name Cathedral on North State Street when gunfire crackled above them. "You better lay down, Willie," the imperturbable Weiss told O'Brien. It was the last thing the gangster ever said. Weiss fell, a bullet in his forehead. O'Brien, wounded in the stomach, chest, and arm, survived, thanks to a two-inch-thick stack of folded papers in his inside coat pocket that kept a bullet from reaching his heart. O'Brien would win the Saltis case, but it proved to be his last major victory. He had begun drinking heavily, causing his wife to walk out on him. He and Stewart ended their partnership, and the big cases stopped coming his way.

In 1932, for reasons he never satisfactorily explained, O'Brien ran for governor of Illinois as an independent and received less than two thousand votes. Four years later, he was disbarred after he was caught trying to remove evidence from the state's attorney's office. The high-profile lawyer who had dazzled juries for years went to work as a salesman for the Midwest Exterminating Company. In 1939, in an attempt to regain his law license, he would testify that he had had "a mental collapse; that . . . he indulged in the use of intoxicating liquors to a considerable extent." He lost his teeth, and his heart started to give him trouble. He claimed that he had "no bank account and no money." In 1944, facing new legal troubles, he disappeared.

William Scott Stewart, like his former partner, also had difficulty holding on to success. In 1929, he was sentenced to three months in the county jail for contempt of court for attempting to prevent a state's witness from appearing in court. Two years later, he beat back a bar recommendation that he receive a one-year suspension for his role in a city corruption case.

Stewart defended gangsters through much of the 1930s, including Roger "the Terrible" Touhy, "Golf Bag" Sam Hunt, and Paul "the Waiter" Ricca. Working for the Mob took its toll. Stewart and his wife divorced in 1945, and he became estranged from his son and daughter. He died of a heart attack in 1964 at the age of seventy-four. The *Tribune* headlined its obituary "William Scott Stewart Dies Broke, Alone."

On June 16, 1924, **Sabella Nitti** was released on bail. She returned to her small farm in Stickney to await retrial, but the second trial never happened. On December 1, the state's attorney's office dropped the charges against her and her husband, Peter Crudelle.

One month after Sabella's release on bail, her lawyer, **Helen Cirese,** scored another unlikely victory: Lela Foster was acquitted of murder. The victory thrilled the young attorney as much as—maybe even more than—it did her client, and her law practice thrived. "'The woman in law'—and straightaway one visualizes a stern, formidable, unromantic person, in a misplaced profession," Cirese wrote in a local women's magazine that November. She didn't consider herself misplaced at all, she insisted. "Have you ever seen the look of hopeless anxiety, of utter misery upon the face of an accused prisoner? Have you, then, seen the looks on that same face when twelve solemn men slowly file in and inform the court their verdict is 'Not Guilty'? The mingled joy, the relief, the moist eyes, the trembling lips, the simple words of thanks—that is truly romance—the romance of law."

After *Revelry,* **Maurine Watkins** never had another play produced on Broadway. In the three years after *Chicago* made her name, she saw a handful of her plays announced, and a couple even went into rehearsal, but none opened in the famed theater district. By the end of the 1920s, frustrated with New York, she moved to Los Angeles to pursue a screenwriting career.

In 1936 Maurine cowrote *Libeled Lady,* which starred Spencer Tracy, Jean Harlow, William Powell, and Myrna Loy. The screwball comedy revolves around a newspaper editor who convinces his girl to marry another man as a means of heading off a libel suit. It was nominated for an Academy Award for Best Picture. In 1981, seeking to revive interest in the movie, *New York Times* film critic Vincent Canby called it "magically funny" and "a comedy to rank alongside such classics as *Twentieth Century, To Be or Not to Be, Pat and Mike* and *The Awful Truth.*"

Canby was right, but *Libeled Lady* proved to be the exception in Maurine's short movie career. With *Chicago,* it turned out, she had said all she had to say about the American experience. The rest was pleasant busywork: straightforward comedies and melodramas that asked no more from an audience than that they show up. For a decade, she produced professionally crafted but uninspired screenplays for forgettable movies, such as *No Man of Her Own,* starring Clark Gable and Carole Lombard, and the Jimmy Durante vehicle *Strictly Dynamite.* Her last screen credit was for 1940's

I Love You Again, which paired her story about a roguish amnesiac and his wife with *Libeled Lady*'s Powell and Loy, this time in a misguided attempt to leech from the movie couple's burgeoning *Thin Man* popularity.

In 1942, fifteen years after Cecil B. DeMille's silent-movie version, Twentieth Century–Fox remade *Chicago* as a talking picture. Starring Ginger Rogers, *Roxie Hart* is a consistently entertaining movie, with a first-rate script by Nunnally Johnson and a naturalistic performance by Rogers. But it strayed a long way from the original play Maurine wrote. Most important of the changes: Rogers's Roxie didn't commit the crime. The Hays Code, which decreed that "no picture shall be produced that will lower the moral standards of those who see it," had come into effect, and so criminals could no longer get away with murder on-screen.

It was at about this time that Maurine quit screenwriting and moved to Florida to be near her retired parents. The move was apparently prompted by her father's poor health. Though she'd had some success publishing short stories in the late twenties, she now effectively stopped writing. She devoted her later years to promoting and funding college scholarships for Greek and Bible studies, and to refusing entreaties to turn *Chicago* into a stage musical. Maurine Watkins died of lung cancer in Jacksonville, Florida, in 1969, at age seventy-three. She never married.

⁂

Maurine's death, of course, was not the end of her story. Her family sold the rights to *Chicago,* and in 1975 a musical adaptation, conceived and directed by groundbreaking choreographer Bob Fosse, reached Broadway. Starring stage legends Gwen Verdon as Roxie and Chita Rivera as Velma, it ran for 936 performances and then went on tour. Twenty years later, the musical returned to the Great White Way, with Fosse's former lover and protégée Ann Reinking as Roxie. Newly relevant again, thanks to the O. J. Simpson and Amy Fisher trials, it took the Tony Award for Best Revival of a Musical and went on to become Broadway's longest-running revival ever. In 2002, *Chicago: The Musical* reached the big screen and won the Academy Award for Best Picture.

In the wake of the musical's mammoth success, a mystique of sorts swallowed *Chicago*'s creator. Maurine Watkins, fans of the musical learned, fled Hollywood in the 1940s and lived out the rest of her life in obscurity, leaving her apartment only after consulting her horoscope. She repeatedly rejected producers' offers to buy her play's rights because she had become a born-again Christian and was horrified that in her youth she had contributed to the acquittals of two murderers and then celebrated them in a wink-and-nod Broadway smash.

This portrait of Maurine comes chiefly from Sheldon Abend, who was president of the American Play Company for more than three decades. Abend, who died in 2003, claimed that Maurine paid the company $500 per year expressly to refuse all offers to revive or adapt *Chicago*. "I believe this gal had a change of heart," Abend told the *Chicago Tribune* in 1997. "She didn't want to accept a dime from *Chicago* because she knew she did the wrong thing. She helped acquit a guilty person." Journalists and theater scholars recycled this view of Maurine for years. University of Delaware professor Thomas H. Pauly, in an introductory essay when *Chicago* was republished in 1997, described her as "an eccentric recluse and born-again Christian" in her later years and stated that she suffered from "a deep-seated guilt that her witty *Chicago Tribune* articles had been responsible for murderesses going free." Rob Marshall, director of the movie musical, also repeated the guilt-ridden, born-again Christian profile in interviews publicizing the movie's release.

It was all myth and misunderstanding. Abend, frustrated at being unable to cash in on one of his fallow properties and put off by her social reserve, reached the wrong conclusions about Maurine. She was never a born-again Christian; she was a practicing Christian for her entire life and a broadly curious theological thinker. In a 1959 letter to an administrator at Abilene Christian College, where she provided scholarship funds, she said that she had read religious texts "widely" and "wildly" throughout her life, "from Harnack's *History of Dogma,* Strong's *Systematic Theology,* and the Jesuits to Martin Buber's disciples and the 'literature' of the Mormons, etc., etc., etc. . . ."

As for having "helped acquit a guilty person," Maurine did no such thing, and there's no evidence to suggest she thought otherwise. Abend may have assumed she'd been a sob sister (it's unlikely he ever read her *Tribune* articles), but of course she wasn't. She never sentimentalized the alleged murderesses she covered, as Hearst's newspapers often did. In her articles for the *Tribune* in the spring and summer of 1924, she did everything she could to see Beulah and Belva convicted, sometimes pushing the bounds of journalistic integrity in an effort to achieve her desired result.

It's possible that, after seeing the liberties taken with *Chicago* on film, Maurine rejected further adaptation offers because she just couldn't bear to have anyone else tinker with her sole successful play. Such reticence certainly would have made sense, especially after *Roxie Hart* turned Maurine's main character into a misunderstood innocent. She also may have been concerned that her play simply had become out-of-date. A 1935 stage revival in London received stinging reviews, with one critic declaring that it had "a flat monotony that produces only boredom and disgust."

That said, Maurine Watkins likely would have approved of the musical adaptation that she had spent more than a decade keeping out of theaters. Bob Fosse had no desire to stage, as he put it himself, "Mary Poppins at lunch in county jail." Unlike Abend, he understood exactly what Maurine was after with *Chicago,* and, finally able to move forward after her death, he stayed true to her desolate, relentlessly cynical spirit for the piece.

This is perhaps best exemplified at the close of the musical. The newly acquitted Roxie and Velma take to the vaudeville stage together, complete with glittery prop guns, working their notoriety for all it's worth. They launch into a lilting, self-congratulatory song-and-dance number. "You know, a lot of people have lost faith in America," Velma tells the audience. "But we are the living examples of what a wonderful country this is." She and Roxie then stride toward the audience, bathing in the applause of the packed house. "*Thank* you, *thank* you," they tell their adoring fans, but there's a hardened gloss to their smiles, a dark glint in their eyes. This is intentional. Fosse told his stars that, though Roxie and Velma are saying "Thank you, thank you" over and over, what they're thinking as the applause thunders down on them is, "Fuck you, fuck you."

Acknowledgments

Jim Donovan, my agent, believed in this book—and in me—from the very start. Without him, *The Girls of Murder City* never would have been written.

Alessandra Lusardi, my editor at Viking, expertly guided this book through every stage of its writing, shaping and fixing it as she went. Her contribution is incalculable.

Many others helped me in various ways during the researching and writing of *The Girls of Murder City*. They include Peter Bhatia, Jerry Casey, Joe Darrow, Nick Fox, Susan Gage, Al Girardi, Jeff Guinn, Aaron Lew, Michael Meggison, Marcia Melton, Maureen Ryan, Michael Walden, and Derek Zeller.

Jeanie Child, of the archives staff at the Office of the Clerk of the Circuit Court of Cook County, went beyond the call of duty on my behalf. I also received valuable assistance from Alan Gornik of the Western Springs Historical Society, Sarah Hutcheson of the Schlesinger Library at Harvard University's Radcliffe Institute, Mollie Eblen and Barbara Grinnell of Transylvania University, and various staff members at the Harold Washington Library, the Chicago History Museum, the Illinois Supreme Court Archives, and the Illinois State Archives.

I would also like to convey my heartfelt appreciation to Wendy Teresi, Katherine Malm's great-granddaughter; Wayne Dickson and Ron Dickson, Ione Quinby's great-nephews; and Helen Del Messier Hachem, Helen Cirese's niece.

Finally, a special thank-you to my wife, Deborah King, for her keen editorial eye, her patient support, and of course her love.

Notes

To tell the stories of Beulah Annan, Belva Gaertner, Maurine Watkins, and the rest of the women and men in these pages, I have relied on a broad swath of primary and secondary sources. (The books and journals used can be found listed in the bibliography.) I constructed many scenes using a combination of sources. Anything between quotation marks comes verbatim from a court transcript, police file, published article or book, personal letter, interview, or other cited source. Every action and event described in *The Girls of Murder City* is thoroughly grounded in documented facts cited here.

The most significant sources of information for this book are the newspapers of the era. In Chicago in the 1920s, there were six daily newspapers, which competed aggressively with each other. The subjects are quoted frequently from newspaper interviews they gave and court testimony published in newspapers. To be sure, what a subject has to say in a contemporary newspaper story should not always be considered his or her exact words. The grammar was typically cleaned up and the phrasing sometimes "goosed" for dramatic effect by both reporters and rewrite men. That said, the city's "respectable" papers—the *Tribune*, the *Daily News*, the *Daily Journal*, and the *Evening Post*—took their journalistic ethics seriously. They did not just make stuff up. To buttress accuracy, I leaned heavily on quotes and descriptions of events that appeared in more than one competing newspaper published on the same day. Newspapers were also a valuable source because they frequently published personal letters, diary entries, and various other primary source materials related to suspects and defendants.

While the reporters and rewrite men of the era did tend to overdramatize events compared to today's journalistic standards, in some ways crime reporting was more accurate in the 1920s. Police reporters were given extraordinary access that is unheard of today. They walked freely through police stations and jails at all hours, sat in on and participated in police interrogations, played cards with prisoners in their cells. They investigated crimes themselves, trying to stay a step ahead of the police, and got so close to the action at crime scenes that they came home with blood on their shoes. They didn't get information from police spokesmen or press releases; they lived their beat.

In the notes for each chapter, after the first reference to a newspaper or magazine article, subsequent citations of the article omit the headline, except when two or more separate articles from the same issue of the same publication are cited in the chapter.

The following newspapers and library holdings are abbreviated throughout:

CDJ = Chicago Daily Journal; CDN = Chicago Daily News; CDT = Chicago Daily Tribune; CEA = Chicago (Evening) American; CEP = Chicago Evening Post; CHE = Chicago Herald and Examiner; LAT = Los Angeles Times; NYT = New York Times; NYW = New York World.

Woollcott = Watkins, Maurine (1708–1712), letters to Alexander Woollcott; Correspondence: Woollcott, Alexander, 1887–1943, Houghton Library, Harvard College Library, Harvard University.

ISA: O'Brien = *In the Matter of W. W. O'Brien (1939)*, Illinois State Archives, Supreme Court of Illinois, vault no. 48400–52602.

Note: In many instances, to make the notes more accessible and to save space, multiple discrete citations for an event or scene have been pulled together into a larger group citation. To see the comprehensive, page-by-page source notes, along with supplementary research information, go to www.douglasperry.net.

Prologue

1   **The radio said so:** "Mrs. Nitti Consoles Beulah: 'Lady Slayer' Told Not to Worry for 'Beauty Will Win,'" *CEA*, Apr. 5, 1924.

1   **Beulah Annan peered through the bars:** The cell number is given in *CEA*, Apr. 5, 1924.

1   **But that was when she was the undisputed:** "Beulah Annan Sobs Regret for Life She Took," *CDT*, Apr. 6, 1924.

1   **Beulah never joined them:** *CEA*, Apr. 5, 1924.

2   **The next day, she sat sidesaddle:** *Chicago Daily News* negatives collection, DN-0076751, Chicago History Museum.

2   **This was the woman who:** "Sleuths Sleuth on Sleuths in Domestic Row," *CEP*, Apr. 9, 1920; "Why the 'Cave-girl' Wants a Third Divorce From Hubby," *Fresno Bee*, Sept. 19, 1926.

2   **"I'm feeling very well":** "Never Threatened Law, Says Divorcee," *CDN*, Mar. 13, 1924.

2   **Faith would see her through this ordeal:** "Mrs. Gaertner Leads Jailed Women in Song," *CDJ*, Mar. 14, 1924.

3   **"Here, Mrs. Gaertner":** "Mrs. Gaertner Lies—Mrs. Law," *CDJ*, Mar. 13, 1924. *CDN* of the same day had Katherine Malm's quote slightly different: "Just pretend it's a beefsteak or a roast chicken, dearie. It makes it easy to swallow."

3   **Then there was Mrs. Elizabeth Unkafer:** "Jail Colony of Women in Chicago Grows," *Danville (VA) Bee*, Apr. 24, 1924.

3   **And Mary Wezenak—"Moonshine Mary":** "Woman on Trial For Moonshine Death," *CDN*, Mar. 11, 1924. Newspapers sometimes spelled her name "Wozemak."

3   **After the police had trundled:** "Feminism Leads Them to Kill, Dean Holds," *Danville (VA) Bee*, Apr. 17, 1924.

4   **Motor cars were so plentiful:** Aylesworth and Aylesworth, 25.

4   **"I am staggered by this state of affairs":** Sullivan, *Rattling the Cup on Chicago Crime*, 27.

4   **Even Oak Park high school girls:** "Mothers Fasten Oak Park Orgies Upon Vamp of 16," *CDT*, Jan. 26, 1923.

5   **Belva, the "queen of the Loop cabarets":** "Why the 'Cave-girl' Wants a Third Divorce From Hubby," *Fresno Bee*, Sept. 19, 1926.

5   **And now that she had grown accustomed to "jail java":** *CEP* photo caption, Mar. 13, 1924.

5   **"How can they?":** "Beulah Annan Sobs Regret for Life She Took," *CDT*, Apr. 6, 1924.

5   **The bare stone walls:** See Lane, *Cook County Jail: Its Physical Characteristics and Living Conditions*.

5   **She took no food and confessed no more:** *CEA*, Apr. 5, 1924.

6   **At one point Sabella Nitti:** Ibid.

6   **"The writer who visits these prisoners week after week":** *Danville (VA) Bee*, Apr. 24, 1924.

6   **Once Beulah's wistful gaze:** "What Life Finally Did to 'the Girl With the Man-Taming Eyes'," *Hamilton (OH) Evening Journal*, May 5, 1928; "Mrs. Annan Has Lonesome Day Behind the Bars," *CDT*, Apr. 7, 1924.

6   **"Sorry? Who wouldn't be?":** *CEA*, Apr. 5, 1924; also "Mrs. Annan Sorry She Won Race for Pistol," *CDN*, Apr. 5, 1924.

7   **Beulah couldn't bear it:** "False Colors of Bohemia Lead to Nowhere—Wanda Stopa Learns Too Late," *CEA*, Apr. 28, 1924.

7   **"Another Chicago girl went gunning":** Quinby, 216.

Chapter 1: A Grand Object Lesson

11   **Out in the hallway:** Robert St. John, who started at the *Chicago Daily News* within weeks of Maurine Watkins joining the *Tribune*, noted that if you dared ask for a raise, your editor would tell you to go take a look at the "fifty or a hundred eager-looking young men and women" waiting out in the corridor every day, hoping to get a chance. "I can hire the best of them for ten dollars a week," the editor would say. See St. John's *This Was My World*, 175. This waiting ritual

among wannabe reporters hadn't changed in a generation. In the early 1890s, Theodore Dreiser stood around in the halls of Chicago newspapers for hours at a time, day after day, hoping to be noticed or tapped for an assignment on a busy day. See Dreiser's *Newspaper Days*, 45–47.

11 **It was the first day of February:** "Murder She Wrote: Tribune Reporter Maurine Watkins Achieved Her Greatest Fame with 'Chicago,' a Play Based on Two Sensational Local Crimes," *CDT*, July 16, 1997; "Women Who've Won: Maurine Watkins," *Syracuse (NY) Herald*, June 26, 1928.

11 **The company had fifteen operators:** *WGN*, 289–90.

12 **The *Tribune* received hundreds of want-ad orders:** For the paper's want-ad operation, see *WGN*, 180–85; Butcher, 109; Wendt, 365.

12 **But Maurine, at twenty-seven years of age:** Watkins, Maurine: Radcliffe College Student Files, 1890–1985, Radcliffe College Archives, Schlesinger Library, Radcliffe Institute, Harvard University. On her graduate-school application, Watkins lists her birthday as July 27, 1896.

12 **Its six stories rose up:** *WGN*, 123. Austin Avenue is now Hubbard Street. After the straightening of the Chicago River, it no longer intersects with St. Clair.

12 **Railroad tracks ran along:** *WGN*, 102–3, 114, 124.

13 **In front of it, facing Michigan Avenue:** Wendt, 488.

13 **"Most of them—the great ones—were ornate":** Dreiser, 5–6.

14 **The *Tribune*'s local room hummed:** *WGN*, 102.

14 **Edward "Teddy" Beck was a Kansan:** Butcher, 40–41; Rascoe, *Before I Forget*, 235.

14 **She had written a letter:** *CDT*, July 16, 1997. See Sullivan, *Chicago Surrenders*, 102, for more information on Robert Lee.

15 **Most of the women who wanted to work:** Ross, 543. Ross described Watkins's colleague at the *Tribune*, Maureen McKernan, as "large and commanding."

15 **Maurine, on the other hand, was tiny:** "Pistol Fire Lights Up 'Chicago'; or, Telling It to the Maurine," *NYW*, Jan. 16, 1927.

15 **Her shyness was palpable:** *Syracuse (NY) Herald*, June 26, 1928.

15 **No, she had never been a reporter before:** Ibid.

15 **"Had any newspaper experience at all?":** "The Author of 'Chicago,'" *NYT*, Jan. 2, 1927.

15 **She was too frightened to answer:** *Syracuse (NY) Herald*, June 26, 1928.

15 **A *Tribune* reporter had famously tracked:** Rascoe, *Before I Forget*, 233.

16 **"I don't believe you'll like newspaper work":** *NYT*, Jan. 2, 1927.

16 **Lee told her she was hired:** *NYW*, Jan. 16, 1927.

16 **The typical job seeker, standing around:** Dreiser, 17.

16 **That was what Maurine liked about it:** *NYW*, Jan. 16, 1927.

16 **Indeed, reporters often impersonated officers:** McPhaul, 8–9, 12.

16 **Or they first proved themselves as picture chasers:** MacAdams, 13–14.

17 **Almost all of the women to be found in newsrooms:** Downs, 27.

17 **The number of killings committed by women:** Adler, "'I Loved Joe, but I Had to Shoot Him': Homicide by Women in Turn-of-the-Century Chicago," 867–78.

17 **Another, far more popular one held that:** Ibid.

18 **They were overwhelmed by alcohol:** Murray, 309.

18 **Hearst hired "sob sisters" like:** Ross, 548. Ross identified Dougherty as Princess Pat.

18 **"It's a grand object lesson":** Gilman, *Sob Sister*, 38.

18 **"I shot him," she wailed:** Lesy, 33–46.

18 **She wasn't a girl from the neighborhood:** Steiner and Gray, 9.

19 **"If more people knew the Greek":** John Elliott, "Tearing Up the Pages," *Portland Review* 29, no. 1, 1983. This article about Maurine Watkins includes an excerpt of correspondence from Dorotha Watkins Jacobsen to Elliott. *Portland Review* is a Portland (Oregon) State University student publication; back issues can be found at the university's Branford P. Millar Library (LH1.P66).

19 **Maurine intended to get an advanced degree:** *NYW*, Jan. 16, 1927.

19 **Walking to and from classes on Radcliffe's verdant campus:** Ibid.

19   **During her high school years and into college, she enjoyed:** "A Roads Scholar Pedals Passion-
       ately Into the Past," *CDT,* Apr. 7, 1986.

19   **Maurine had always felt easily overwhelmed:** In the 1920s, in a letter to her friend Alexander
       Woollcott, she wrote about her social anxiety, insisting that she was "by nature a recluse." See
       Woollcott.

20   **Living on the East Coast for the first time:** Letter from Maurine Watkins to W. R. Smith, Dec. 7,
       1959, William Roy Smith: Vice President of Abilene Christian College, 1940–1962 (MS9), Mil-
       liken Special Collections, Abilene Christian University Library.

20   **She was convinced "the only thing that will cure":** *NYW,* Jan. 16, 1927.

20   **Art was an obligation, Baker told her:** Kinne, xiv.

20   **He advocated finding out about "your great":** Kinne, 99.

20   **Once that seed had been planted:** Another reason Chicago called to her was that the celebrated
       stage actor Leo Ditrichstein, with whom Maurine sought to place a play, was there. Ditrich-
       stein apparently showed some interest in working with her, but he soon left the city for Europe,
       abandoning the idea. See *NYT,* Jan. 2, 1927.

20   **It was a city, Theodore Dreiser wrote:** Dreiser, 3.

20   **She picked out an apartment to rent:** *CDT,* July 16, 1997.

21   **St. Chrysostom's was a gem:** Author's visit.

21   **She needed a murder:** *NYW,* Jan. 16, 1927.

21   **"Being a conscientious person I never prayed":** Ibid.

Chapter 2: *The Variable Feminine Mechanism*

The narrative for Walter Law and Belva Gaertner's last night together—and Belva's subsequent arrest—draws from the following key sources: "Bootlegger Had No Pints," *Iowa City
Press Citizen,* Mar. 15, 1924; "One-Gun Duel Tragedy Told By Woman," *CDN,* Mar. 12, 1924;
"Never Threatened Law, Says Divorcee," *CDN,* Mar. 13, 1924; "Mystery Victim Is Robert Law;
Hold Divorcee," *CDT,* Mar. 12, 1924; "Hold Divorcee as Slayer of Auto Salesman," *CDT,* Mar.
13, 1924; "Mrs. Gaertner Lies—Mrs. Law," *CDJ,* Mar. 13, 1924; "Mrs. Gaertner in Cell for Slaying Is No Longer Gay," *CEP,* Mar. 13, 1924; "Gamble with Death Excuse for Killing," *NYT,* Mar.
13, 1924. Descriptions of the neighborhood are derived from Holt and Pacyga, 8–9, 133.

23   **Later, she realized the quart:** *CEP,* Mar. 13, 1924; Sullivan, *Rattling the Cup on Chicago Crime,*
       91–92.

23   **The orchestra had been playing:** "Jury Holds Belva's Fate," *CDN,* June 5, 1924.

23   **She stared at the blood-soaked clothes:** Lesy, 199.

23   **The caracul coat bothered her:** "Belle Bemoans Ruined Coat," *CDJ,* Mar. 13, 1924.

24   **Belva had never been able to count on:** Illinois Soldiers' and Sailors' Orphans' Home Records,
       1900 (255.004-008), Illinois State Archives, Margaret Cross Norton Bldg., Springfield, Illinois.
       Belva's mother deposited her two children in the state orphanage when times got tough for her.
       Belva's father died when Belva was four years old.

24   **He had just won the Franklin Institute Gold Medal:** "Here and There," *Scientific American,*
       Apr. 1924.

24   **The room was stuffed:** *CDT,* Mar. 12, 1924; Case S-443652 (*Gaertner* v. *Gaertner,* 1926), Office of
       the Clerk of the Circuit Court of Cook County.

25   **"He gave me that coat, too":** Lesy, 199. Also see "Gin Bottle and Slippers Shown at Belva's Trial,"
       CEP, June 5, 1924.

26   **In her first few weeks:** "Women Who've Won: Maurine Watkins," *Syracuse (NY) Herald,* June
       26, 1928; "Pistol Fire Lights Up 'Chicago'; or, Telling It to the Maurine," *NYW,* Jan. 16, 1927.

26   **After only a few days on the job:** "Young Lady," *New Yorker,* Jan. 29, 1927, 18.

26   **If she were lucky, she might:** "Bobbed Wig or Wigged Bobs Is Fashion Decree," *CDT,* Apr. 24,
       1924.

26   **It hardly helped to know:** Rascoe, *Before I Forget,* 242.

26 The newsroom's majordomo was a profane: Rascoe, *Before I Forget*, 235.

27 "The prima donna is one who will": *WGN*, 132.

27 When the country committed to the World War: *WGN*, 85.

28 Serious journals called the Hearst style: See Pelizzon and West.

28 His papers also vocally supported him: Murray, 55.

28 The hardball tactics in the circulation war: Nash, *Makers and Breakers of Chicago: From Long John Wentworth to Richard J. Daley*, 30–31.

29 Howey's charge was, "Beat the *Trib*": Murray, 120.

29 "Don't ever fake a story": Rascoe, *Before I Forget*, 236.

29 In contrast to the *Tribune*'s culture: Murray, 67–74.

29 Editors at the two newspapers worked: Wendt, 451.

29 They bribed officers to sit in on: Murray, 206; Hecht, *Gaily, Gaily*, 35–36.

30 Howey's most memorable physical characteristic: Hecht, *Charlie: The Improbable Life and Times of Charlie MacArthur*, 49–50.

30 "What do you mean, the man": Murray, 35–36.

30 "A newspaper man need have only a spoonful": *WGN*, 133.

31 It was after one in the morning: *WGN*, 159; "Mystery Victim Is Robert Law; Hold Divorcee," *CDT*, Mar. 12, 1924.

31 She and Walter were so drunk: "One-Gun Duel Tragedy Told by Woman," *CDN*, Mar. 12, 1924, and *CDT*, Mar. 12, 1924.

32 The papers would refer to her: "'Flip Coin' Murderess Acquitted by Chicago Jury on Eighth Ballot," *Waterloo (IA) Evening Courier*, June 6, 1924.

32 "Mr. Law said something about hold-up men": Lesy, 199.

33 A girl reporter simply couldn't be counted on: Ross, 6.

33 Despite the dramatic rise in "gun girls": Dornfeld, 189.

33 "I would rather see my daughter starve": Ross, 22.

33 The *Tribune*, at least, wanted a true: Butcher, 208.

33 On her first assignment, Fanny Butcher: Butcher, 205–6.

33 She had to listen, she said, "to the intimate": Ibid.

34 "Mrs. Belle Brown Overbeck Gaertner": *CDT*, Mar. 12, 1924.

35 The story had been designated: *WGN*, 102, 159, 236, 242, 252.

37 Every crime story was instantly recognizable: Gilman, "The Truth Behind the News," 1–4. Sabella Nitti was designated "Senora Sabelle" in "Dialect Jargon Makes 'Em Dizzy at Nitti Trial," *CDT*, July 7, 1923.

38 "Call William," Belva had pleaded: Lesy, 199.

Chapter 3: One-Gun Duel

The chief sources of information for William and Belva Gaertner's life together are court documents from their second divorce, in 1926, and their aborted annulment case, in 1917: Case S-331246 (*Gaertner* v. *Gaertner*, 1917) and case S-443652 (*Gaertner* v. *Gaertner*, 1926). These case files reside in the archives of the Cook County Clerk of the Circuit Court in Chicago. Page numbers are not listed because each case's documents, compiled over many weeks or months, are out of order and mostly unnumbered. The case files are not overwhelming in size, however. Anyone going through them in the Circuit Court archives can easily find my trail.

39 The horses had almost made the marriage: "Finds Liberty as Taxi Driver," *Waterloo (IA) Evening Courier and Reporter*, Aug. 4, 1920; "Riding to a Fall," *CDT*, Sept. 16, 1917.

39 One observer noted that the "suppleness": *Evening Courier and Reporter*, Aug. 4, 1920.

39 William gave her a present during their courtship: "Sleuths Sleuth on Sleuths in Domestic Row," *CEP*, Apr. 9, 1920.

39 With her trim torso and her penchant: Holt and Pacyga, 73–79, 95–96.

40 The parks, opined a visitor: Pierce, 398.
41 That was the name she had been using: *CDT*, in its September 16, 1917, report, suggests that the couple met on the city's South Side bridle paths. The *Fresno Bee* of September 19, 1926, in "Why the 'Cave-Girl' Wants a Third Divorce from Hubby," describes William Gaertner meeting Belva in a Loop cabaret, where William "had the habit of seeking diversion from the cares of his business." Considering their respective stations in society and William's taste in women, it is likely that the initial meeting was in a cabaret. William treasured the portrait he had commissioned of her in cabaret dress, so he clearly had seen her on stage, and it made an impression. The "revelations of the female form" quote comes from Rascoe's *Before I Forget*, 297.
41 Here, wearing molded breastplates: Lesy, 196. Belva Gaertner's age is listed in Illinois Soldiers' and Sailors' Orphans' Home Records, 1900 (255.004-008), Illinois State Archives, Margaret Cross Norton Bldg., Springfield, Illinois. She was born September 14, 1885.
42 He soon discovered her given name: Case S-331246 (*Gaertner* v. *Gaertner*, 1917). Also see: case S-327058 (*Oberbeck* v. *Oberbeck*, 1917), Cook County Clerk of the Circuit Court.
42 Belva, it turned out, was easy to have: Belva and William Gaertner married for the first time on June 4, 1917. But William had another longtime mistress, Helen LaFontaine, and when LaFontaine found out about the marriage, she threatened William's reputation. Within days of the ceremony, William told Belva the marriage was over. On August 3, he filed a bill of complaint in the Cook County Superior Court seeking an annulment. Then somewhere between October 1917 and the following March, the newlyweds reconciled. In August 1918, just over a year after their ill-fated first marriage, William and Belva married again. See case S-331246 (*Gaertner* v. *Gaertner*, 1917). Also see "Riding to a Fall," *CDT*, Sept. 16, 1917, and "Gaertners Jog Apart as Court Cuts the Reins," *CDT*, May 7, 1920.
42 He controlled the universe: "New Camera to Take Mars," *NYT*, May 9, 1907.
43 "You are one husband in a million": "The Matrimonial Worm That Turned at Last," *San Antonio Light*, Jan. 9, 1927.
43 On top of such frivolities: "Are Chicago Women Slaves to Corsets? Well—Yes and No," *CDT*, June 8, 1921.
43 "Thanks for the advice": *San Antonio Light*, Jan. 9, 1927.
44 "It wasn't unusual for him": "Belva Gaertner Will Fight Rich Husband's Suit," *CDT*, Aug. 2, 1926.
44 He hired celebrated detective W. C. Dannenberg: The Gaertner divorce and the events leading up to it are detailed in "Sleuths Lose Jobs as Woman Gets Divorce," *CEP*, May 7, 1920; "Gaertners' Life Just One Sleuth After Another," *CDT*, Apr. 9, 1920; "Gaertners Jog Apart as Court Cuts the Reins," *CDT*, May 7, 1920; "Detectives Bind Wife in Hyde Park Home; Ratio is 16 to 1," *CEA*, Apr. 12, 1920. Also see case S-443652 (*Gaertner* v. *Gaertner*, 1926).
44 The neighborhoods to the west: Holt and Pacyga, 95–98.
45 Belva munched a sandwich: Descriptions and dialogue from the inquest come from the following sources: "One-Gun Duel Tragedy Told by Woman," *CDN*, Mar. 12, 1924; "Belle Bemoans Ruined Coat," *CDJ*, Mar. 13, 1924; "Other Woman's Gems Shine as Widow Sneers," *CDT*, Mar. 13, 1924; "Hold Divorcee as Slayer of Auto Salesman," *CDT*, Mar. 13, 1924; "Gamble with Death Excuse for Killing," *NYT*, Mar. 13, 1924; "Never Threatened Law, Says Divorcee," *CDN*, Mar. 13, 1924; "Mrs. Gaertner Lies—Mrs. Law," *CDJ*, Mar. 13, 1924; "Mrs. Gaertner in Cell for Slaying Is No Longer Gay," *CEP*, Mar. 13, 1924; "Gaertner Trial Starts," *CDN*, June 4, 1924. Additional information came from Lesy, 200; and Aylesworth and Aylesworth, 22.
51 The day after William caught her in bed: William and Belva's face-off on this day is chronicled in the *Evening Courier and Reporter*, Aug. 4, 1920.
53 Wags called the Gaertner estate: "She's Taxi Driver Now—Her Own Boss," *CDT*, July 10, 1920.
54 The whip would be presented: "Sleuths Sleuth on Sleuths in Domestic Row," *CEP*, Apr. 9, 1920.
54 "Sure, I whipped my millionaire husband": *Fresno Bee*, Sept. 19, 1926.
55 She had married William because: *CEA*, Apr. 12, 1920.
56 "Me threaten him with a knife?": "Other Woman's Gems Shine as Widow Sneers," *CDT*, Mar. 13, 1924.

56   Belva was the only inmate "dressed up": "Belle Bemoans Ruined Coat," *CDJ*, Mar. 13, 1924; "Mrs. Gaertner Lies—Mrs. Law," *CDJ*, Mar. 13, 1924.

56   "It gives me an awfully blank feeling": "Mrs. Gaertner Lies—Mrs. Law," *CDJ*, Mar. 13, 1924.

56   "You see, they have taken away": Ibid.

56   "I hope they won't put me to work": Ibid.

Chapter 4: Hang Me? That's a Joke

57   When the jail matrons brought Belva in: "Never Threatened Law, Says Divorcee," *CDN*, Mar. 13, 1924; "Mrs. Gaertner Lies—Mrs. Law," *CDJ*, Mar. 13, 1924.

57   The streak had stood at twenty-nine: Lesy, 154.

57–58   In the *Tribune*, Genevieve Forbes derided: "Dialect Jargon Makes 'Em Dizzy at Nitti Trial," *CDT*, July 7, 1923; "Death for 2 Women Slayers," *CDT*, July 10, 1923.

58   There was simply no comparison: Katherine Malm was actually a native of Austria. But she emigrated with her family at age seven, and her look and accent were thoroughly American.

58   There'd never been a time when it was easy: The best source of information on the difficulties in convicting women, especially husband-killers, in Cook County is Adler's "'I Loved Joe, but I Had to Shoot Him': Homicide by Women in Turn-of-the-Century Chicago," 883–86.

58   At fourteen, Belva found herself dumped: Illinois Soldiers' and Sailors' Children's School, Record Group 255.004, Illinois State Archives. Also see Cmiel, 26–27.

58   Kitty dropped out of the fifth grade: "Ladies in Crime," *CDT*, Mar. 27, 1927.

58   She'd married Otto Malm illegally: "Kitty Malm's Legal Husband Seeks Divorce," *CDT*, Mar. 13, 1924.

58   "Defendant Katherine Baluk": Superior Court of Cook County, chancery no. 400645, *Baluk* v. *Baluk*, May 31, 1924.

58   This shouldn't have surprised her: "Suspends Police Blamed for Gun Girl's Escape; Mrs. Malm's Love for Baby May Trap Her," *CDT*, Nov. 26, 1923.

59   Max now claimed: Superior Court of Cook County, chancery no. 400645, *Baluk* v. *Baluk*, May 31, 1924.

59   "Fellows, always fellows": "Ladies in Crime," *CDT*, Mar. 27, 1927.

59   Soon Belva and Kitty were playing cards: "Three Women Smilingly Awaiting Trials That May Cost Their Lives," *Elyria (OH) Chronicle-Telegram*, Mar. 19, 1924.

59   "You can now tell them": "Malm Woman's 'Death Notes' Are Plea for Her Baby," *CEP*, Dec. 1, 1923.

59   He quickly adjusted his memory: There is no evidence that Kitty Malm carried a gun that night or knew how to use a gun. It was clear even to the prosecutors that Otto's claim that Kitty fired the fatal bullet into Edward Lehman was a transparent attempt to save himself from the gallows. See "Confession of Slayer Clears Man in Cell; *CDT*, Nov. 24, 1923; "Blames Escape of Mrs. Malm on Policemen," *CDT*, Nov. 25, 1923; "Expect Pistol Fight in Capture of Malm's Wife," *CEP*, Nov. 26, 1923.

60   The lawyer figured Kitty would be free: "Ex-'Tiger Girl,' Kitty Malm, to Ask for Parole," *CDT*, Oct. 10, 1932.

60   "Say, nobody in the world": "'I'm Not Scare't,' Says Kitty, but She Cries a Bit," *CDT*, Feb. 24, 1924. For more background information on Kitty Malm, see "Savage Mother Cries Out from Gun Girl's Soul," *CDT*, Nov. 29, 1923.

60   "She flopped her abundant fur wrap": "Angel Wings for Malm If I Hang, Says Lone Kitty," *CDT*, Feb. 19, 1924.

61   "Mrs. Malm is the hardest woman": Descriptions of Kitty Malm's trial and its aftermath come from: "Jury Completed to Decide Fate of Kitty Malm," *CDT*, Feb. 21, 1924; "Girl in Court on Cot Exposes Mrs. Malm," *CDN*, Feb. 21, 1924; "Mrs. Malm Has Collapse After State Surprise," *CDT*, Feb. 22, 1924; "Mrs. Malm Pale and Broken as Trial Resumes," *CEP*, Feb. 23, 1924; "New Surprise Witness in Malm Case Promised," *CEP*, Feb. 25, 1924; "Kitty Malm, Two-Gun Girl, on Stand," *CDN*, Feb. 25, 1924; "Mrs. Malm Trial Ending," *CDN*, Feb. 26, 1924; "'Tiger Girl,' On

Stand, Accuses Malm of Killing," *CDT*, Feb. 26, 1924; "Kitty, Witness, Accuses Malm," *CDJ*, Feb. 25, 1924; "Guilty; Malm Girl Gets Life," *CDT*, Feb. 27, 1924; "Mrs. Malm Gets Life; Mate Hears His Fate Mar. 8," *CEP*, Feb. 27, 1924.

63 Forbes, in the *Tribune*: *CDT*, Feb. 22, 1924. Maurine Watkins would steal the phrase two years later for a fictional "Tiger Girl." Her Kitty Baxter would say of herself, "Say, for the last ten years I've carried a gun where most girls carry a powder-puff." See Watkins, 67.

63 Kitty read some of the coverage: "Mrs. Malm Is Resting in Cell After Collapse," *CEP*, Feb. 22, 1924.

65 They were "physically and mentally": Israel, 121.

65 The social activist Belle Moskowitz: Ibid.

66 Her attitude and language: "Mrs. Malm Surrenders; Admits Share in Slaying," *CDT*, Nov. 28, 1923; "Quiz 'Killers' Face to Face," *CDT*, Nov. 29, 1923.

66 Two weeks after convicting Kitty: "Mrs. Gaertner Has 'Class' as She Faces Jury," *CDT*, June 4, 1924.

66 But the *Tribune* stated the situation: "Beulah Annan Awaits Stork, Murder Trial," *CDT*, May 9, 1924.

66 "My experience makes me know": "Wants Jury of 'Worldly Men,'" *Danville (VA) Bee*, Mar. 28, 1924.

66 Asked by newspapers to examine photographs: "Women That Shoot Men True to Type," *Fresno Bee*, Apr. 19, 1924.

Chapter 5: No Sweetheart in the World Is Worth Killing

68 Maurine's desk sat on the east side: *Chicago Tribune* photo files; *WGN*, 135.

68 Maurine was "so lovely": Butcher, 40–41.

69 Maurine had never even seen a poker game: "The Talk of the Town," *New Yorker*, May 21, 1927.

69 She didn't drink: "Alimony," *Hearst's International Cosmopolitan*, July 1927. See the author's biography accompanying the story.

69 Teddy Beck, the managing editor: Butcher, 40–41.

69 One of the few other women: Butcher, 41.

69 The 1920s began, wrote Burton: Rascoe, *We Were Interrupted*, 3.

70 Gangsters funneled a million dollars: Murray, 309.

70 Fred Lovering, of the *Daily Journal*, foolishly: Dornfeld, 137.

70 Maurine was stunned to learn: "Chicago," *NYW*, Jan. 16, 1927. Letter to the "dramatics editor" by Maurine Watkins.

70 Sitting in a cell less than forty-eight hours: "Jail Java Instead of Gin for Divorcee," *CEP* photo caption, Mar. 13, 1924.

71 "One number on the programme": "Mrs. Gaertner Leads Jailed Women in Song," *CDJ*, Mar. 14, 1924.

71 "Law is to blame for the trouble": "Mrs. Gaertner Lies—Mrs. Law," *CDJ*, Mar. 13, 1924.

72 In the original photos from the night: *Chicago Tribune* photography archives; *Chicago Daily News* negatives collection, DN-0076750, Chicago History Museum.

72 Worse, the fusel oil and industrial: Sullivan, *Rattling the Cup on Chicago Crime*, 90–92.

72 The typical murderess, one panel exclaimed: "False Colors of Bohemia Lead to Nowhere—Wanda Stopa Learns Too Late," *CEA*, Apr. 28, 1924.

72 Her colleague at the paper, Genevieve Forbes: See Genevieve Forbes file, in Women Building Chicago 1790–1990, Special Collections, University of Illinois at Chicago.

73 "When they talked of gin and blood, Mrs. Law": "Other Woman's Gems Shine as Widow Sneers," *CDT*, Mar. 13, 1924.

74 "No sweetheart in the world": "No Sweetheart Worth Killing—Mrs. Gaertner," *CDT*, Mar. 14, 1924.

76   **There'd been hundreds of brothels:** 1929 Illinois Crime Survey, 845–50.

76   **The 1911 Vice Commission calculated:** Wendt and Kogan, 294.

76   **In her purse, unknown to her employer:** St. John, 159.

76   **Quinby had a way, a colleague:** Ibid.

77   **She'd march through the *Post*'s newsroom:** Author interview with Jackie Loohauis-Bennett, May 8, 2008. Loohauis-Bennett worked and became friends with Quinby during Quinby's last years at the *Milwaukee Journal* in the 1970s and early 1980s.

77   **One fellow scribe remarked:** Newspaper clipping, headlined "Meeting Queen Marie, Lunching with Film Stars All in Day's Work." Undated, paper of origin unknown, in Ione Quinby Papers, Western Springs (Illinois) Historical Society.

77   **Indeed, back then, just before:** "Finds Liberty as Taxi Driver," *Waterloo (IA) Evening Courier and Reporter,* Aug. 4, 1920.

77   **Instead, she undertook a new career:** Ibid.

77   **"Well, I just can't take orders":** "She's Taxi Driver Now—Her Own Boss," *CDT,* July 10, 1920.

77   **Any man walking by the taxi stand:** "Finds Liberty as Taxi Driver," *Waterloo (IA) Evening Courier and Reporter,* Aug. 4, 1920.

78   **In the spring of 1920, Belva:** Israel, 128.

78   **It was, said one commentator:** Israel, 120.

78   **Doctors warned that the "flapper":** Israel, 136.

78   **School boards across the country:** "Roused Teachers Plan Convention Aimed at 'Blue Laws,'" *Davenport (IA) Democrat and Leader,* Apr. 5, 1928.

78   **The *Evening American* reported that:** Kahn, 292.

79   **Already Maurine had decided that she would make:** In correspondence with the writer John Elliott, Dorotha Watkins recalled her cousin Maurine ending a marriage engagement when she was about twenty-four because she was convinced her dedication to work would make her a terrible wife. See Elliott, "Tearing Up the Pages," *Portland Review.*

79   **Soon after starting at the *Tribune*:** "Pioneer in Birth Control Tells How Holland Profited," *CDT,* May 17, 1924.

79   **Maurine knew all about how birth control:** Israel, 109; Morris, *Theodore Rex,* 224.

79   **She also attended a conference:** "Pacifists Turn to Socialists for Their Guides," *CDT,* May 21, 1924.

79   **Maurine decided that murder was more:** "Chicago," *NYW,* Jan. 16, 1927.

79   **Chicagoans rejected the notion:** "Pistol Fire Lights Up 'Chicago'; or, Telling It to the Maurine," *NYW,* Jan. 16, 1927.

80   **One of Maurine's early assignments:** "Jurors Clear Boy Who Killed Brutal Father," *CDT,* Apr. 25, 1924.

80   **In Chicago, the young reporter had noticed:** "Pistol Fire Lights Up 'Chicago'; or, Telling It to the Maurine," *NYW,* Jan. 16, 1927.

80   **To get star treatment in "Murder City":** "Chicago," *NYW,* Jan. 16, 1927.

80   **She would even develop a kind of crush:** "Pistol Fire Lights Up 'Chicago'; or, Telling It to the Maurine," *NYW,* Jan. 16, 1927.

80   **"I had to ask him a lot of questions that":** Ibid.

80   **The gangster's matter-of-fact attitude:** Woollcott. As an example of her need to idealize, in one letter to Woollcott, Watkins goes on at some length about her adolescent hero worship of former U.S. senator Albert Beveridge.

81   **"Gunmen are just divine . . .":** "Pistol Fire Lights Up 'Chicago'; or, Telling It to the Maurine," *NYW,* Jan. 16, 1927.

81   **Standing around at the Criminal Courts Building:** "Miss Watkins Suggests Press Agent for Gray," *New York Telegram,* Apr. 18, 1927.

81   **The British war hero Ian Hay Beith:** Duncombe and Mattson, 16–17.

Chapter 6: The Kind of Gal Who Never Could Be True

The engine of this chapter's narrative is Beulah Annan's Midnight Confession, which she gave after prosecutors took her back to her apartment after having first questioned her at the Hyde Park police station. Her initial claims to police that Harry Kalstedt was a stranger who broke in and tried to rape her are patently false. The story she told in later days and weeks—that Harry had arrived drunk and bolted for Al's gun after she told him their relationship was over—surfaced only after her lawyers entered the picture. The Midnight Confession, however, has the ring of truth throughout. The mask is gone; Beulah, sobered up, is remorseful and distraught and answers questions with specifics in a free-flowing way. This confession also matches up with key facts established at the inquest and with other details brought out at the trial. See "Woman in Salome Dance After Killing," *CDN*, Apr. 4, 1924; "Gin Killing is Re-enacted in Cell in Jail," *CDJ*, Apr. 5, 1924; "Mrs. Nitti Consoles Beulah," *CEA*, Apr. 5, 1924; "What Life Finally Did to 'the Girl with the Man-Taming Eyes,'" *Hamilton (OH) Evening Journal*, May 5, 1928; "Judge Admits All of Beulah's Killing Stories," *CDT*, May 24, 1924; "Tried to Kill Me, Says Beulah Annan on Stand" (jump-page headline), *CEA*, May 24, 1924; "'Shot to Save My Own Life,' Says Beulah on Stand," *CEP*, May 24, 1924.

83 **The *Tribune* that morning carried:** Bergreen, 109.

83 **Already, truckloads of flowers:** Ibid, 110.

84 **Back in October, when Beulah:** *Hamilton (OH) Evening Journal*, May 5, 1928.

84 **She knew a doctor who'd give her morphine:** Ibid.

84 **She felt it was a woman's prerogative:** "Annan Killing to Grand Jury," *CDJ*, Apr. 7, 1924.

84 **She looked at the flowered paper:** Watkins, 3. Watkins's scene description of Roxie and Amos's fictional flat mirrored Beulah and Al's real one.

85 ***There's another man*, she said:** "Mrs. Annan Says She Is Glad She Killed Kalstedt," *CEP*, Apr. 4, 1924; *CDN*, Apr. 4, 1924.

85 **"If that's the kind of a woman":** "'Glad,' Says Jazz Slayer," *CEA*, Apr. 4, 1924.

86 **She'd been dancing around:** "Spurns Husband Who Saved Her from Gallows," *Washington Post*, July 13, 1924.

86 ***Why, you're nothing but a dirty:*** *Hamilton Evening Journal*, May 5, 1928. The paper quotes her as saying, "Why, you're nothing but a four-flusher and a jail bird!" In her trial testimony, it came out that she also used an expletive.

86 **"Come home, I've shot a man":** *CDN*, Apr. 4, 1924.

87 **"Where is the gun?":** *CDT*, May 24, 1924.

87 **When he came in the door, the first thing:** *CEA*, May 24, 1924; "Jury Finds Beulah Annan Is 'Not Guilty,'" *CDT*, May 25, 1924.

87 **When a voice tweeted over the line:** "Woman Plays Jazz Air as Victim Dies," *CDT*, Apr. 4, 1924. This quote comes from Watkins's first story about Beulah. In later reports, in newspapers throughout the country, the quote was typically relayed as: "I've just killed a man!"

87 **The nearness of wealthy Hyde Park and Kenwood:** Holt and Pacyga, 87–88.

88 **Fighting raged for days:** Ciccone, 168; Wendt, 464–65.

88 **"This will get us by," he said:** Nash, *Makers and Breakers of Chicago: From Long John Wentworth to Richard J. Daley*, 52. Nash writes that the motorcycle's driver was Dean O' Banion. O'Banion would later become one of the city's foremost bootleggers.

89 **"Midnight was like day":** Ward and Burns, 87.

89 **One of the officers, Sergeant Malachi Murphy:** *CEA*, May 24, 1924.

89 **"I came home and found this guy":** *San Antonio Light*, Dec. 21, 1947. The headline is illegible on the University of Texas Library microfilm. The byline is Peter Levins.

89 **"I am going to quit you":** *CEP*, Apr. 4, 1924.

89 **"I told him I would shoot":** *San Antonio Light*, Dec. 21, 1947.

89 **She dropped—a dead-away faint:** *CDT*, May 24, 1924; "Beulah on Stand Fails to Keep Out Her Confession," *CEP*, May 23, 1924.

90 "Don't you know me?": *CDT*, May 24, 1924; *CDT*, May 25, 1924.
90 Albert Allen, the stenographer there to record: *CEP*, May 23, 1924.

Chapter 7: A Modern Salome

91 "I've been a sucker, that's all!": "Demand Noose for 'Prettiest' Woman Slayer," *CDT*, Apr. 5, 1924; Pauly, 128.
91 "I guess I was too slow for her": "Hold Mrs. Annan for Murder," *CDJ*, Apr. 4, 1924.
91 The young, slender woman, with "wide blue eyes": Quoted section from "Select Jury to Pronounce Fate of Beulah Annan," *CDT*, May 23, 1924. The description of how Beulah Annan was dressed comes from *CDN* negatives collection, images DN-0076797 and DN-0076798, Chicago History Museum, and *CDJ*, Apr. 4, 1924.
92 "He came into my apartment this afternoon": "Woman Plays Jazz Air as Victim Dies," *CDT*, Apr. 4, 1924; Pauly, 123.
92 "I didn't know—I didn't realize": *CEA*, Apr. 4, 1924.
92 She said the same thing over and over: *CDT*, Apr. 4, 1924.
92 Harry's voice hung in the air: *San Antonio Light*, Dec. 21, 1947; Pauly, 125.
92 Photographs of the suspect in her revealing attire: *CDJ*, Apr. 4, 1924; "Will Her Red Head Vamp the Jury?" *CDN*, Apr. 4, 1924; "'Glad,' Says Jazz Slayer," *CEA*, Apr. 4, 1924.
93 "You are right, I haven't been telling": Pauly, 122; *CDT*, Apr. 4, 1924.
93 After the shooting, she became "distracted": Untitled clipping, *Lincoln State Journal*, Apr. 4, 1924, Quinby Papers, Western Springs Historical Society.
93 "How much did you drink?" they asked: Pauly, 137; "Judge Admits All of Beulah's Killing Stories," *CDT*, May 24, 1924.
94 It wasn't because she was giving them: Ibid. W. W. Wilcox described her as "smiling most of the time" that night.
95 Back at the station, flush with pride: *CDN*, Apr. 4, 1924.
95 "Harry was my greatest love": "Mrs. Annan Says She is Glad She Killed Kalstedt," *CEP*, Apr. 4, 1924.
95 "I am glad I did it," she said: Ibid. Also see *CEA*, Apr. 4, 1924.
95 "Mrs. Beulah Annan, termed by her questioners": *CDN*, Apr. 4, 1924.
95 In the *Tribune*, Maurine wrote that the popular: *CDT*, Apr. 4, 1924; Pauly, 123.
96 It borrowed from Edgar Allan Poe: *CEA*, Apr. 4, 1924.
96 "A grotesque dance over the body": "Dances Over Body of Man She Kills," *Davenport (IA) Democrat and Leader*, Apr. 6, 1924.
97 Sometimes it seemed that running down payment: Stewart, *Stewart on Trial Strategy*, 60.
97 He was so successful with murder cases: "William Scott Stewart Dies Broke, Alone," *CDT*, Mar. 20, 1964.
97 Wanderer was a veteran of the World War: Lesy, 9–15.
97 So did the hanging, when Wanderer: Murray, 240–241.
98 He prepared for each court appearance: Stewart, *Stewart on Trial Strategy*, 109–10.
98 "I am a great believer in original": Ibid., 568.
98 He married a performer, Louise Dolly: ISA: O'Brien, 31.
98 In 1922, he married a third time: Case B-121999 (*O'Brien, William and Zoe*, 1925), Office of the Clerk of the Circuit Court of Cook County.
99 In 1922, two assistant state's attorneys accused: "2 Bribe Efforts Cited in Charges Against O'Brien," *CDT*, Oct. 5, 1922; "Seek to Disbar W. W. O'Brien on Bribery Charge," *CDT*, Oct. 3, 1922.
99 Two years later, it happened again: ISA: O'Brien, 32.
99 "I haven't much money," he told reporters: "'I'd Rather Be Dead,' Mrs. Annan Sobs as She Prays," *CEP*, Apr. 5, 1924.
99 "Beulah wanted a gay life": "Beulah, the Beautiful Killer!" *CDT*, Dec. 30, 1951.
100 She wore a light brown dress, a darker brown coat: *CDT*, Apr. 5, 1924.

100 From the next room could be heard strains of: Ibid.
100 "I wish they'd let me see him": Ibid.
100 She had a seven-year-old son: Ibid.
100 She had married that first time: "Mrs. Annan Sorry She Won Race for Pistol," *CDN*, Apr. 5, 1924.
100 "I didn't love Harry so much": *CDN*, Apr. 4, 1924.
101 "They say she's the prettiest woman ever accused": *CDT*, Apr. 5, 1924.
101 "Both went for the gun!": Ibid.
101 The inquest dragged on, and Beulah grew: *CDT*, Apr. 5, 1924; *CDJ*, Apr. 5, 1924.
102 "He pressed a $5 bill into her hand": *CDJ*, Apr. 5, 1924.
102 After the inquest, the police moved Beulah: *CDN*, Apr. 5, 1924.
102 "Murderesses have such lovely names": "Pistol Fire Lights Up 'Chicago'; or, Telling It to the Maurine," *NYW*, Jan. 16, 1927.
102 In the morning, Sabella clomped past the cell: *CEA*, Apr. 5, 1924.
103 "You pretty-pretty," she croaked: Ibid.
103 When the Italian immigrant was convicted, Forbes: "Death for 2 Women Slayers," *CDT*, July 10, 1923.
103 "Mrs. Nitti Consoles Beulah": *CEA*, Apr. 5, 1924.

Chapter 8: Her Mind Works Vagrantly

104 "Twenty-three, not twenty-nine": "Gin Killing Is Re-enacted in Cell in Jail," *CDJ*, Apr. 5, 1924.
104 "Harry said, 'You won't call me a name like that'": "Woman in Salome Dance After Killing," *CDN*, Apr., 4, 1924.
105 She suggested they have a picture taken: Pauly, xvi.
105 "No, no, no. It would choke me": "'I'd Rather Be Dead,' Mrs. Annan Sobs as She Prays," *CEP*, Apr. 5, 1924.
105 The thought of what she'd done to her husband: What Beulah said is paraphrased in *CDJ*, Apr. 5, 1924.
105 "My husband says he'll see me through": "Mrs. Nitti Consoles Beulah," *CEA*, Apr. 5, 1924.
105 "I suppose it is true that a man may drift": "'Too Slow' for the Wife He Fought for in the Gallows' Shadow," *Fresno Bee*, Aug. 8, 1926.
105 He had refused to talk to reporters at the inquest: "Demand Noose for 'Prettiest' Woman Slayer," *CDT*, Apr. 5, 1924.
105 "I can't believe it, I can't": "Mrs. Nitti Consoles Beulah," *CEA*, Apr. 5, 1924.
106 A part of her believed Al had made her cheat: *CEP*, Apr. 5, 1924; "Beulah Annan Sobs Regret for Life She Took," *CDT*, Apr. 6, 1924.
106 "Sun. Oct. 7: Daddy and I had an argument": "What Life Finally Did to 'the Girl with the Man-Taming Eyes,'" *Hamilton (OH) Evening Journal*, May 5, 1928. The newspaper published a photostat of a page from Beulah's diary, which ran alongside the article.
107 Two years ago, she and Al had taken a trip: *CDJ*, Apr. 5, 1924.
107 "I didn't want to hurt Albert," she said: "Annan Killing to Grand Jury," *CDJ*, Apr. 7, 1924.
108 They stared at her, followed her, told stupid jokes: *Hamilton (OH) Evening Journal*, May 5, 1928.
108 She and Perry were just teenagers when: Spencer County (IN) Index to Marriage Records 1850–1920, Spencer County Clerk's Office, ancestry.com.
108 A year and a half later, she gave birth: Kentucky Birth Index, 1911–1999, Kentucky Department for Libraries and Archives.
108 "There will always be temptations": *CEA*, Apr. 4, 1924.
108 "If I hadn't been working, I'd never have met": *CEP*, Apr. 5, 1924.
108 Quinby had waited an hour: Ibid.

109 "Well, thinking it all over, I think": "Mrs. Annan Sorry She Won Race for Pistol," *CDN*, Apr. 5, 1924.
109 "I am just a fool," she said: *CEP*, Apr. 5, 1924.
109 "I had never shot a gun but once": "Mrs. Nitti Consoles Beulah," *CEA*, Apr. 5, 1924.
110 "Will Her Red Head Vamp the Jury?": Headline of large photograph accompanying "Woman in Salome Dance After Killing," *CDN*, Apr. 4, 1924.
110 "Forty hours of questioning and cogitation": *CEP*, Apr. 5, 1924.
110 "Stunned—almost to the point of desperation": "Mrs. Nitti Consoles Beulah," *CEA*, Apr. 5, 1924.
110–111 "A noose around that white neck with Venus lines": Ibid.
111 Alone among the reporters, she wrote that: Pauly, 126; *CDT*, Apr. 5, 1924.
111 Men "gazed at photographs of her lovely": *Hamilton (OH) Evening Journal*, May 5, 1928.
112 That first day behind bars she received a beautiful red: "Mrs. Nitti Consoles Beulah," *CEA*, Apr. 5, 1924.
112 The next day, somebody sent her "a juicy steak": "Mrs. Annan Has Lonesome Day Behind the Bars," *CDT*, Apr. 7, 1924.
112 Letters began to show up at the jail, dozens of them: *Hamilton (OH) Evening Journal*, May 5, 1928.
112 Nash pushed the trial date back: Pauly, xviii, xxxi.

Chapter 9: Jail School

113 The *Evening Post* announced that April 21: "Five Women Are in Court Today on Murder Charges," *CEP*, Apr. 21, 1924.
114 The Broadway star Mae West had been hired: Watts, 65.
114 "They got up from the tables": Watts, 49.
114 She'd been relegated to a minor-league vaudeville: Watts, 65.
114 "I think in most cases where a man is shot": "Wants Jury of 'Worldly Men,'" *Danville (VA) Bee*, Mar. 28, 1924.
115 Maurine Watkins, witnessing this response to Beulah: "Chicago" (letter to drama editor), *NYW*, Jan. 16, 1927.
115 Five people—three generations of the family: "Montana Boy On Stand Tells of Killing 'Cop,'" *CEP*, Apr. 24, 1924.
115 Photographers surrounded Beulah, Belva, and Sabella: "Jail Beauties Face Court in Easter Garb," *CEA*, Apr. 21, 1924; uncategorized notes, Ione Quinby Papers, Western Springs Historical Society.
115 she was now seeking bail: "Mrs. Nitti May Be Free on Bond," *CEP*, Apr. 28, 1924. Bail for Sabella was set at $12,500.
116 "Beulah has been told she's beautiful": "Least Stylish of Court Ladies Only Happy One," *CDT*, Apr. 22, 1924.
116 The person most responsible for Sabella Nitti's makeover: Helen Cirese's decision to open her own practice because no law firm would hire her comes from an author interview with Cirese's niece, Helen Del Messier Hachem, Oct. 23, 2008.
117 Tall and slender, she wore a white blouse: "Slayer Gets Stay of Execution": Undated *CDT* photo and caption, Series I: Personal Papers: Folder 9, Helen Cirese Papers, University of Illinois at Chicago Special Collections.
117 Chicago's police chief declared that when women: Lesy, 156.
117 The next day, when the police told her: "Uproar in Nitti Murder Trial," *CDJ*, July 7, 1923.
117 The father of children ranging in age: Overview of Nitti case comes from case 15740 (1923), Supreme Court of Illinois, Illinois State Archives, Springfield, Illinois.
118 The next day, when an interpreter informed her: "Mrs. Nitti's Tragedy Melts Hearts of Women in Jail," *CDT*, July 12, 1923.
118 "For the first time in the history of Illinois": "To Hang Illinois Woman," *LAT*, July 10, 1923.

118   The wife of one of the jurors soon announced: "Murderess Tries Suicide," *LAT,* July 12, 1923.
118   After weeks of being ignored by her fellow inmates: "Informally: Jail Can Really Do a Lot for a Woman," *CDT,* July 3, 1927.
118   The *Los Angeles Times* dramatically undercounted: Adler, "'I Loved Joe, but I Had to Shoot Him': Homicide by Women in Turn-of-the-Century Chicago," 883–84.
119   "Me choke," she told anyone: Pauly, 156; "Murderess Row Loses Class as Belva Is Freed," *CDT,* June 7, 1924.
119   "This takes from eight to fourteen minutes": MacAdams, 18.
120   Judge Joseph B. David postponed the execution: "See Hope for Nitti New Trial," *CDJ,* Aug. 4, 1923; "5 Lawyers Make New Attempt to Save Mrs. Nitti," *CDT,* Aug. 5, 1923.
120   They insisted that Sabella, whose court request: Hope Sheldon, untitled biographical essay on Helen Mathilde Cirese (RES.3/17/99 Wd. Ct. 2800), Women Building Chicago 1790–1990, Special Collections, University of Illinois at Chicago.
120   "Nice face—swell clothes—shoot man": *CDT,* July 12, 1923.
121   "Her cheap, faded blouse hikes up": "Dialect Jargon Makes 'Em Dizzy at Nitti Trial," *CDT,* July 7, 1923.
121   A group of them wrote a letter to the *Tribune: CDT,* July 12, 1923.
121   "A jury isn't blind, and a pretty woman's never": "Beulah Annan Awaits Stork, Murder Trial," *CDT,* May 9, 1924.
121   "If Mrs. Sabella Nitti-Crudelle ever gets out of prison": "Nitti-Crudelli Benefited by Prison Period," *Davenport (IA) Democrat and Leader,* Mar. 21, 1924.
122   "We simply reconditioned her": "Beauty Aids Saved Woman's Life," *Philadelphia Evening Bulletin,* Sept. 6, 1940.
122   "When she came to the county jail, she appeared": *Davenport (IA) Democrat and Leader,* Mar. 21, 1924.
123   The fear of miscegenation was so great: "White Wife Is Freed as Killer of Negro Mate," *CDT,* July 17, 1924.
123   One Virginia newspaper, commenting on: "A Woman Jury to Try Women Slayers Urged," *Danville (VA) Bee,* June 12, 1924.
123   "Women make good law students": Stewart, *Stewart on Trial Strategy,* 573.
124   She had, after all, said she'd killed: "This Thing and That Thing of the Theater," *CDT,* Oct. 16, 1927.
124   The inmate the *American* had derided as a "bent old woman": *CEA,* Apr. 21, 1924.
125   "A horrible looking creature she was": *CDT,* July 3, 1927.
125   "They study every effect, turn, and change": *CDT,* June 7, 1924.
125   "Colorful clothes would mark her as a brazen hussy": "'Chair Too Good for Them,' Says 'Gentle Sex' Which Is Ready to Save State's Time," *New York Telegram,* Apr. 20, 1927.
125   The women, "all man-killers," wrote one: "1924: Jail Cabaret," In "Our Pages: 100, 75 and 50 Years Ago," *NYT,* May 24, 1999.
125   Belva offered fashion tips and gave: *CDT,* July 3, 1927.
126   "Love-Foiled Girl Seeks Man's Life": *CEP,* Apr. 24, 1924.
126   Only an hour after the unfortunate caretaker fell: Quinby, 216.
126   The story was an instant sensation: Ibid.

Chapter 10: The Love-Foiled Girl & Chapter 11: It's Terrible, but It's Better

The best single source of information on Wanda Stopa's background, her relationships, her time in New York, her final days, and her funeral is the chapter on Stopa in Ione Quinby's excellent nonfiction book about women murderers, *Murder for Love,* pages 199–229. The daily news coverage of Stopa also was remarkably detailed and comprehensive. In chapters 10 and 11, material was used from the following newspaper articles: "Love-Foiled Girl Seeks Man's Life; Kills Caretaker," *CEP,* Apr. 24, 1924; "Wanda Was Known as Wild Little Woman by Federal Office Associates," *CEA,* Apr. 24, 1924; "Smith About 40 and of Iron-Gray-Haired

Type Women Call Interesting," *CEA*, Apr. 24, 1924; "Brother Tells How She Came to Live in Studios While Home Was Closed," *CEA*, Apr. 24, 1924; "Girl Lawyer Shoots at Wife of 'Friend,' Kills Old Man," *CEA*, Apr. 24, 1924; "Seize Chauffeur Who Drove Wanda to Slaying Scene," *CEP*, Apr. 25, 1924; "Love-Mad Pleading of Wanda Stopa in Her Letters," *CEA*, Apr. 25, 1924; "Seek Girl Slayer in Vain," *CDT*, Apr. 25, 1924; "Wed, Then I Met My True Love, Says Wanda," *CEA*, Apr. 25, 1924; "Dope Changed Wanda, Is Cry of Saddened Mother," *CEA*, Apr. 25, 1924; "Wanda Stopa Found—Dead," *CDT*, Apr. 26, 1924; "Wanda's Family Marked for Death; Husband Sought," *CEP*, Apr. 26, 1924; "Knew She'd Do It—Smith; I Love Kenley—Wife," *CEA*, Apr. 26, 1924; "Woman Murderer Suicide in Detroit," *NYT*, Apr. 26, 1924; "Says Glascow Was Evil Influence," *NYT*, Apr. 27, 1924; "'Mother' Is Last Spectacle of Wanda Dream," *CDT*, Apr. 27, 1924; "Wanda's Funeral Tomorrow; Crowd Passes by Coffin," *CEP*, Apr. 28, 1924; "False Colors of Bohemia Lead to Nowhere—Wanda Stopa Learns Too Late," *CEA*, Apr. 28, 1924; "No Friends on Hand to Meet Body of Wanda," *CDT*, Apr. 28, 1924; "Finale Soon to Girl's Tragedy," *LAT*, Apr. 28, 1924; "Police Break Up Morbid Mob at Stopa Home," *CDT*, Apr. 29, 1924; "Battle Crowds at Wanda Rites," *CEA*, Apr. 29, 1924; "Morbid Thousands Assemble at Funeral of Wanda Stopa," *CDT*, Apr. 30, 1924; "Wandering Wanda," *CDT*, Jan. 12, 1947.

129   **Visitors to the city described it as "a dense":** Pierce, 277, 409.
129   **They spoke of its aggressive nature:** Pierce, 411.
129   **Chicagoans called the problem the "smoke horror":** Wendt, 462.
129   **Chicago had become too cultured and prosperous:** Pierce, 481.
139   **The Smiths had a history of giving shelter:** Mellow, 137.
139   **Hemingway claimed that Doodles, whom he found:** Ibid.
144   **Epilepsy, the *Tribune* wrote:** *CDT*, Apr. 26, 1924.
149   **The problem wasn't so much public attitudes toward crime:** "Pistol Fire Lights Up 'Chicago'; or, Telling It to the Maurine," *NYW*, Jan. 16, 1927.
150   **The small group of mourners did their best to concentrate:** Quinby, 227; Ross, 544.

Chapter 12: What Fooled Everybody

153   **Thomas Nash, a former alderman:** "Who's Who in New City Council," *CDT*, Apr. 2, 1913; "Litsinger Reads Nash Record in Freeing Killers," *CDT*, Oct. 30, 1928.
153   **On May 7, a jury convicted Elizabeth Unkafer:** "Woman Given Life in Jail as Murderess," *CDT*, May 8, 1924.
153   **Lizzie was a loon; she'd said she committed:** "This Thing and That Thing of the Theater," Oct. 16, 1927.
153   **Before "Moonshine Mary," Kitty Malm was sent:** "Beulah Annan Awaits Stork, Murder Trial," *CDT*, May 9, 1924; Pauly, 134–35.
155   **The "forbidden cabinet," the one that:** "Mrs. Gaertner's Powder Puff Is Seen Victory Aid," *CEP*, June 4, 1924. Reporter Ione Quinby labeled it the forbidden cabinet.
155   **"Belva has her powder puff again":** Ibid.
155   **Maurine, knowing full well that everyone was talking:** "Beulah Annan Sobs Regret for Life She Took," *CDT*, Apr. 6, 1924.
155   **On May 8, the day after Unkafer's conviction:** *CDT*, May 9, 1924.
156   **"Mrs. Beulah Annan, young and beautiful slayer":** "Beulah Sorry World Knows About Stork," *CEA*, May 9, 1924.
156   **The day after she disclosed the pregnancy:** "Beulah Wants No Delay of Murder Trial," *CDT*, May 10, 1924.
156   **The pregnancy revelation surprised Maurine:** Pauly, xviii.
157   **"What counts with a jury when a woman":** Pauly, 133–35; *CDT*, May 9, 1924.
157   **The official line from William Scott Stewart:** Ibid.
158   **The story became so big that twenty-four-year-old:** Mellow, 278.
158   **"Pity the female Polak lawyer couldn't shoot":** Baker, 130.

158   The Palos Park shooting and its circumstances: Mellow, 278.
158   "I love it. I love it. I love it": Ibid.
158   "What fooled everybody when I told them": "Beulah Annan Credits Babe with Melting Jury's Heart," *Atlanta Constitution,* May 26, 1924.
159   "Albert probably won't want me back": *CDT,* Apr. 6, 1924.
159   A rumor floated around the city's newsrooms: "Spurns Husband Who Saved Her from Gallows," *Washington Post,* July 13, 1924.
159   The boxing champion Jack Dempsey: Kahn, 110.

Chapter 13: A Modest Little Housewife

160   Reporters took up most of the first handful of rows: "Pick 12 Jurors in Annan Trial," *CDJ,* May 22, 1924.
160   Al leaned forward in his seat, twisting his cap: Ibid.
160   She did not meet his eyes: "Beauty Faces Murder Trial," *LAT,* May 23, 1924.
160   "The courtroom was full of appreciative smiles": "Blonde Beauty Acquitted After Killing Lover," *Syracuse Herald,* Mar. 1, 1925.
160   "Slightly pale from her recent illness but blossoming": *CDJ,* May 22, 1924.
161   The "boarding-school girl" look: Dunlop, 153–56.
161   The *Post* alluded to a metaphor by Alexander Pope: "Beulah on Stand Fails to Keep Out Her Confession," *CEP,* May 23, 1924.
162   What any decent defense attorney in Chicago wanted: "Choose Morons on Jury, Advice of Playwright," *New York Telegram,* Apr. 19, 1927.
162   So far they'd never lost a case: McConnell, 62.
162   They'd had such success that they were about to: ISA: O'Brien, 35–36.
162   He had a propensity for going on: Case B-121999 (*O'Brien, William and Zoe,* 1925), Office of the Clerk of the Circuit Court of Cook County.
162   A journalist labeled the always well-dressed Stewart: McConnell, 62.
162   "There is an atmosphere around every law office": Stewart, *Stewart on Trial Strategy,* 576–78.
163   They were each making at least $20,000: *CDT,* July 11, 1925.
163   Stewart liked to say that: William Scott Stewart, *Stewart on Trial Strategy,* 7.
163   "When your client claims to be": Ibid., 439.
163   "In Chicago," Stewart pointed out: Ibid., 283.
163   He would represent thirteen female murder: ISA: O'Brien, 34.
163   He planned to argue that Beulah was a "virtuous working girl": "Judge Admits All of Beulah's Killing Stories," *CDT,* May 24, 1924; Pauly, 142.
164   "Too damned many women gettin' away with murder": *CDT,* May 23, 1924.
164   The men accepted by the defense, Maurine wrote: Ibid.
164   The jury selection moved along slowly: *CDJ,* May 22, 1924.
164   She "leaned wearily on one white hand": *CDT,* May 23, 1924.
164   "Would the fact that the defendant and the deceased": *CDT,* May 23, 1924; *CDJ,* May 22, 1924.
165   Three days earlier, federal agents had raided: Higdon, 29.
165   In a follow-up raid, this one at the Stock Yards Inn: "Rifles Close Beer Parlor," *CDJ,* May 24, 1924.
165   Worse yet, as jury selection for Beulah's trial: Higdon, 44.
165   The *Tribune* immediately offered $5,000: Higdon, 50.
165   They would prove, the prosecutors told the newly impaneled jury: *CDT,* May 23, 1924.
166   That the defense "favored bachelors": "Beulah, the Beautiful Killer!" *CDT,* Dec. 30, 1951.
166   "We are not relying on the beauty of this woman": *CEP,* May 23, 1924.
166   Right off, Beulah was called to the stand: "Judge Puts Proof Up to Defense," *CEA,* May 23, 1924.
166   Before the trial could get under way, Judge Lindsay: *CEP,* May 23, 1924.

166   Patricia Dougherty, writing as Princess Pat: *CEA*, May 23, 1924.
166   "We're not trying a case of adultery": *CDT*, May 24, 1924.
167   Responding to a question from Stewart, Beulah said: *CEA*, May 23, 1924.
167   "Who was the first person to arrive": *CEP*, May 23, 1924.
167-68   "The luck," the *Evening Post* wrote, "seemed to be going": *CEP*, May 23, 1924.
168   "Her statements are entirely too vague": *CDT*, May 24, 1924.
168   "I believe the statements are competent and admissible": *CEA*, May 23, 1924.
168   Woods's conversation with Beulah in her kitchen: "Beulah, on Stand, Tells Wine Killing," *CDJ*, May 24, 1924; Stewart, *Stewart on Trial Strategy*, 92.
168   Stewart viewed it as a victory: Stewart, *Stewart on Trial Strategy*, 92.
168   He also believed that if he and O'Brien played it right: Ibid.
169   "It is true that a jazz record was being played": *CEA*, May 23, 1924.
169   "Kalstedt forced his way into her apartment": *CEA*, May 23, 1924.
169   Maurine noted that "Tears slowly came to Beulah's": *CDT*, May 24, 1924.
169   "At three in the afternoon," O'Brien continued: *CEA*, May 23, 1924.
169   "She foolishly took a drink": *CDT*, May 24, 1924.
170   "Fascinated, the jury followed him down the path": *CDT*, May 24, 1924.
170   "He put on a jazz record and made advances": *CEA*, May 23, 1924.
171   "Both reached for the gun," he said: Ibid.
171   "However, she tried to get it": *CDT*, May 24, 1924.
171   "He was in the St. Cloud reformatory": *CDT*, May 24, 1924.
172   Betty Bergman, Beulah's boss, took the stand: Ibid.
172   He read Beulah's words from his notes: *CEP*, May 23, 1924.
172   He insisted that Woods had never promised: *CEP*, May 23, 1924.
173   "In news articles, you are not allowed to write editorials": "Pistol Fire Lights Up 'Chicago'; or, Telling It to the Maurine," *NYW*, Jan. 16, 1927.
173   "'Beautiful' Beulah Annan's chance for freedom": *CDT*, May 24, 1924.

Chapter 14: Anne, You Have Killed Me

This chapter was chiefly drawn from the following four articles: "Beulah, on Stand, Tells Wine Killing," *CDJ*, May 24, 1924; "Tried to Kill Me, Says Beulah Annan on Stand," *CEA*, May 24, 1924; "'Shot to Save My Own Life,' Says Beulah on Stand," *CEP*, May 24, 1924; "Jury Finds Beulah Annan Is 'Not Guilty,'" *CDT*, May 25, 1924. These reports include extensive excerpts from Beulah Annan's trial testimony, with the *American* printing virtually all of it. The transcriptions closely mirror each other, though the wording of the same questions and answers occasionally differs to a minor degree from one newspaper to the next. I have synthesized this published testimony as seamlessly as possible. Unless otherwise indicated, Beulah Annan's trial testimony and details related to the testimony come from these sources. The official court records for the trial were destroyed years ago.

175   *"Her name was Hula Lou"*: "'Glad,' Says Jazz Slayer," *CEA*, Apr. 4, 1924.
175   Outside, on the sidewalk: "'Glad,' Says Jazz Slayer," *CEA*, Apr. 4, 1924; "Dances over Body of Man She Kills," *Davenport (IA) Democrat and Leader*, Apr. 6, 1924; "Woman in Salome Dance After Killing," *CDN*, Apr. 4, 1924.
176   "The case of Beulah Annan is one of the most remarkable": "Spurns Husband Who Saved Her from Gallows," *Washington Post*, July 13, 1924.
177   "All you have to do is to tell the truth": Stewart, *Stewart on Trial Strategy*, 170.
178   Maurine, well on her way to becoming a court expert: "Maurine Watkins Stirred by 'Old Fashioned Girl's' Sin and Sashweight Story," *New York Telegram*, Apr. 30, 1927.
178   The *Daily News* noted that Beulah: The *Daily News* story is quoted in "The Truth Behind 'Chicago' Glitz Was Fleeting for the Real Women of 'Murderess Row,'" *Chicago Sun-Times*, Mar. 23, 2003.
183   There had never been a "more dramatic story": Ibid.

Chapter 15: Beautiful—but Not Dumb!

191   In his closing argument, Assistant State's Attorney William McLaughlin: "Jury Finds Beulah Annan Is 'Not Guilty'", *CDT*, May 25, 1924; Pauly, 148.

191   "No woman living would have stayed in that apartment": "Beulah, on Stand, Tells Wine Killing," *CDJ*, May 24, 1924.

191   "You have seen that face, gentlemen": *CDT*, May 25, 1924; "Tried to Kill Me, Says Beulah Annan on Stand" (jump-page headline), *CEA*, May 24, 1924.

191   Beulah, nervous now that her part in the drama: *CDT*, May 25, 1924.

191   He told the jury that if they believed she lied: *CEA*, May 24, 1924.

192   "The verdict is in your hands": *CDT*, May 25, 1924

192   He laid into McLaughlin for using: *CDJ*, May 24, 1924.

192   "Every defense counsel knows the value": "Playwright Says Parents of 2 Murder Defendants Have No Monopoly on Sobs," *New York Telegram*, Apr. 25, 1927.

192   "She had played the Victrola while the man": *CDT*, May 25, 1924.

193   "Will this woman be convicted, or will her looks": "Beauty in the Courts," *Decatur (IL) Review*, May 25, 1924.

194   An observer watched as Beulah "wrung her hands": "Beulah Annan Credits Babe with Melting Jury's Heart," *Atlanta Constitution*, May 26, 1924.

194   "Oh, I can't thank you!": *CDT*, May 25, 1924.

194   She kissed a juror: "Spurns Husband Who Saved Her from Gallows," *Washington Post*, July 13, 1924.

195   She grasped the jury foreman's hand: "Beulah, the Beautiful Killer!" *CDT*, Dec. 30, 1951.

195   "Beulah Annan, whose pursuit of wine": Pauly, 143–44; *CDT*, May 25, 1924.

196   "Men on a jury generously make allowance": "'Chair Too Good for Them,' Says 'Gentle Sex' Which Is Ready to Save State's Time," *New York Telegram*, Apr. 20, 1927.

196   "Mrs. Beulah Annan, Chicago's prettiest slayer": "Beulah Annan Fades Away to Seclusion," *CDT*, May 26, 1924.

197   "It was the baby—not me," she told: *Atlanta Constitution*, May 26, 1924.

197   She told another reporter that "I know now better": "'Too Slow' for the Wife He Fought for in the Gallows' Shadow," *Fresno Bee*, Aug. 8, 1926.

198   Beulah and Al must have had a terrible fight: *Washington Post*, July 13, 1924.

198   "He doesn't want me to have a good time": *Washington Post*, July 13, 1924.

198   "I want lights, music and good times": Ibid.

198   News of Beulah's acquittal received: *CDT*, May 25, 1924; Pauly, xix.

199   When introduced to another reveler: Higdon, 63.

Chapter 16: The Tides of Hell

200   The mood also was completely different: "Lilacs Mock Home, Tomb of Sorrow," *CEA*, May 23, 1924.

200   For much of the morning, as family friends: *CEA*, May 23, 1924.

200   As she did in her report on Wanda: "Simple Funeral Service Is Held for Franks Boy," *CDT*, May 26, 1924.

201   "Only relatives, a few close friends, and": *CDT*, May 26, 1924.

202   "How and why was Robert Franks, a fourteen-year-old heir": Higdon, 68.

203   "He caught them lightly and deftly": "Big Experience Either Way, Is Nathan's View," *CDT*, May 31, 1924.

203   "While it is a terrible ordeal both to my boy and": Higdon, 89.

204   Kitty Malm, the most famous gun girl: "Kitty Malm Starts Serving Life Term," *CEA*, May 29, 1924.

204 "You'll not find me making any trouble": "Kitty Admits She Expected 'Rope' Verdict," *CDT,*
Feb. 28, 1924.

204 "Some other woman might get off": "Life Term for 'Tiger' Woman," *Lincoln (NE) Sunday
Star,* Mar. 9, 1924.

204 "Goodbye, Kitty, and good luck": "Kitty Malm Sobs as She Starts to Begin Life Term," *CEP,*
May 29, 1924.

205 Reporter Owen Scott, seeing Kitty carted: "A Woman Jury to Try Women Slayers Urged,"
Danville (VA) Bee, June 12, 1924.

205 She was intent on doing "a character analysis": "Pistol Fire Lights Up 'Chicago'; or, Telling It
to the Maurine," *NYW,* Jan. 16, 1927.

206 "In clear, precise language," Maurine wrote: *CDT,* May 31, 1924.

208 "The Franks murder mystery has been solved": Higdon, 112.

208 "Anyone who had ever spoken to either of them": *NYW,* Jan. 16, 1927.

209 "He couldn't have done it": "'Dick Innocent,' Loebs Protest; Plan Defense," *CDT,* June 1, 1924.

209 "This thing will be the making of me": Higdon, 127.

Chapter 17: Hatproof, Sexproof, and Damp

As with Beulah Annan, Chicago's daily newspapers captured every detail and utterance
at Belva Gaertner's trial. Unless otherwise indicated, material for this chapter comes from
the following articles: "Belva Gaertner Goes to Trial on Murder Charge," *CEP,* June 3, 1924;
"Mrs. Gaertner on Trial," *CDN,* June 3, 1924; "Mrs. Gaertner Has 'Class' as She Faces Jury,"
CDT, June 4, 1924; "Complete Jury in Belva Case," *CDJ,* June 4, 1924; "Mrs. Gaertner's Powder
Puff Is Seen Victory Aid," *CEP,* June 4, 1924; "Gaertner Trial Starts," *CDN,* June 4, 1924; *CDJ,*
June 4, 1924; "Jury Holds Belva's Fate," *CDN,* June 5, 1924; "Gin Bottle and Slippers Shown at
Belva's Trial," *CEP,* June 5, 1924; "State Launches Trial of Belva for Law Killing," *CDT,* June
5, 1924; "Gaertner Case Given to Jury; See Acquittal," *CDJ,* June 5, 1924; "Jury Finds Mrs.
Gaertner Not Guilty," *CDT,* June 6, 1924; "Mrs. Gaertner Found Innocent of Slaying," *CDN,*
June 6, 1924; "Belva 'Checks Out' of Jail," *CDJ,* June 6, 1924; "Mrs. Gaertner Given Freedom
on Murder Charge," *CEP,* June 6, 1924; "Murderess Row Loses Class as Belva Is Freed," *CDT,*
June 7, 1924. Also see Pauly, 149–57.

210 He was considered the "ace": Higdon, 50.

213 Nash had made a name for himself: "Who's Who in New City Council," *CDT,* Apr. 2, 1913; "Thomas
Nash, Long in City Politics, Dies," *CDT,* Apr. 12, 1955.

213 "The list of Tom Nash's clients reads": "Litsinger Reads Nash Record in Freeing Killers," *CDT,*
Oct. 30, 1928.

213 He took seriously his client's preference: "Wants Jury of 'Worldly Men,'" *Danville (VA) Bee,*
Mar. 28, 1924.

214 "She's wrong," one policeman told: Ibid.

214 There also was one more consideration: "Jury Finds Beulah Annan Is 'Not Guilty,'" *CDT,* May 25,
1924.

215 Though she joked about it in the *Tribune:* "Pistol Fire Lights Up 'Chicago'; or, Telling It to
the Maurine," *NYW,* Jan. 16, 1927.

215 "The essence of Christianity": Ibid.

218 A reporter from the *Atlanta Constitution:* "Another Woman Acquitted of Murder by Chicago
Jury," *Atlanta Constitution,* June 6, 1924.

Chapter 18: A Grand and Gorgeous Show

224 Said Loeb, "I know I should feel sorry": Higdon, 141.

224 The approach apparently worked: Higdon, 305.

224   The reporter, taking a shot at Leopold's atheism: "Leopold, Loeb Trial Set for Monday, Aug. 4,"
      CDT, June 12, 1924.
225   "Why come to me?" he croaked: Higdon, 139.
225   "The judge entered; Superior Court, criminal branch": *CDT,* June 12, 1924.
226   "The case was really ridiculous": "Pistol Fire Lights Up 'Chicago'; or, Telling It to the Mau-
      rine," *NYW,* June 16, 1927.
228   By the middle of 1924, after having interviewed: "Women Who've Won: Maurine Watkins,"
      Syracuse (NY) Herald, June 26, 1928; *NYW,* June 16, 1927.
228   The *American* called the *Tribune*'s broadcast: Higdon, 159–67.
229   She wrote that Pola Negri had: "Negri's Art Shines Through Sordid Plot," *CDT,* July 27, 1924;
      "Fine Storm Washes Away All Their Sins," *CDT,* July 30, 1924.
229   She reported on child star Jackie Coogan's: "Jackie Coogan Is Mayor for Ten Minutes," *CDT,* Aug.
      7, 1924.
229   Covering a society yacht party: Author interview with former *Milwaukee Journal* editor in chief
      Dick Leonard, May 2, 2008.

Chapter 19: Entirely Too Vile

230   "The finer the spirit of the young artist": Kinne, 266.
231   "Nobody but a newspaper worker knows": "Feminine Punch Is Knockout," *CHE,* Sept. 18, 1927.
231   "Who knows you now? Nobody": Watkins, 15.
231   The Victorian writer George Meredith wrote: Kaplan, 541.
232   Expanding on Meredith's writing, Baker added: Kinne, 93–94.
232   "Oh, I feel so sorry for her when I think": Watkins, 43.
233   Baker taught classical Greek comedy: Kinne, 92.
233   In October, the *New Yorker:* "Chicago," *New Yorker,* Oct. 2, 1926.
234   She had put down on the page: "Pistol Fire Lights Up 'Chicago'; or, Telling It to the Maurine,"
      NYW, Jan. 16, 1927.
234   "It seems to me that the purpose and treatment": Ibid.
234   "You wrote something that might have an effect": Kinne, 267.
234   One prominent playgoer at its pre-Broadway: Pauly, x.
235   "I quite agree with Professor Archer": *Chicago* file, Katherine Cornell Library for the Perform-
      ing Arts at Lincoln Center.
235   "Liquor runs deep down the course": "Blind-Pigs in Clover," *Vanity Fair,* Apr., 1927.
235   The jury quickly attacked West's off-Broadway play: Mantle, 3–5.
236   When *SEX* went to trial, in February 1927: Watts, 90–92.
236   "Here, take these, too!": Watkins, 47–48.
236   The New York correspondent for: "Chicago's Lady Killers Theme of New Play," *CDT,* Dec. 31, 1926.
237   "My hat is off to the genius of": "Hughes Lauds Play for Baring 'Ghastly Farce' of Courts," *San Anto-
      nio Light,* Mar. 13, 1927.
237   Two months after the play opened, humorist: "How a Murder Should Be Advertised," *Western
      Weekly,* Feb. 6, 1927.
238   The *New York Times,* in profiling: "The Author of 'Chicago,'" *NYT,* Jan. 2, 1927.
238   A *New York World* feature on Maurine: "Pistol Fire Lights Up 'Chicago'; or, Telling It to the
      Maurine," *NYW,* Jan. 16, 1927.
239   Velma is described as being in her "late thirties": Watkins, 24.
239   Maurine even offered herself up: Watkins, 41.
239   The furthest she went in acknowledging: "Chicago," *NYW,* Jan. 16, 1927.

Chapter 20: The Most Monotonous City on Earth

240   The train swung north into Chicago's sprawling: Pierce, 504.
240   The traveler coming into Chicago for the first time: Pierce, 430.

240 Once the train settled into LaSalle: "Girl Author Pays 'Chicago' Surprise Visit," *CEP*, Oct. 11, 1927.
240 *Chicago*'s press agent planned: Ibid.
241 The best available seat at this late hour: Ibid.
242 Eddie Kitt, the manager, smiled at her approach: Ibid.
243 She'd been a reliable background player: Ibid.
243 New York was surprisingly tame: Lesy, 304.
243 At one point, Maurine took a trip to supposedly: Woollcott.
243 Haver would admit that herself, saying: "Roxie Kept Her Jumping," *LAT*, Feb. 26, 1928.
243 "Miss Watkins is uncannily keen": "'Chicago' Is a Murder Dance in Jazz Time," *CEP*, Sept. 12, 1927.
244 The *American* observed that "Good-natured": "Women Can't 'Go Hang' in Chicago, It Seems," *CEA*, Sept. 12, 1927.
244 "Gee, this play's sure got our number": "Murder She Wrote," *CDT*, July 16, 1997.
244 "Roxie Hart's supposed to be Beulah Annan": Pauly, xxvi.
244 *Chicago* was indeed filled with awful: "Those Playwrights," *NYT*, May 26, 1929; also "Theater," *Oakland (CA) Tribune*, Nov. 10, 1926.
245 O'Brien, recognizing his own words: Pauly, xxvii.
245 The production recalled gayer journalistic: "This Thing and That Thing of the Theater," *CDT*, Oct. 16, 1927.
245 It had been incorrectly "whispered about": *CEA*, Sept. 12, 1927.
246 After *Chicago* opened, the magazine weighed in: "Young Lady," *New Yorker*, Jan. 29, 1927.
246 That other popular stage authoress: Chandler, 2.
246 *Vanity Fair* thrilled to this "seraphic": *Vanity Fair*, Apr., 1927; "Pistol Fire Lights Up 'Chicago'; or, Telling It to the Maurine," *NYW*, Jan. 16, 1927.
246–47 The *New York Times*'s theater correspondent: *NYT*, Jan. 2, 1927.
247 Frances Browning was the sixteen-year-old: "Browning's Wife Tells Her Story," *NYT*, Jan. 26, 1927.
247 A swarming crowd gave him an ovation: "Legal Veil of Secrecy May Dim Dramatics out of Browning Case," *NYW*, Jan. 25, 1927.
247 An editor's note pointed out that: "Our 'Peaches' Has Got to Have a Jury!" *NYW*, Jan. 30, 1927.
248 Among those who signed up to cover the trial: "Maurine Watkins Sees Frustrated Ambition in Woman's Bitter Reviling," *New York Telegram*, Apr. 21, 1927; "The Olympian Eye," *New Yorker*, Apr. 30, 1927.
249 *Time* magazine pointed out that the "details": "Carnival," *Time*, Apr. 25, 1927.
249 "Strike up the band, for the show starts": "Playwright Says Dislikes Couple Didn't Realize Now Flame into Open Hate," *New York Telegram*, May 6, 1927.
249 More than a hundred seats in the courthouse: "Miss Watkins Suggests Press Agent for Gray," *New York Telegram*, Apr. 18, 1927.
250 "Feel depressed," she wrote: Woollcott.
250 On the first day of the trial, Maurine highlighted: MacKellar, 112.
251 In Philadelphia, the play was withdrawn: "'Revelry' Withdrawn from Philadelphia Stage; 'Unpatriotic,'" *CDT*, Sept. 7, 1927.
251 "The play that Miss Watkins fashioned is": "Wild Men," *New Republic*, Sept. 28, 1927.
252 George Jean Nathan, in the *American*: "The Theatre," *American Mercury*, Nov. 1927.
252 "Does your department pay damages to": Woollcott.
252 Nelson B. Bell, a *Washington Post* film: "Offerings at the Theaters: Rialto," *Washington Post*, Mar. 5, 1928.
253 The *Chicago Tribune* reported that: "Theater," *CDT*, Dec. 6, 1927.
253 Baker wrote to Maurine from Yale: Kinne, 268.
253 "I expect it will be the making of me": Watts, 92.
254 "I am not coming for a drink today": Woollcott.
254 But her themes and subjects changed little: See *Hearst's International Cosmopolitan*, July, Nov. 1927; July, Sept., Dec. 1928; Jan. 1929.

254   One, "Butterfly Goes Home," once again: "Real 'Chicago' Play Heroine Dies Unknown," *Oakland (CA) Tribune*, Mar. 14, 1928.

254   Instead she had come to believe that "the feminine": "'Chair Too Good for Them,' Says 'Gentle Sex' Which is Ready to Save State's Time," *New York Telegram*, Apr. 20, 1927.

Epilogue

256   "A Woman Jury to Try Women Slayers": *Danville (VA) Bee*, June 12, 1924.

256   Seven years later, in 1931, Illinois voters: "Women Juror Law Held Void by High Court," *CDT*, May 1, 1931.

256   Finally, in 1939, fifteen years after Beulah: "Women to Start Serving on Juries in September," *CDT*, July 9, 1939.

256   "Chicago men have suddenly become delighted": "Men Now Eager to Get on Jury; Reason: Women," *CDT*, Jan. 13, 1940.

257   "It was with a gesture of contempt": "Spurns Husband Who Saved Her from Gallows," *Washington Post*, July 13, 1924.

257   In January 1927, six months after her divorce: "Beulah Annan, Beauty Freed of Murder, Is Bride," *CDT*, Jan. 19, 1927.

257   At a divorce hearing Beulah told of "blackened": "'Beautiful Slayer' Fails to Get Decree," *Washington Post*, May 8, 1927.

257   "She wasn't very beautiful": *Oakland (CA) Tribune*, Mar. 14, 1928.

257   On March 14, 1928, the *Tribune* wrote: "Beulah Annan, Chicago's Jazz Killer, Is Dead," *CDT*, Mar. 14, 1928.

258   "I cannot make myself realize that Beulah has given": *Washington Post*, July 13, 1924.

258   She mused publicly that Al's willingness to endure: "'Chair Too Good for Them,' Says 'Gentle Sex' Which Is Ready to Save State's Time," *New York Telegram*, Apr. 20, 1927.

258   Ten years after Beulah left him, Al, now: "Dead Woman Linked with Stoll Kidnap," *Brownsville (TX) Herald*, Oct. 10, 1934.

258   The judge granted a request for a new trial: "Annan Goes Free in Party Slaying of Woman Guest," *CDT*, Dec. 29, 1934.

258   After moving into a luxurious: "Husband Sues Belva Gaertner, Freed in Murder," *CDT*, Aug. 1, 1926; Case S-443652 (*Gaertner v. Gaertner*, 1926).

259   This cowardice apparently infuriated Belva: "The Matrimonial Worm That Turned at Last," *San Antonio Light*, Jan. 9, 1927.

259   Another paper referred to her as: "Why the 'Cave-girl' Wants a Third Divorce from Hubby," *Fresno Bee*, Sept. 19, 1926.

259   She traveled to New York, Europe, and Cuba: Ship manifests, ancestry.com.

259   When William Gaertner died in 1948: "Business Left to Chicago U.," *NYT*, Dec. 15, 1948; Belva E. Gaertner probate notice, *Pasadena Star-News*, May 26, 1965.

259   Katherine Malm was a model prisoner: "Kitty Malm, 'Tiger Girl' of Sensational Murder Case, Is Dead," *CDT*, Dec. 28, 1932.

259   "Each time," the reporter recalled: "Dear Mrs. Griggs," a reprint of a five-part series that appeared in the *Milwaukee Journal* in March 1980, Ione Quinby Papers, Western Springs Historical Society.

259   Kitty tried to win early release in 1930: Joliet Penitentiary Record for Katherine Baluk (no. 418-9185), Illinois State Archives, Margaret Cross Norton Building, Springfield, Illinois.

259   In response, Quinby began to agitate: "May Free Convict," *Charleston (SC) Gazette*, July 19, 1931.

260   Elsie Walther, a prisoner advocate working for: "Ex-'Tiger Girl,' Kitty Malm, to Ask for Parole," *CDT*, Oct. 10, 1932.

260   In 1931, he was involved in riots: "Fear New Riots at Joliet; Tell Guards to Shoot," *CDT*, Mar. 25, 1931.

260 She soon began an advice column: "Angel of the Green Sheet," *Coronet*, Sept. 1953; "Mrs.Griggs," Mar., 1980.

260 "Whenever we had a tour come through": Author interview with Jackie Loohauis-Bennet, May 8, 2008.

261 Convinced she was failing: "Informally: Feminine Fallacies in Newspaper Work," *CDT*, July 17, 1927; Steiner and Gray, 14.

261 The following year, in 1926, O'Brien: "Noted Lawyer Shot in Chicago Gang War; 2 Killed, 3 Wounded," *NYT*, Oct. 10, 1926.

261 "You better lay down, Willie": ISA: O'Brien, 33.

261 O'Brien, wounded in the stomach: "Chicago Police War upon Bandits," *NYT*, Oct. 14, 1926.

262 O'Brien would win the Saltis case: ISA: O'Brien, 33.

262 He had begun drinking heavily: Case B-121999 (*O'Brien, William and Zoe*, 1925).

262 Four years later, he was disbarred: ISA: O'Brien, 30–40.

262 In 1939, in an attempt to regain: ISA: O'Brien, 27–29.

262 In 1944, facing new legal troubles: "William W. O'Brien Disbarred 2d Time; Five Others Banned," *CDT*, May 13, 1944.

262 In 1929, he was sentenced to three months: "Scott Stewart Ordered to Jail by High Court," *CDT*, Dec. 21, 1929.

262 Two years later, he beat back: McConnell, 136.

262 Stewart defended gangsters through much of the 1930s: "William Scott Stewart Dies Broke, Alone," *CDT*, Mar. 20, 1964.

262 On June 16, 1924, Sabella Nitti was released: "Mrs. Crudelle, Back on Nitti Farm, Rejoices," *CDT*, June 17, 1924; "Drop Charge of Murder Against Two Crudelles," *CDT*, Dec. 2, 1924.

263 " 'The woman in law'—and straightaway": "The Woman in Law," *Viewpoints* magazine, Nov. 1924, series 3, folder 72, Helen Cirese Papers, Special Collections, University of Illinois at Chicago.

263 In the three years after *Chicago* made: "Theater," *CDT*, Dec. 6, 1927; "News and Gossip of the Times Square Sector," *NYT*, Aug. 25, 1929, Sept. 17, 1929; Woollcott.

263 In 1981, seeking to revive interest: "How a 1936 Screwball Comedy Illuminates Movie History," *NYT*, Feb. 1, 1981.

264 Maurine Watkins died of lung cancer: Letter from Fred J. Thompson to Mr. J. E. Smith, Oct. 9, 1969, William Roy Smith: Vice President of Abilene Christian College, 1940–1962 (MS9), Milliken Special Collections, Abilene Christian University Library.

265 Abend, who died in 2003, claimed: "Murder She Wrote," *CDT*, July 16, 1997.

265 "She didn't want to accept a dime": *CDT*, July 16, 1997; also see "Pssstttt! 'Chicago' Has a Secret Past," *USA Today*, Mar. 25, 2003.

265 Journalists and theater scholars recycled: Grubb, 193; Pauly, xiii.

265 University of Delaware professor: Pauly, xiii, xxix.

265 In a 1959 letter to an administrator: Letter from Maurine Watkins to W. R. Smith, Dec. 7, 1959, William Roy Smith: Vice President of Abilene Christian College, 1940–1962 (MS9), Milliken Special Collections, Abilene Christian University Library.

266 A 1935 stage revival in London: "London Dislikes Watkins Play," *NYT*, Mar. 14, 1935.

266 Bob Fosse had no desire to stage: Grubb, 201–3.

266 Fosse told his stars that, though Roxie and Velma: Ibid.

Bibliography

BOOKS

Abbott, George. *"Mister Abbott."* New York: Random House, 1963.

Adler, Jeffrey S. *First in Violence, Deepest in Dirt: Homicide in Chicago, 1875–1920.* Cambridge, MA: Harvard University Press, 2006.

Anderson, Sherwood. *Mid-American Chants.* New York: John Lane, 1918.

Asinof, Eliot. *Eight Men Out: The Black Sox and the 1919 World Series.* New York: Henry Holt, 1987.

Aylesworth, Thomas G., and Virginia L. Aylesworth. *Chicago: The Glamour Years (1919–1941).* Lincoln, NE: Bison Books, 1986.

Baker, Carlos, ed. *Ernest Hemingway: Selected Letters, 1917–1961.* New York: Scribner's, 1981.

Bergreen, Laurence. *Capone: The Man and the Era.* New York: Simon & Schuster, 1996.

Birchard, Robert S. *Cecil B. DeMille's Hollywood.* Lexington: University Press of Kentucky, 2004.

Bronte, Patricia. *Vittles and Vice.* Chicago: Henry Regnery, 1952.

Butcher, Fanny. *Many Lives, One Love.* New York: Harper & Row, 1972.

Campbell, Joseph W. *The Year That Defined Journalism: 1897 and the Clash of Paradigms.* New York: Routledge, 2006.

Chandler, Charlotte. *She Always Knew How: Mae West, a Personal Biography.* New York: Simon & Schuster, 2009.

Chicago Vice Commission. *The Social Evil in Chicago.* 1911.

Ciccone, F. Richard. *Mike Royko: A Life in Print.* New York: PublicAffairs, 2001.

Cmiel, Kenneth. *A Home of Another Kind.* University of Chicago Press, 1995.

Dornfeld, A. A. *"Hello Sweetheart, Get Me Rewrite!": The Story of the City News Bureau of Chicago.* Academy Chicago, 1988.

Downs, M. Catherine. *Becoming Modern: Willa Cather's Journalism.* Selinsgrove, PA: Susquehanna University Press, 1999.

Dreiser, Theodore. *Newspaper Days: An Autobiography.* Santa Rosa, CA: Black Sparrow Books, 2001.

Duncombe, Stephen, and Andrew Mattson. *The Bobbed Haired Bandit: A True Story of Crime and Celebrity in 1920s New York.* New York University Press, 2006.

Dunlop, M. H. *Gilded City: Scandal and Sensation in Turn-of-the-Century New York.* New York: HarperCollins Perennial, 2000.

Federal Writers' Project of the Work Projects Administration. *Kentucky: A Guide to the Bluegrass State.* New York: Hastings House, 1954.

Gilman, Mildred. *Sob Sister.* New York: Jonathan Cape & Harrison Smith, 1931.

Grubb, Kevin Boyd. *Razzle Dazzle: The Life and Work of Bob Fosse.* New York: St. Martin's, 1989.

Hecht, Ben. *Charlie: The Improbable Life and Times of Charles MacArthur.* New York: Harper & Bros., 1957.

———. *Gaily, Gaily.* Garden City, NY: Doubleday, 1963.

Higdon, Hal. *Leopold and Loeb and the Crime of the Century.* Champaign: University of Illinois Press, 1999.

Holt, Glen E., and Dominic A. Pacyga. *Chicago: A Historical Guide to the Neighborhoods—the Loop and South Side.* Chicago Historical Society, 1979.

Israel, Betsy. *Bachelor Girl: 100 Years of Breaking the Rules—a Social History.* New York: Harper-Collins Perennial, 2002.

Johnson, Curt. *Wicked City: Chicago from Kenna to Capone.* New York: Da Capo Press, 1998.

Kahn, Roger. *A Flame of Pure Fire: Jack Dempsey and the Roaring '20s.* New York: Harcourt, 1999.

Kaplan, Justin, ed. *Bartlett's Familiar Quotations,* 17th ed. Boston: Little, Brown, 2002.

Kinne, Wisner Payne. *George Pierce Baker and the American Theatre.* Cambridge, MA: Harvard University Press, 1954.

Kobler, John. *Capone: The Life and World of Al Capone.* New York: Da Capo Press, 1992.

Kogan, Herman, and Lloyd Wendt. *Bosses in Lusty Chicago.* Bloomington: Indiana University Press, 1967.

Lane, Winthrop D. *Cook County Jail: Its Physical Characteristics and Living Conditions.* Chicago Community Trust, 1923. See alchemyofbones.com/stories/jail.htm.

Lesy, Michael. *Murder City: The Bloody History of Chicago in the Twenties.* New York: Norton, 2007.

Lewis, Lloyd, and Henry Justin Smith. *Chicago: The History of Its Reputation.* New York: Harcourt, Brace, 1929.

MacAdams, William. *Ben Hecht: The Man Behind the Legend.* New York: Scribner's, 1990.

MacKellar, Landis. *The "Double Indemnity" Murder: Ruth Snyder, Judd Gray and New York's Crime of the Century.* Syracuse University Press, 2006.

Madison, James H. *The Indiana Way: A State History.* Bloomington: Indiana University Press, 1990.

Mantle, Burns, ed. *The Best Plays of 1926–27 and the Yearbook of the Drama in America.* New York: Dodd, Mead, 1927.

Masters, Edgar Lee. *The Tale of Chicago.* New York: Putnam's, 1933.

McConnell, Virginia A. *Fatal Fortune: The Death of Chicago's Millionaire Orphan.* Westport, CT: Praeger, 2005.

McPhaul, John J. *Deadlines and Monkeyshines: The Fabled World of Chicago Journalism.* Englewood Cliffs, NJ: Prentice-Hall, 1962.

Mellow, James R. *Hemingway: A Life Without Consequences.* New York: Da Capo Press, 1993.

Morris, Edmund. *The Rise of Theodore Roosevelt.* New York: Ballantine, 1980.

———. *Theodore Rex.* New York: Random House, 2001.

Murray, George. *Madhouse on Madison Street.* Chicago: Follett, 1965.

Nash, Jay Robert. *Makers and Breakers of Chicago: From Long John Wentworth to Richard J. Daley.* Academy Chicago, 1985.

———. *World Encyclopedia of Organized Crime.* New York: Paragon House, 1992.

Newton, Eric. *Crusaders, Scoundrels, Journalists: The Newseum's Most Intriguing Newspeople.* New York: Times Books, 1999.

Nicholson, Virginia. *Among the Bohemians: Experiments in Living, 1900–1939.* New York: William Morrow, 2002.

Pasley, Fred. *Al Capone: The Biography of a Self-made Man.* New York: Ives Washburn, 1930.

Pauly, Thomas H., ed. *"Chicago": With the* Chicago Tribune *Articles That Inspired It.* Carbondale: Southern Illinois University Press, 1997.

Pierce, Bessie Louise, ed. *As Others See Chicago: Impressions of Visitors, 1673–1933.* University of Chicago Press, 2004.

Quinby, Ione. *Murder for Love.* New York: Covici Friede, 1931.

Raab, Selwyn. *Five Families: The Rise, Decline and Resurgence of America's Most Powerful Mafia Empires.* New York: St. Martin's Griffin/Thomas Dunne, 2006.

Raiff, Janice L., Ann Durkin Keating, and James R. Grossman. *The Encyclopedia of Chicago.* Chicago History Museum, online edition: www.encyclopedia.chicagohistory.org.

Rascoe, Burton. *Before I Forget.* Garden City, NY: Doubleday, Doran, 1937.

———. *We Were Interrupted.* Garden City, NY: Doubleday, 1947.

Ross, Ishbel. *Ladies of the Press: The Story of Women in Journalism by an Insider.* New York: Harper & Bros., 1936.

Sandburg, Carl. *Chicago Poems.* Whitefish, MT: Kessinger, 2004.

Schultz, Rima Lunin, and Adele Hast. *Women Building Chicago 1790–1990.* Bloomington: Indiana University Press, 2001.

Smith, Alston. *Chicago's Left Bank.* Chicago: Henry Regnery, 1953.

Spinney, Robert G. *City of Big Shoulders: A History of Chicago.* DeKalb: Northern Illinois University Press, 2000.

Spivak, Lawrence E., ed. *The American Mercury Reader.* Whitefish, MT: Kessinger, 1944.

St. John, Robert. *This Was My World.* Garden City, NY: Doubleday, 1953.

Stewart, William Scott. *Stewart on Trial Strategy.* Chicago: Flood, 1940.

Sullivan, Edward Dean. *Chicago Surrenders.* New York: Vanguard, 1930.

———. *Rattling the Cup on Chicago Crime.* New York: Vanguard, 1929.

Terkel, Studs. *Chicago.* New York: Pantheon, 1986.

———. *Touch and Go.* New York: New Press, 2007.

Ward, Geoffrey C., and Ken Burns. *Jazz: A History of America's Music.* New York: Knopf, 2000.

Watts, Jill. *Mae West: An Icon in Black and White.* New York: Oxford University Press, 2001.

Watkins, Maurine. *Chicago.* New York: Knopf, 1927.

———. *"Chicago": With the* Chicago Tribune *Articles That Inspired It,* ed. Thomas H. Pauly. Carbondale: Southern Illinois University Press, 1997.

Wendt, Lloyd. Chicago Tribune: *The Rise of a Great American Newspaper.* Chicago: Rand McNally, 1979.

Wetzsteon, Ross. *Republic of Dreams: The American Bohemia, 1910–1960.* New York: Simon & Schuster, 2003.

The WGN: A Handbook of Newspaper Administration. Chicago: Tribune Company, 1922.

Zorbaugh, Harvey, and Howard P. Chudacoff. *The Gold Coast and the Slum: A Sociological Study of Chicago's Near North Side.* University of Chicago Press, 1983.

JOURNALS

Adler, Jeffrey S. "'I Loved Joe, but I Had to Shoot Him': Homicide by Women in Turn-of-the-Century Chicago." *Journal of Criminal Law & Criminology* 92, no. 3–4, 2003.

Elliott, John. "Tearing Up the Pages." *Portland Review* 29, no. 1, 1983. Portland (Oregon) State University Library (LH1.P66).

Gilman, Mildred. "The Truth Behind the News." *American Mercury* 29, no. 6, 1933.

Pelizzon, Penelope V., and Nancy M. West. "Multiple Indemnity: Film Noir, James M. Cain and the Adaptations of a Tabloid Case." *Narrative* 13, no. 3, 2005.

Steiner, Linda, and Susanne Gray. "Genevieve Forbes Herrick: A Front-Page Reporter Pleased to Write About Women." *Journalism History,* Spring 1985.

Stewart, William Scott. "A Criticism of the Public Defender System." *John Marshall Law Quarterly,* no. 2, 1936.

Index